Lathes and Turning
Techniques

Lathes and Turning
Techniques

The Best Of Fine WoodWorking

The Taunton Press

Cover photo by Mark A. Knudsen

The Taunton Press
Inspiration for hands-on living™

10 9 8 7 6 5
Printed in the United States of America

A FINE WOODWORKING Book

FINE WOODWORKING® is a trademark of The Taunton Press, Inc.,
registered in the U.S. Patent and Trademark Office.

The Taunton Press, Inc.
63 South Main Street
PO Box 5506
Newtown, Connecticut 06470-5506
e-mail: tp@taunton.com
Distributed by Publishers Group West

Library of Congress Cataloging-in-Publication Data

The Best of fine woodworking. Lathes and turning techniques:
 36 article / selected by the editors of Fine woodworking
 magazine
     p. cm.
   "A Fine woodworking book" — T.p. verso.
   Includes index.
   ISBN 1-56158-021-X
   1. Turning.   2. Lathes.   I. Fine woodworking
   II. Title: Lathes and turning techniques.
TT201.B43   1991
684'.083 — dc20   91-17307
                                                              CIP

Contents

Introduction

athe work is both the most accessible and the most diverse woodworking specialty. With one machine, a half-dozen chisels and a few sticks of lumber, you can turn all the parts for a chair, the legs for a table, or a dozen candlesticks. From a little larger chunk of wood, possibly salvaged from your backyard, you can hollow out a bowl, fashion a vase or turn a shape meant only to show off the beauty of a unique piece of wood.

The 36 articles in this book, selected from back issues of *Fine Woodworking* magazine, touch on nearly every facet of woodturning. Whether you're a professional turner, someone who turns occasionally as part of your other woodworking activities or a novice just picking up the craft, there's something here for you. You'll find tips on spindle turning for beginners and for advanced architectural turners, as well as articles about chucks, chisels and lathes themselves. In addition, experienced turners share some of their favorite techniques and projects—everything from traditional nutcrackers to 3-ft.-wide burl platters. And finally, as an inspiration to turners working at all levels, there are reviews of regional and international exhibitions showcasing some of the best woodturning of the last few years.

—*Jim Boesel, executive editor*

The "Best of *Fine Woodworking*" series spans issues 46 through 80 of *Fine Woodworking* magazine, originally published between mid-1984 and the end of 1989. *(Lathes and Turning Techniques* contains a number of articles from earlier and later issues.) There is no duplication between these books and the popular *"Fine Woodworking* on..." series. A footnote with each article gives the date of first publication; product availability, suppliers' addresses and prices may have changed since then.

In the last fifty years, Rude Osolnik has produ— thousands of turnings, like this rhododendron weed pot, that highlight the natural beauty of w— grains and the elegance of simple lines.

Spindle Turning
Fine points for the beginner

by Rude Osolnik

I always enjoy teaching spindle turning because any well-coordinated person can pick up the rudiments of the craft so quickly. Unlike so many woodworking disciplines, spindle turning doesn't demand a long apprenticeship. Almost from the start, good students begin exploring an endless variety of shapes, wood grains, colors and textures, and injecting their own feelings and personality into their work. This personal involvement is what makes the craft so fascinating for me year after year.

If you want to learn spindle turning, don't even think about duplicating the complex spindles you see in books. That copying has given spindle turning a reputation as a boring, repetitive task. Relax, and concentrate on cutting a nice, free shape. I encourage beginners to start with simple shapes, like the weed pot shown in the picture series, and to work with found wood, which is cheap and often stunning. If you buy expensive wood, you'll be too worried about the money to learn how to handle your tools and master the basic cuts. The secret to spindle turning is locating the highs and lows, which is a matter of measurements, then connecting those points with shoulders (flat areas), coves (hollows) and beads (round or oval swellings). These shapes are cut with a parting tool and a shallow fluted gouge, with the same techniques used to shape the weed pot.

Since so many good turnings are designed to showcase the natural beauty of woods, searching for wood is a good way to start thinking about turning. Good sources for hardwoods include the firewood pile, trees knocked down by storms or old age, and fallen branches. Look for sections with curvy undulations to the bark, or with burls, bubulous growths often having spectacular, distorted grain patterns. Spalting, the dark-line patterns caused by mineral stains and fungus infestation as wood decays, is very pretty. Wood with wormholes, cracks and interesting bark also is good.

Generally, dead limbs are pretty dry, but if the wood feels wet, I stack it out of direct sunlight for a few months to get rid of excess moisture. I might rough-turn a wet piece and put it into a plastic bag for a week before finishing it. I don't use chemicals like polyethelene glycol (PEG) to stabilize wet wood. I tried it once, but the turning never felt dry. One thing that sells turnings is the warmth you feel when you pick up a piece. If a turning feels clammy, it won't sell. That's why wood doesn't sell well on a rainy day when it can absorb environmental moisture.

If your found wood doesn't have an exceptional grain or spalted pattern, it's crucial that its turned form be attractive. This means a turning has to be balanced, well-proportioned, and have pleasing lines. That's an intimidating roadblock for many beginners. Get around it by working from nature. Natural objects frequently have an attractive shape—an onion is a good example. Fruit forms are also good. The designing is all done—you just need to extract some of the lines. Also, get into the habit of cutting pieces to different lengths. The size variations will force you to think of different forms, shapes and proportions.

When you see a pleasing shape, scribble that form on a scratch pad and build an inventory of shapes. Look for simple lines that don't detract from the natural flow of the wood grain. Pieces should look as if they're rising out of the surfaces they rest on. Note how slender, delicate sections create a distinctive elegance. I've also found that if a piece looks good, it feels good. If your hands flow smoothly over the piece, it's good.

Another thing that hampers beginners is that they have too many tools. My tool kit is pretty small, only five tools—a square-nose parting tool; three homemade gouge/skew combinations (¾ in., ½ in. and ¼ in.), and a large gouge about 2 in. wide. I always show how I use my tools, but nobody needs tools like mine. All you need are a parting tool and a couple of gouges. The Superflute gouges, available at local outlets and mail-order supply houses, work well for spindle turning. The point is, almost any tool will work well if you learn how to hold it properly.

I don't spend a lot of time preparing turning stock, especially for simple shapes like the weed pots, but it's wise to bandsaw off any lopsided corners and protuberances that will get in the way when you rough-turn the piece. Perfect balance isn't necessary. I usually locate one of the spurs to the side of the heart of a limb section, which throws the piece out of balance anyway. This produces an interesting star effect on the side of the turning. I often try four or five centers on a piece before getting the effect I want. It's a good way to manipulate the emerging grain patterns. Because of the out-of-balance pieces, don't turn at the higher RPMs, especially when roughing out. Ninety percent of my work, anything up to 5 in. to 6 in. in diameter, is done at 1,800 RPM. For pieces more than 6 in. in diameter, I slow down to 600 RPM.

To shape the weed pot shown, I mount a chunk of oak between centers and rotate the spindle by hand a couple of times to seat the centers. Since my centers are small and sharp, they penetrate easily, but you may want to drill a center hole for heavy centers with thick spurs. If a piece is very irregular, I sometimes begin with the heavier centers, then shift to the smaller ones, once the spindle is balanced. Rotating the spindles is also a good way to check if the turning clears the tool rest, which should be about ⅛ in. from the turning. The tool rest should be slightly below the center of the turning, so the cutting edge of your tool will be just above the center, as shown below. Remember, you will be cutting with a small section of the bevel near the point of the tool, or slightly to the right or the left of center, and that part of the chisel should be above center. Concentrate on the relationship between the edge and the work. Take a ¾-in. gouge and try cutting with the lathe off, turning the stock by hand so you can see how the gouge rides on its bevel and can be lowered or rotated to the right or left until the cutting edge contacts the wood and begins to remove stock. Always try to set the bevel first, then bring the cutting edge down, rather

Practice cutting with the lathe off, rotating the wood by hand, until you understand how the tool rides on its bevel as it cuts.

To shape a weed pot, begin with the gouge on its side, left, and reduce the diameter of the vessel's neck. Don't try to cut the shape all at once, but make several passes. Final cuts, center, are very light, aimed at minimizing the amount of sanding needed to polish the surface. On the bottom, work the point of your gouge or parting tool in to form a concave surface, right, which will help ensure that the pot's base will be true enough to sit on a flat surface without rocking.

than jamming in the point of the tool, which could catch.

I rough out pieces with a 2-in. gouge, making a shearing cut down the cylinder, but a ¾-in. gouge will work. This is one of the most difficult parts of turning, because the out-of-balance stock produces quite a bit of vibration and the larger tool will absorb some of this. Because of the great amount of material removed during roughing out, I also wear a glove to prevent chips and bark from cutting my hands. A face shield is advisable.

Once the stock is turned to a fairly true cylinder, try to visualize a shape that best shows off the wood's natural beauty. My general strategy is to shape the base of the turning first, to eliminate excess waste and give myself more room to work, then do the top near the tailstock. Most of my weed pots are cut with a ¾-in. or ½-in. gouge, but I will use a narrower gouge for tight curves. The general rule is to cut in from the greatest diameter to the smallest, as shown. Begin your cuts with the gouge fairly high and the flute of the tool pointing up. Then, as you go to the smaller diameter, bring the cutting edge down and rotate your wrist so it's almost at a right angle to the spinning, above, left. Keep the tool riding on its bevel. Don't rely only on your hands to move the gouge. The smoothest turning motion involves swaying back and forth with your body, rather than a hand movement. Keep your arms close to your body and move your arms and body together. Don't use a white-knuckle grip on the tool. As you get toward the final shape you want, take finer and finer cuts, above, center, to produce the smoothest surface possible.

Bark left on the turning can provide an interesting texture, but if it comes loose, stop the lathe and squirt in Hot Stuff, a syrupy cyanoacrylate glue which dries almost instantly. It's available from Craft Supplies USA, 1644 S. State St., Provo, Utah 84601 (they also sell Osolnik's turning tools and urethane oil), and Conover Woodcraft Specialties, Inc., 18125 Madison Rd., Parkman, Ohio 44080.

Before cutting off or parting the top and bottom, I shape the ends of the turning to facilitate cleanup. On the top, I cut an inverted cone with a stem slightly thinner than the drill bit used to bore out the center of the pot. The drill will neatly pop off the waste as it goes into the main body of the pot. On the bottom, I work the gouge in to create a concave surface, above, right. I cut nearly through, then sever the last bit with the lathe turned off.

I bore the pilot hole in the weed pot with a brad point drill in a Jacobs chuck mounted in the headstock. You can also use a drill press. The best way to finish the hole is to modify regular spade bits, which are available from any hardware store. Grind the center to make a long, slender brad point and taper the main body of the bit to shape the rim of the original hole, as shown. I wrap the center bit with enough tape to make it fit snugly and run true down the drilled hole.

Forming the concave surface on the pot makes it easy to level the bottom, since the center bump left in parting off is recessed so it can't make the pot rock. To sand this surface, I mount a mandrel with a 1-in.-dia. sanding disc in my drill press, far left, and hold the turning under the spinning disc. With a little practice, you'll find you can manipulate the turning to produce a smooth bottom. To prevent the paper from grabbing, I glue a thin piece of foam to the disc, then glue sandpaper to the pad.

After you've made a few weed pots, try a simple stool with turned posts, as shown in figure 3, p. 11. Make the beads, coves and shoulders with the same cutting techniques you used on the weed pot. Chuck a 2-in. turning square between centers and

Sand bottom of the pot by rotating it freehand against a foam-backed sanding disc mounted on a mandrel chucked in a drill press.

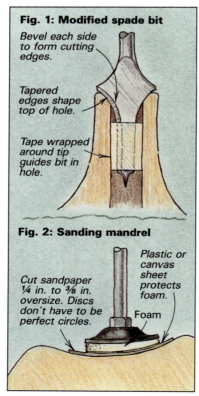

Fig. 1: Modified spade bit

Bevel each side to form cutting edges.

Tapered edges shape top of hole.

Tape wrapped around tip guides bit in hole.

Fig. 2: Sanding mandrel

Plastic or canvas sheet protects foam.

Cut sandpaper ¼ in. to ⅜ in. oversize. Discs don't have to be perfect circles.

Foam

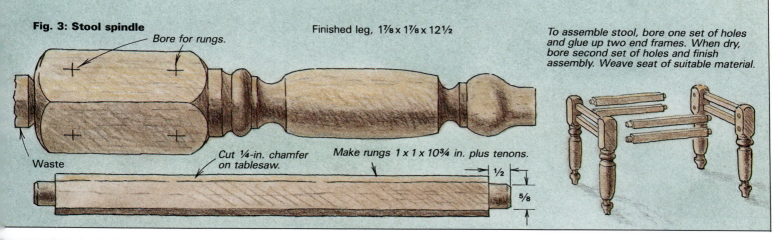

Fig. 3: Stool spindle

Bore for rungs.

Finished leg, 1⅞ x 1⅞ x 12½

To assemble stool, bore one set of holes and glue up two end frames. When dry, bore second set of holes and finish assembly. Weave seat of suitable material.

Waste

Cut ¼-in. chamfer on tablesaw.

Make rungs 1 x 1 x 10¾ in. plus tenons.

½

⅝

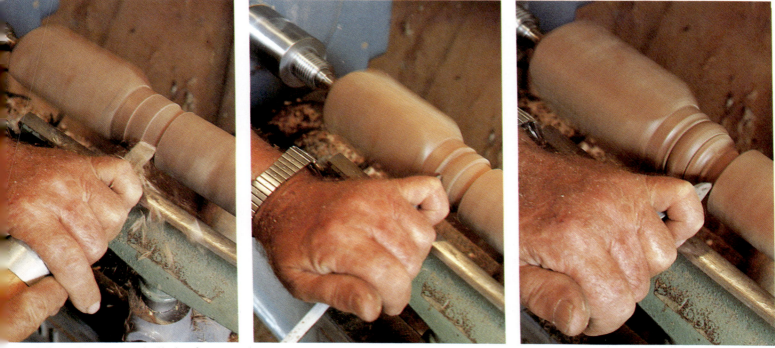

When shaping a spindle leg for a stool, use a parting tool to set the depths of the coves, left. After setting the depths, roll the gouge down each side of the flat band to create a bead, center.

To cut the cove, right, roll the gouge down from each high point to hollow the section between the shoulders. Always cut downhill, toward the middle of the hollow.

For a napkin ring, fit a block on a mandrel, left. Cut beads by rolling a gouge over the shoulders formed with a parting tool, right.

rough-turn a cylinder, as before. Use your parting tool to set the depths, then round the shoulders with a ½-in. gouge. To avoid tearing the corners below the top square, I score the area with the point of my gouge, then cut from right to left and left to right with the gouge to clear out about ½ in. of wood. Then, I lower the depth with a parting tool. In addition to the depth below the top square, you must establish the flat below the narrow top bead and the bottom of the top cove. Again, use the narrow gouge to round over the square shoulders left by the parting tool to form the bead or hollow out the cove. The bottom section is done the same way. Set the flats, then shape between the flats. Use the point of a gouge or a parting tool to crisply cut the small flat areas and cut sharp lines bordering the beads and coves. You can size the coves and beads with calipers, if you like. For the rungs of the stool, I turn ⅝-in. tenons on the stretchers and chamfer the pieces on a tablesaw.

To expand your technique experiment with mandrels. Basically, they're plugs that support stock that would be awkward to mount between centers. To make a napkin ring with a 1½-in. hole, for example, turn a 6- to 7-in.-long plug that's 1½ in. in diameter. The plug is just a holding device, so don't worry about producing a perfectly flat surface. Now, drill a 1½-in. hole through a 2-in.-thick block of walnut and friction-fit the block on the plug, as shown at bottom left on p. 11. To turn the ring, use a parting tool to lower the center of the ring, then a small gouge to round the end sections.

Another mandrel makes it easy to turn salt and pepper shakers. Since I make a lot of these, I've modified a drill to cut the three-step hole in one pass, figure 4, but you could use three different drills. The larger hole is ¾ in., and is later plugged with a small cork. After I bore out the walnut blank, I turn a three-step plug to fit inside. Then, the blank slides over the mandrel, the tailstock is brought up and the outside of the shaker turned to shape, sanded and finished. Drill the top for salt and pepper holes.

Bracelets are always a nice gift, and an excuse to try pressure turning. Turn the two fixtures shown at bottom right, which resemble two 3-in.-dia. bottles set opening-to-opening. Glue sandpaper to the ends of the fixtures, mount a 5-in.-dia., ½-in.-thick disc between them as shown and turn the bracelet shape. Free it with the tool shown in figure 5. You can re-turn the small disc to make a napkin ring.

It's annoying how many people ruin good turnings by sanding. They forget that clear, sharp lines make the spindle look nice. I cut 100-grit garnet paper into strips about 2½ in. wide, and fold them lengthwise. I wrap the strips around my fingers or use parts of the strip, whatever I have to do to make the paper follow the lines of the piece and not dub off the sharp shoulders. Don't ever flatten out a wide sheet with your hand and sand. That's how beginners sand bowls to create razor-sharp rims. After sanding with 100 grit, I progress to 150, 220, then 320. As you sand, check to get rid of the smear wood, torn chalky-looking fibers. Sand until these fibers have a glazed look.

For a good, quick finish, apply a coat of Deft clear sanding sealer and let stand until tacky. Then saturate a pad of 0000 steel wool with urethane oil, and use the pad to apply the urethane while the turning is spinning slowly on the lathe. Buff the turning on the lathe with a cloth. □

Rude Osolnik has been turning wood for more than 50 years. He retired as head of the woodworking program at Berea College in Kentucky in 1978, but still conducts turning seminars at his home and in workshops across the country.

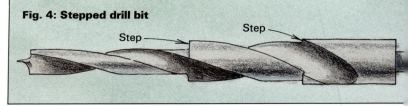

Fig. 4: Stepped drill bit

Step — Step

Turn plug to match three-stepped hole bored with modified twist drill, top. Hole could also be bored with three separate drills. Then, fit salt shaker blank on plug and mount it on lathe.

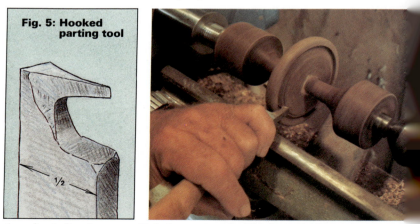

Fig. 5: Hooked parting tool

½

A walnut disc pressure-fit between two bottle-shaped plugs can be shaped to form bracelet. Free bracelet by working in hook-shaped tool, shown above, left, from both sides of disc.

Working with an old-time turner

by Dick Burrows

Working with Rude Osolnik is a delight—he's the fastest, and probably cleverest turner I've ever seen, a great storyteller and, even after 50 years as a woodworker, just plain excited about wood. When he was showing me how to turn a weed pot, he abruptly shut off the lathe, moved the light up and said, "Isn't that pretty?" It was, but what's more important, he reminded me why I wanted to be a woodworker in the first place.

Wood is everywhere in Rude's world. There are piles of it near the nine lathes in the two shops next to his house. The house itself could be a craft museum. Bowls and pots ready to go to the Benchmark Gallery, which his son runs in Berea; carvings, ceramics and other objects he traded his work for; even a handmade Windsor chair built by his wife, Daphne. During a tour of the neighboring countryside, he showed me another barn full of his wood. Across the road is another complete shop, now unused, where he and his sons used to mass-produce wooden letters, stools and other gift items for companies in New York and other big-city markets. Nearby are more sheds full of wood, some of it dark with dust and age, but Rude identified the rosewood, walnut and rhododendron without hesitation. Each wood cache also prompted a story about bargains, sly trading and people trying to take the country boy to the cleaners.

Rude never wastes a chance for a story or a humorous ruse. Due to a reservation mixup at the car agency, I drove to Berea in a shiny, metallic-blue Toyota MR2, a hot little sportscar that seemed a little out of place in the quiet college town. Rudy just had to borrow it. "There are some old guys I have coffee with every day. I'm going to drive up and tell them it's my car. Shake 'em up a little." They believed him, for a while at least, and marched out to admire the car, talk about cylinders and gears, while commenting about old goats who won't grow up.

Later, Daphne asked how he was going to explain the car's absence when I left. "I'm going to tell them you made me take it back. They'll believe that." Afterward, he admitted he probably gave everything away when he answered a question about the cost of the car with "I'd give my pickup for the car and $200."

I had hoped to meet Rude ever since I began teaching myself turning in North Carolina about 15 years ago. His work was pictured in magazines or shown in the Southern Highlands Guild shops, and I knew he was making a living at it, just as I wanted to do. I copied some of his plywood-lamination bowls and rolling pins, and his distinctive candleholders, but I

To make a distinctively Osolnik-style candlestick, form two cones, cutting in from each end toward the narrow stem. The top cone is one-third the length of the stock, which should be straight-grained to prevent the stem from breaking.

never got the candlesticks right.

The difference, Rude told me, is that he shaves the stems thinner than his imitators and cuts a slight curve on the top and bottom cones. He's made at least 150,000 of these candlesticks, which helped pay his children's college tuitions. The design is simple—the top cone is one-third the length of the stock, the bottom two-thirds, but each one is a little different and has a little different shape. Rude consistently turns one every five minutes. He often began turning at 4 AM, four hours before he had to leave to teach his first class, and he knew the time was up when he'd finished 48 candlesticks. (Incidentally, be careful if he says, "we'll get an early start in the morning." He means it.) To save time on spindles like the candlesticks, Rude doesn't even stop the lathe to remove and chuck on new pieces. The secret is in having a delicate touch and using a fine spur center. He made a believer of me, and I'm going to try it again, as soon as my fingers stop stinging.

Little details like the stem of the candlestick—the elegance of a slender form, a subtle curve or line cut to reveal the natural beauty of the wood—abound in Rude's work. His output as a turner over the years is astounding, yet each piece has a certain individuality that comes from Rude's enthusiasm for the wood and his joy in revealing its beauty. He's a craftsman's production turner. Not only is he enthusiastic about the work he produces, he delights in the process and coming up with clever ways to produce. There was no pretentious posturing, no art babble—just two guys

who like wood enjoying the work. That's a feeling I often find stifled in a world of art objects and woodworkers who pride themselves on working within tolerances that would challenge a machinist.

Rude has no secrets. He'll show you every technique he knows, if you're interested, all the while stressing there's no one right way to do any turning. Experiment and have fun as you develop your own style and technique. Don't do too much measuring. Use reference points on your tools, such as the distance from the bandsaw table edge to the blade, or the length of your thumb or the width of your hand instead of rulers. If the diameter of your lathe's tailstock is ½ in., use that as a guide for estimating spindle diameters. When making duplicates, use completed objects to guide your eye, rather than taking measurements. Simple, commonsense tricks. Try them and see how relaxing spindle turning becomes, and how much more of you goes into the turning.

Be warned though. Rude makes everything seem easier than it is. He's been at it a long time. He grinds high-speed steel bars to make his own turning tools, for example. Each tool looks like a roundnose scraper with a 30° bevel on the bottom and a flute cut into the top to help clear shavings. In Rude's hands they cut, not scrape, and they do everything effortlessly. When I tried it, though, I found the long bevel a little awkward and caught the tool a couple of times. I discovered it pulled and tore much the way a badly placed skew did. The tool's so versatile that it's worth a little practice.

One thing I like about Rude's tools is their beefy 1½-in.-dia. handles. Rude explained that a small handle encourages you to clench the tool tightly and this hampers smooth cutting. If you hold the tool as if you were shaking hands with a person, with your thumb on the top of the tool, and relax your grip, you'll do better work with less effort. Little pointers like that kept cropping up all day long. One of his former students, a woodworker in Berea, told me Rude had always been like that. He continually came up with efficient, if somewhat unorthodox, methods to get the job done.

One day a pickup drove up to Rude's shop and a man and his wife got out. Folks downtown had given them directions and said Rude wouldn't mind seeing him. The man had an idea for a new sharpening system. As Rude was talking to the man, his wife softly said "My husband thinks it's an honor to walk on the same concrete as that man." That about sums it up. □

Dick Burrows is an associate editor of Fine Woodworking.

Diameters can be cut using calipers and a parting tool. Short sleeves are safer, because a hidden defect or split in the work can catch fabric. As the production run proceeds, diameters can be gauged visually, according to how deep the tool penetrates the work.

Production Tips from an Architectural Turner

Working fast without sacrificing quality

by Mark A. Knudsen

What's an architectural turner? That's a question I would hardly have known to ask when I first started turning 20 years ago. Today, I'd say it's someone who turns parts of buildings—work ranging from thimble-size multiples to columns 16 in. in diameter and 15 ft. long. In this article, I'd like to focus on some of the fine points I've learned about architectural turning—an overview of the ways a production turner thinks about his work, his time and his tools.

The challenge in this craft is not ultimate workmanship and technique. You are not turning status pieces or something to go into a display case in a museum. In fact, the opposite can be true. One time I decided to turn a set of stair balusters with a perfect, skew-burnished surface from one end to the other. My aim was to match the surface I'd read about in books and seen on some decorative turnings. I felt pretty proud of myself when the work was picked up, but I heard about it in a hurry from the finishers. They couldn't get the stain to penetrate the burnished

surface, they suspected that not even paint would stick, and they thought I'd lost my mind to turn like that.

In short, architectural woodturning is a craft where your artistic sensibilities are mostly directed toward rescaling proportions and making faithful copies of existing work. The name of the game is economy—in every stage of the operation—from handling stock and laying out, to making the best use of your tools, to knowing when the job is done. Much of the success in production turning relates directly to the first things beginning turners learn: Keep your bevel rubbing and your tool edge sharp. When you forget one of the basics, you are asking for spoiled work. Inspiration? Pick up your tools and work.

False economy—Every client has a budget, and this determines how much time can be spent for turning. It also affects how accurately you lay out and center the stock, and how precisely you can afford to duplicate the pattern. You also have to account for

From *Fine Woodworking* magazine (January 1988) 68:48-51

he time needed to prepare the stock from planks, including rips to the lumberyard. As long as you can get the client to understand the compromises involved, there should be no problems. But don't try to save money in the wrong place, in using low-quality wood. This will detract from the look of the finished work, take longer to prepare and turn, and result in much more waste. Many times, poor wood is full of tension that is released when the lumber is sawn into turning squares. The piece bows, turns rough, costs more in sandpaper and requires more time all along the line.

In any case, when sizing wood I usually allow some extra all around the square for bowing, which may be caused by uneven moisture content and/or internal tension. This might be as much as 3/16 in. for long oak balusters; for nice walnut or pine, it might be just a planing allowance. If the first cut from the edge of a board bows a lot, I'll flip the board over and rip from the other edge. It is best to let the wood rest a couple of days after sawing so it can stabilize before planing, although deadlines don't always allow this luxury. A way around the problem is to cut an hour's worth of wood at a time. It will not spring too much in an hour, although it may after it's been turned.

Preliminary marking—The baluster in this article exhibits typical features: There are square pummels at the ends, a center ball and symmetrical vase shapes. These elements are separated by coves and lists, which are also called listels or fillets. To mark out where the pummels end, I line up a number of blanks evenly, then use a carpenter's square to mark them all at once. To be sure the line shows clearly when the work turns, I usually rotate each piece 90° and mark a second side the same way.

It's necessary to center the work accurately, so the turned parts of the spindle will line up evenly with the pummels. For most work, you can do this simply by holding a pencil in your fingers and marking in from all four sides to draw a little box in the center. Then fit the work on the headstock and tailstock by eye. For most woods used in this trade—cherry, walnut, poplar, maple, basswood and the even-grained pines—you don't have to drill center holes. The exception is when diameters are very small and precise and/or you are turning a wood like oak, with alternating hard and soft grain that may cause the headstock and tailstock to drift off center.

Snug the work up in the lathe by cranking the tailstock until the drive spurs hold without chattering. Do this with the lathe running; the vibration seems to help seat the spurs. When you get the hang of it, you won't bother to turn the lathe off when removing one piece and mounting another—the trick is not to drill the centerholes. As soon as the points of the headstock and tailstock grip, let go of the work and it will slowly begin to pick up speed. If it looks off-center, this is the time to knock it true. Then snug the tailstock to engage the drive spurs. Don't overdo the tailstock pressure—too much will cause the work to bow when it gets toward final size, and this will promote the washboard surface called ribbing, or roping. Also, on a light-duty lathe, you might push the bearings right out of the headstock.

If I'm starting a design from scratch, I draw the shapes carefully full-size on a wooden pattern so the client has something to verify and I have something to take dimensions from with calipers. If I have an existing baluster to duplicate, however, I make a very simple pattern, as shown in figure 1 on the next page. It makes sense to draw as few reference lines as possible. If you have too many lines on a pattern, it is easy to cut to the wrong one.

I mark the low and high points on the vases and the areas that will be wasted for the lists and coves. The exact sizes of the minor elements in the design can be gauged by eye very accurately by comparing them to the sizes of the tool used to cut them.

My shopmade spindle lathe has speeds from 400 RPM to 1400 RPM. General turning, such as a porch baluster, is done in the 900 RPM to 1000 RPM range. After years of turning for a living, I turn at the slowest speed that will let me take wood off quickly. High-speed turning tends to reduce the feel of the cut so that, without realizing it, you may slip into taking a rough, scraping cut rather than shearing the wood cleanly. This risks tearout and will dull tools quickly.

Similarly, practice on poplar or maple to learn. You can push softer woods around and think you are doing things right, but poplar or maple will show you the truth. Practice with carbon steel tools, not high-speed steel—you'll burn them blue until you learn to cut correctly, but at least they will be quick to resharpen, and that's something you have to practice as well.

Sharpening—I don't like to grind right up to the cutting edge so that the sparks dance on it. I'm sure these sparks soften the steel. I stop a little short so the steel is left hard, and then whet to the edge with a small medium-grit stone.

I vary the bevel shapes on my gouges according to what woods I'm turning–longer for pine, shorter for oak. It is important that the bevel be smooth and unfaceted. Otherwise, the cutting will be erratic when the gouge is rolled, and you will subject yourself to many mysterious catches. For the same reason, file out any nicks in your tool rest and round the long bottom edges on your skews so they slide freely.

I make it a point to keep all my skew chisels at the same bevel angle, 25°. If the bevel angles vary, each skew will cut a little differently, and you'll never get the hang of cutting with any of them. A skew has to be razor sharp to work, and you might have to touch the edge up once a minute on some jobs. I've seen guys hone a skew edge to perfect sharpness, but then use the tool until it starts to smoke and the edge turns blue. There's no sense in that—if you have to push a skew, stop to hone it. Spit on your whetstone, refresh the edge, and get back to turning. The few seconds this takes may just save you all the time you have invested in the piece already.

I keep my whetstone handy in the breast pocket of my jacket. I used to wear a regular apron, but then I discovered pharmacists' jackets. They have a flap that closes tight around the front of your neck to keep shavings out. You can get them in a variety of styles—short-sleeve/long-sleeve, cotton/nylon, all colors—for about $12 at uniform stores. They have designs with side pockets as well, but these fill up with shavings too fast. I also keep a chunk of paraffin in the pocket—if you rub the tool rest and the tool with paraffin, it will feel like your tool just got sharper.

Use a tool rest as long as the work whenever possible, and be sure it is parallel to the work so you can use it as a reference point to gauge how uniform a cylinder is. Another benefit of a long tool rest is that for some jobs you can mark the pattern lines directly on the rest with fine-tipped markers—in which case, you don't need to make a pattern.

Feeling the cut—The pummels are cut with a skew in a series of V-cuts, made by arcing the long point into the work. You should not have to gauge the depth of the cut with calipers or by stopping the lathe to look. Instead, just listen and feel the cutting action: It starts as a series of tick-tick-tick cuts, with the point of the skew hitting the corners of the wood. As soon as the ticking smooths out to a steady cut, you have cut down to the round. With a ¾-in. to 1¼-in. roughing gouge, now round the cylinder down evenly from one end to the other. In many common designs, the diameter of this cylinder will be the diameter of all the high spots in the finished turning. This means that your roughing gouge should be kept sharp, because any tearout may show in the finished turning. Again, don't stop the lathe to check for roundness, just lay the back of the gouge on top of the work and listen for clicks. Next, place the pattern up against the rotating work and mark the reference diameters with a pencil.

With calipers set to the diameter, use a parting tool to cut the profile depths at the center of the work. If you have only a few turnings to do, with a number of different diameters, it pays to have plenty of calipers, laid out in the order of use. Color-code them with paint or bands of tape so you can tell which is which; you can color-code the pattern too. If you have several dozen of the same part to turn, however, you should be able to dispense with calipers after turning the first few—just note how deep the parting tool goes, then use that as your gauge.

The reason to start in the center is that after the ends have been turned down, the work will be much more likely to whip. So turn the ball, then turn the adjacent ends of the vases. Leave the coves surrounding the ball until the baluster is almost completely turned. There's no sense in making the workpiece too thin so early. The coves will be a light, last cut, and you can hold the turning to stabilize it. If you examine the photographs, you'll see there is no one way to hold your tools. Most times, on long work, I'll be holding the wood as it turns. This dampens vibrations and allows a surer cut.

Getting the most from your tools—By changing your grip and supporting the work, you can do a surprising variety of work with any tool. A roughing-out gouge can take a smooth shearing cut in the manner of a skew, and a skew can make square wood round. This last operation can be dangerous, however, so I wouldn't advise beginners to try it. Wear all your safety gear, too.

Parting tools can turn beads like a skew: You roll the tool over so the axis of the tool points right at the center of the work. If your parting tool is tall in relation to its cutting width, as most narrow parting tools are, the job is more difficult because the cutting edge pivots away from its point of contact with the tool rest—but it can still be done and it's worth practicing. Similarly, skew can be used in the same manner as a parting tool, removing an incredible amount of wood very quickly. Practice this with small skews at first, because a catch can knock the wood right out of the lathe. Another idea is to turn with the long point leading; this requires that the tool be almost parallel to the work. The cut is useful when you are having trouble with ribbing.

The idea behind tool versatility is dexterity, not strength. Get the tool pointed in the right direction, and change the angles to keep it pointing in the right directions as the shapes emerge.

Don't look at the edge of the tool, but at the top profile of the turning, so you can see how the profile is developing. You wouldn't look right in front of the tires when you were driving, would you? When you watch the top, you can see the form take shape in relation to the whole as well as the individual section. You can learn to know what is going on at the cutting edge of the tool by the sound and the feel, provided you learn to hold the tool lightly.

If you have to fight any tool, you are doing something wrong. Keep a light grip with both hands. I've thought a long time about exactly how to describe the amount of grip needed. I've come up with three ways, and you can choose the one that makes the most sense to you: Squeeze about as hard as you would dare to squeeze a rotten egg; or about as hard as you would screw in the last bit of a turn when changing a light bulb; or, for the engineers among the readers, about as hard as you can squeeze a Kellogg's shredded wheat bisquit before it crumbles.

Good technique produces good surfaces. I'm not sure what the standards are in other parts of the country, but when I send out work that's to be stained, it's ready to be stained; if it's to be painted, it's ready to paint. I generally don't send out work with any tearout. If a rough spot won't sand out, I'll fill it myself with wood putty. If a piece is to be stained and I catch my tool in it, I've bought it. If the wood is not really bad, my failure rate is about three pieces in 100, which I feel is a good compromise between speed and accuracy.

There are exceptions to a good finish. I've seen some restoration jobs where the new work was so much better than the old

Staff

Fig. 1: Simplifying production turning

1. Cut pummels with skew.
2. Turn to cylinder with roughing gouge.
3. Waste to diameter of center fillets with parting tool.
4. Turn ball and ends of vases with skew.
5. Part to low point (LP) diameter on vase.
6. Turn vase with roughing gouge and skew.
7. Waste to fillets at ends with parting tool.
8. Shape with parting tool.
9. Turn remaining beads and coves with ¼-in. gouge.

Undercut listels so paint will not fill and soften profiles.

High points along this design are full diameter of roughed-out cylinder.

Place pencil in notches to mark reference points on cylinder.

Pattern is cut ¼ in. shorter than distance between pummels so it can be held against turning cylinder without catching.

Hand positions

Left, on long work with small diameters near the center, it is best to cut the main shapes at the center first, then work toward the ends. If the ends were cut to size first, then the work would whip. The author steadies his hand against the tool rest for extra control.

The roughing gouge, right, takes a paring cut that will later be cleaned lightly with a skew. Note that the gouge, with the tool rest acting as fulcrum, is levered against the forearm, while the right hand damps vibration in the work. This forearm support helps avoid a ribbed, or washboard, cut by relieving much of the pressure between the gouge's bevel and the work.

Lower left, fingers extended under the tool rest and wrapped behind the work help to dampen vibration. In addition to backing up the work, the author's fingers can gauge the roughness or smoothness of the surface being turned.

Below is shown yet another grip; the tool is controlled by both hands and the left forearm. This is the final truing and undercutting of the listels, or fillets, at each side of the center coves. A light sanding will finish the job and leave a uniform surface properly textured for painting.

that it stood right out from 20 feet away. When I do a restoration job, I try to get a look at the site to see the standards the work was turned to originally. If there are skew marks and tearout, then that's what I give the customer.

Finishing up—My final surface for most painted work comes from 100-grit or 150-grit sandpaper—not regular production paper, but a type called metalcloth P 100-J (available from Econ-Abrasives, P.O. Box 865021, Plano, Tex. 75086; 800-367-4101, 214-377-9779). It's resin-bonded and cloth-backed for durability. I'd say it outlasts paperbacked sandpaper 10 to one. But the real reason I like it is because the grit size is very uniform—that's what the "P" in the code means; the "J" refers to the cloth back. The 100-grit cuts fast, but leaves a surface you'd expect from ordinary 150-grit paper; the 150-grit is like 220-grit production paper.

To use the sandpaper, you have to soften the backing so it will conform to the curves in the work: I cut a strip about 2 in. wide, then pull the backing over the edge of my tool rest at a variety of angles to break it in. When I'm sanding, I usually keep a small, hard kitchen sponge in my hand to back up the paper and put the pressure where it's needed. To make a hard kitchen sponge, wet one then let it dry out. The sponge flattens out to about ⅛ in. in thickness after a while. If you fold the sandpaper over the sponge's edge, it will conform to a very small cove shape. You can fold the sponge double or triple for whatever other coves are in the work, then all the coves will sand out uniformly.

In closing, I'd like to add a story proving that if you can't win them all, you can at least try. One time I was asked to turn a set of spindles with ½-in.-dia. tenons on the ends, which I did. The next day I got a call from the job foreman: The tenons didn't fit the ½-in. holes, and the carpenters were all spending time shaving them down. I didn't feel I could be responsible for what every manufacturer's ½-in. drill bit actually was, and even less so for the size hole it cut after resharpening or getting bent. So these days I insist that anybody asking for a particular diameter tenon send me a few holes with the order—a piece of the same wood as the job, drilled by the carpenter who would do the work, using the bit he'd use on the job. Haven't had a complaint since. □

Mark A. Knudsen's shop is in Des Moines, Iowa.

Turning Thin and Finishing with Epoxy

by David Lory

My turning tools are made from an Armalloy alloy. I get the bits from the Richard Ela Co., 744 Williamson St., Madison, Wis. 53703. I grind them to a 15° relief angle and secure them in long, square-sectioned shafts with two allen screws (photo, below). I have two tools, one a roundnose and the other a spearpoint chisel. They require honing several times during the course of turning a single bowl.

I do all of my turning on the outboard side of the lathe. I get the block rounded at the slowest speed. Then, still working on the outside, I shape the plug into the largest bowl possible. Moving my tool rest around, I turn the inside. On larger and deeper bowls I use a ½-in. electric drill with a 2½-in. wood bit to drill out the center before turning it. When turning the inside, I cut from the rim toward the center. This compresses the wood fibers and allows me to turn the bowl to a finished thickness of ⅛ in. I stop at stages to examine the grain, so I can work with it and bring out the best it has to offer. Fancy cuts detract from its natural flow. The interior grain generally determines the shape of a bowl, as

that's its most visible part. I then return to the outside and reshape it to follow the contour of the inside. On these last cuts the lathe is speeded up as much as possible without the wood chattering.

To prevent checking and to reduce tear-out and pecking, I turn the bowl as quickly as possible. And once I begin, I carry through to the end without interruption. If I have to put my work aside temporarily, I cover the bowl with a wet cloth to keep it from drying out.

Bowls can fly apart while being turned. Some break because of unseen flaws in the wood; others may break apart if they're gouged too deeply. Excessive dryness may cause some to crack while being sanded. Some bowls will fly apart for no apparent reason. The turner should take every precaution in selecting his blanks, in controlling their moisture content and in properly tooling the rotating plug.

After a bowl is turned to shape, I sand the outside, starting with 80 grit and working up to 220. I return to the inside, make the finishing cut, and sand it. The bowl should be ⅛ in. thick at the sides and ³⁄₁₆ in. to ¼ in. thick at the

base. This thickness is important because its uniformity helps prevent checking when it's dried to about 0% moisture. I cut the bowl off the glue block with a handsaw, leaving the bottom somewhat thicker so if it does warp I can sand it flat without ruining the bowl. If I did a good job of turning, the bowl will not need any hand-sanding.

Now the bowl is ready to be finished. Instead of the usual oils and varnishes, I use a heavy-duty epoxy-resin paint, No. 100 Clear Epoxy (Peterson Chemical Corp., 1104 S. River St., Sheboygan, Wis. 53081). It comes in two parts—paint and hardener. When it dries it doesn't become brittle, and bowls will flex rather than break. It is clear and there is no discoloration of the wood. It meets federal requirements for use with food, and hot (up to 250°F) and cold foods can be served without bad effects. This finish is resistant to acids, detergents and alcohol. To prepare the bowls for the application of epoxy, I put them in the oven for five hours at 150°. Some of them will warp greatly during the baking; all of them will warp in different ways and to differ-

Square-sectioned steel shaft securely holds replaceable metalcutting tool bits. Armalloy is harder than ordinary high-speed steel and will hold a sharp edge longer. You can grind it on a fine aluminum-oxide wheel.

Some of Lory's bowls turned from locally available burls and stumps. Epoxy finish, which completely penetrates the ⅛-in. thick walls, makes the bowls flexible and durable.

Using a steel-hafted chisel, Lory takes a cut off a rotating bowl blank. Tooling the alternating long and short-grain surfaces produces both shavings and dust.

ent extents. This gives each piece character and life.

After the baking, I resand the bottoms on a belt sander to make them flat. Because the bowls may pick up moisture, I rebake them. Then I take a few out of the oven at a time and epoxy them with a 1-in. brush, which minimizes runs. For durability, I use four or five coats. The first is mixed with 40% A (paint), 40% B (hardener) and 20% thinner. The thinner makes for deeper penetration, but any more than 20% would make the mixture useless. For subsequent coats I use 50% A and 50% B. These coats are applied every other day with a light sanding (using 320-grit aluminum-oxide paper) in between. I apply the epoxy to the inside of the bowl first, and when that is dry to the touch, I do the outside. Good ventilation and a mask are important. Though the toxicity is low, it can be irritating. At 75°F and 60% relative humidity, the finish will dry dust-free in 30 minutes. It will dry to touch in two hours and cure hard in seven days. To speed up curing time, place the bowl in an oven five minutes after applying the finish, and bake it for 20 minutes at 180°F.

The epoxy leaves a high-gloss finish when it hardens, and I feel this detracts from the natural beauty of the wood. To get back the natural patina and glow of the wood, I spend several hours rubbing down each bowl by hand. The epoxy finish is not easy to sand because special care must be taken not to sand through the fourth layer into the third. If this happens, a dull spot will appear and the bowl must be repainted. I rub the bowl with 320-grit aluminum-oxide paper, 00 steel wool, 0000 steel wool and then with rottenstone. Rubbing brings out the true beauty of the wood. Epoxy makes the wood stronger than it was before and much more useful. The combination of beauty and practicality make the bowls truly functional pieces of art, which I believe will last well beyond my lifetime. □

Tool Rests and Turning Tactics

by Bob Gilson

Turner Harry Nohr showed me how to make a tool support for outboard turning from a brake drum with three feet welded onto it. The vertical post can be 2-in. steel pipe with a ½-in. by 1-in. by 12-in. steel tool rest welded to the top. Make your cuts toward the lathe, from the rim to the base of the bowl, to load the wood compressively and reduce chatter. Good lathe speeds for bowls are 900 RPM for a 6-in. turning, 600 RPM for 12-in., and 350 RPM for 18-in. bowls. At this point you will find out how solidly your lathe is mounted to the floor or wall (yes, wall). Sometimes it is necessary to run a brace from the lathe table behind the headstock to the wall to reduce vibration. If your lathe has enough power and is well mounted, it is possible to remove ¼ in. at a pass, but this isn't necessary. As you make the first cuts, the outside of the bowl will be out of round from sawing and mounting. Take care to avoid too heavy a cut on the invisible spinning projections. The angle of the tool relative to the cut should remain constant, with the trailing edge clearing the work by ¹⁄₁₆ in. As the inside corners are turned, it is important to be aware at all times of the clearance to prevent the heel of the tool from catching the work. The smaller the clearance without catching, the smoother the cut. The finish cut with these tools is not as smooth as from a regular woodturning tool, but they make possible the thin sections. When using a floor tripod, it is usually necessary to plant one of your own feet on it to hold it in place.

The following steps will help you avoid most problems of warpage and vibration when turning a bowl 12 in. or larger. Rough out the outside of the bowl to within ⅛ in. of the desired shape. Then rough out the inside, leaving a wall thickness of 1 in. (The outside may be out of round at this point.) Next, sharpen the tool and take a finish cut of ¹⁄₁₆ in. on the outside. Rough-sand the outside with a glass-foam sanding block (a respirator should be worn), and then fine-sand in stages from 120 to 280 grit. Now turn the inside of the bowl ¼ in. thick to a depth of about 2½ in. The wall should be slightly thicker at the end of the cut to allow for blending with the next cut. Then sand the same as the outside.

On a larger bowl another 2½-in. step would be turned, but on a 12-in. bowl the rest of the inside may now be turned to ¼ in. to blend with the previous cut. Start by removing the wood nearest the lip. A caliper is useful for measuring wall and bottom thicknesses. The two cuts are blended with the sanding block and then finish-sanded in stages. The outside of the bowl may be ¼ in. or more out of round at this point as the wood dries. The bowl is then sawn off the mounting block as close to the base as possible. For a beginner the total time for turning a 12-in. bowl might by 4½ hours. With experience, and a good wood like shagbark hickory, you may cut the time down to 2 hours. Once you take a finish cut, the bowl should be completely turned as quickly as possible, as there is the likelihood that it will warp overnight, even if covered with a plastic

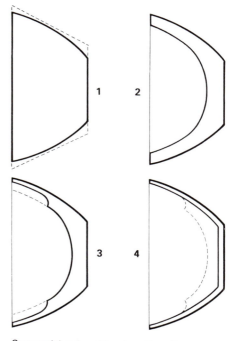

Sequential order of turning. Centrifugal forces might cause the bowl to distort or even to fly apart if the rim is not cut first, leaving mass of turning in center.

bag that has moistened wood chips in it.

The bowl at this time may have a 20% moisture content. Bowls that will fit into an oven should be baked at 150° for two hours to dry them completely. Larger bowls must be left several months to air-dry. The remainder of the mounting block is then sanded off and the bottom sanded flat. If there are any flaws, such as those that frequently occur in a burl, fill them with a filler, then sand.

Finish the bowl with four coats of clear epoxy varnish. After the epoxy has cured for about four weeks, sand it with 240-grit paper (for light woods) or 360 (for darker woods) to smooth out any irregularities and take off the gloss. Then continue to polish with steel wool and pumice followed with rottenstone. □

Turning chair and stool spindles

by Mac Campbell

Turning spindles and rungs between centers is difficult because their thin diameter makes them whip badly. Furthermore, they have to be virtually identical, otherwise you'll get bogged down in a nightmare of tedious fitting on each chair or stool at assembly.

I avoid this problem and speed up the process by using shopmade dowel cutters to rough the spindles or rungs to a consistent size, then finish turn them with a block plane followed by sanding. My dowel cutters are simply rectangular wooden blocks with a hole bored through one edge to allow the dowel blank to be fed through. An angled rabbet cut into one face of the block opens up a slot, allowing the cutting edge (a bench chisel clamped to the jig) to do its work. The dowel cutter can be hand-fed or guided along the lathe's tool rest.

To bore the hole, I mount the block on a faceplate and bore with a bit equal to the diameter of the finished dowel. Then, I use a square-edge scraper to enlarge the opening, creating a cone-shaped entrance hole slightly larger than the diameter of the turning blank I'll be using. The angled rabbet, shown at right, is cut on the tablesaw with the blade tipped at an angle equal to the slope of the cone.

I made one dowel cutter that accepts a square ¾-in. blank on one end and reduces it to an ¹¹⁄₁₆-in. dia. To produce the ½-in.-dia. tenons on the end of these turnings, I made another dowel cutter that has an alignment block mounted to it with an ¹¹⁄₁₆-in.-dia. hole bored through it (see figure 1). This hole is centered over the ½-in.-dia. exit hole to ensure proper alignment as the tenon is cut. To help align the exit hole with the hole in the block, turn a spindle ½-in.-dia. on one end and ¹¹⁄₁₆-in.-dia. on the other. Slip the spindle into the dowel cutter, then slip the alignment block over it. A screw that runs through the top of the dowel cutter stops the dowel's passage through the cutter, forming the tenon on its end. A third dowel cutter reduces ¹¹⁄₁₆-in.-dia. turnings to ⅜ in. dia. for tapering chair spindles or dowels on stool rungs.

To turn the dowel blank as the cutter is fed along its length, I've built some drive centers that attach to the lathe's headstock. These are basically simple wooden chucks. Each consists of a wooden block screwed to a faceplate. For the largest one, I chop a square hole to accept a square dowel blank. A smaller drive center has a stepped hole made by first boring a ½-in. hole followed by a ¹⁵⁄₃₂-in. hole. To keep the blank

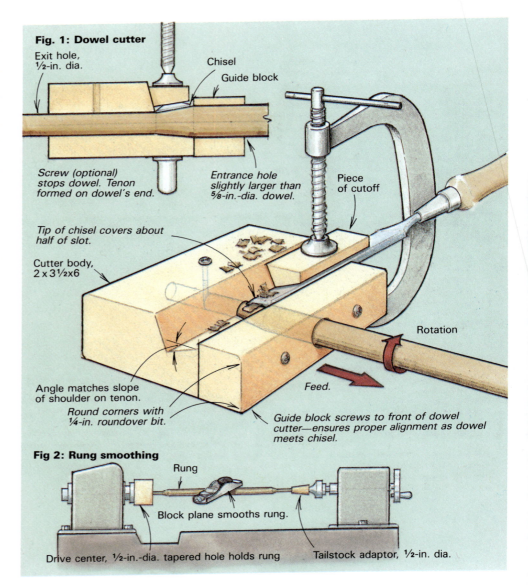

Fig. 1: Dowel cutter

Exit hole, ½-in. dia.

Chisel

Guide block

Screw (optional) stops dowel. Tenon formed on dowel's end.

Entrance hole slightly larger than ⅝-in.-dia. dowel.

Piece of cutoff

Tip of chisel covers about half of slot.

Cutter body, 2 x 3½ x 6

Angle matches slope of shoulder on tenon.

Round corners with ¼-in. roundover bit.

Rotation

Feed.

Guide block screws to front of dowel cutter—ensures proper alignment as dowel meets chisel.

Fig 2: Rung smoothing

Rung

Block plane smooths rung.

Drive center, ½-in.-dia. tapered hole holds rung

Tailstock adaptor, ½-in. dia.

firmly on the tailstock, I made a tailstock adaptor from a 2-in.-long wood plug, with a ½-in.-dia. hole bored in one end.

This is how the setup works. I prefer to split turning blanks from the tree, but if I can't use split stock, I mill the blanks to ¾-in. square and cut them to length. A C-clamp holds the chisel to the cutter and should be set to cover about half the slot. With the lathe set at about 1,350 RPM, I insert a blank into the square drive center and hold up the blank's other end with the dowel cutter. I turn the lathe on and, reaching over the turning with my right hand, feed the cutter down the turning. This isn't as risky as it sounds; I've found that after some practice, I could turn the spindle down freehand, that is without supporting the dowel cutter on the tool rest. Feed the cutter down the blank until it hits the drive center. If the cutter is sup-

ported, you can go just about up to the drive center. If the turning jams in the cutter's exit hole, knock the chisel in a little deeper. If that doesn't work, slice off a little more of the cone on the tablesaw or shave it down with a rabbet plane and try the setup again.

Stop the lathe, remove the dowel cutter and, using the same procedure, cut the ½-in. tenon on the end of the turning. Work up a batch of these turnings and then clamp the ¹¹⁄₁₆-in. cutter to the workbench with the exit hole facing you, and clamp down the ½-in. cutter. Feed the turning through the cutter, grip its tenon in a portable drill, reverse the drill and draw the remaining length of the turning through the cutter. Only a very short length of the dowel should remain to be turned—the portion of the dowel inside the drive center and the length of dowel

From *Fine Woodworking* magazine (March 1988) 69:45-47

For boring rung holes, Campbell uses a 2x4 with a hole bored through it as a guide for his drill. Demonstrated here on a Windsor chair, the technique works on stools too. To avoid splintering, the auger bit (extended by a pipe welded to it) is retracted when the pilot screw breaks through. The holes are then finished by boring from the other side.

inside the cutter that the chisel could not reach.

I reverse the drill and feed the far end of each turning into the cutter to produce the ½-in. tenon on the other end. Next, using the ½-in. tailstock adaptor, and the lathe running at 2,200 RPM, I smooth the turning with a block plane and finish surfacing it with a belt sander and 120-grit paper.

You can also use this method to produce spindles that taper from their midpoint to the tenons by cutting ⅜-in. tenons on the ends of the $^{11}/_{16}$-in. turnings, then tapering the turnings with the block plane.

When I have to bore the holes for rungs,

Gallery of stools

The dictionary describes a stool as a seat, usually without back or arms, supported by a pedestal or three or four legs. But in reality, stools come in all shapes and sizes and can be built for any purpose using almost any kind of joinery and finish. Once you've abandoned a preconceived idea of what a stool should look like (it has three or four skinny legs and a round seat), the design possibilities broaden considerably. The photos here show some of the stools we've encountered recently and are a good cross section of recent stool design.

Built for sitting at a 42-in.-tall counter, the cherry stool at left was built by James Hutchinson of Mohnton, Penn. Its back legs are bent from tapered laminations, while its front legs are bandsawn from 8/4 stock. The crown rail is splined and mitered, and the stretchers are bandsawn and assembled with mortise-and-tenon joints. Its seat is 18 in. wide and 10 in. deep. "Seating Planes" is the title of these stools, above, built by Fred Puksta of Rochester, N.Y. The stool on the left is made of white ash with ebony inlay. Puksta built the stool on the right with ebonized cherry, then inlaid the legs with a line of multi-colored telephone wire. Both are 30 in. tall, with 24-in. by 24-in. bases. The rungs are ash covered with rubber tubing, and the stools are assembled with bridle and mortise-and-tenon joints.

I revert to a tool I last used for log-cabin building. It is a ½-in. auger bit welded onto the end of a ⅜-in. OD steel rod. The whole setup, about 20 in. long, is chucked into my drill.

Here's how I use it. I dry assemble the chair or stool right-side-up on my bench. With a pair of dividers, I measure the rung's hole positions relative to the benchtop and then poke a mark at the correct location. I turn a 2x4 scrap into a boring guide by boring through its wide face with the extended auger bit. With the guide block clamped in my vise, I line up the bit—sighting along the shaft for the right angle—and begin boring the rung hole. I stop boring just as the auger's lead-screw breaks through the leg. I turn the piece around and bore through the other three legs, stopping each time as the pilot breaks through. I go back and finish boring the holes from the other side. The difference in angle when you approach the hole from the other side makes no difference if you put the auger's leadscrew in the exit hole.

After all the rung holes are bored, I remove the front or back legs, insert the rungs and reassemble. I then turn the chair 90° and bore for the center rung.

This system is for through-wedged joints; if you prefer a blind or fox-wedged joint, set a depth stop on the auger bit.

The setup is very accurate and nearly foolproof. One caution, however: Because the leg you are boring into is at an angle, file back the auger bit's cutting lip. Otherwise, the cutting lip will contact the downhill side of the leg first and start cutting before the spurs have a chance to score ahead of it, tearing out the hole instead of cutting cleanly. □

Mac Campbell builds custom furniture in Harvey Station, N.B., Canada.

Photo: Charlie Swanson

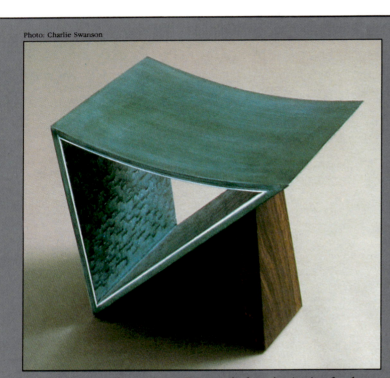

Photo: D'Wayne Blackdog

Charlie Swanson of Providence, R.I., used a bent lamination for the seat of his 17-in.-tall stool, above. He covered the seat with gesso and then textured it with a rubber stamp. To create the luminescent-band edge treatment, Swanson wiped away the Japan-color surface paint, revealing the gesso beneath. Bill Sloane's stool, below left, took 200 hours to build; it was the first piece of furniture he built. It's 20 in. tall and has legs tenoned into the slats of its 14-in. by 14-in. seat. The stool's seat and legs are maple; the stretchers, cherry. It's finished with linseed oil and turpentine. The 4-legged cherry stool, below right, was built as a one-day project by Stephen Proctor, dean of woodworking at the Wendell Castle School in Scottsville, N.Y. Proctor used it to demonstrate shaper techniques to his students. The legs were profiled on the shaper using a flush trim bit guided by a template and then tapered on the planer. With a felt-tipped pen, Proctor sketched in the ballet slippers on the legs.

Robert Sonday of Free Union, Va., made this traditional Shaker weaver's stool from untraditional Wenge and then gave it an oil finish. The stool is 38 in. high, 19½ in. wide and 14¾ in. deep with a 26-in.-high seat woven with cotton tape.

The Granville Mill
Turning out bowls by the bunch

by Richard Ewald

Stuart Boudwell begins removing the bowl blank from a chunk of maple mounted on a bowl lathe that was built when the plant was founded in the 1860s and that has been in continuous production ever since.

A mechanical bowl machine can be a depressing sight for one-of-a-kind bowl turners. Theoretically, with the pneumatic-powered concentric cutters of a lathe, like the one shown above, you can turn a maple log into a roughed-out 22-in. bowl in about two minutes. In the next three minutes, you could be looking at five more bowls, all from the same chunk of wood, and each 2 in. smaller in diameter than the one that preceded it, like the bowls shown in the right photo on p. 25. In practice, it takes a little longer than that at Granville Manufacturing. But not much.

A short article in a Boston, Mass., newspaper about the 132-year-old bowl manufacturing plant in Granville, Vt., aroused my curiosity as to how the company produced a bowl every two minutes. It was late spring when I drove from my home in southern Vermont through the sparsely populated Rochester Valley into the north-central part of the state. I arrived at the Granville Mill and watched what may be the most crudely efficient and simple woodworking machine ever devised for making bowls.

A three-man crew has no problem averaging 350 bowls per eight-hour shift. Subtracting a half-hour for lunch, that breaks down to almost 47 bowls an hour, or a bowl about every minute and a quarter. With a projected total production this year of 150,000 bowls, Granville is probably the country's leading manufacturer of one-piece hardwood bowls. Looking at numbers like this over a period of more than 130 years, it's not difficult to believe that more one-piece wooden bowls have been turned on this spot than anywhere else.

This may sound very efficiently modern and high tech, but the bowl operation at Granville Manufacturing still has more of the flavor of a backwoods sawmill than a contemporary woodworking shop. Sixteen-foot maple and yellow birch logs are rolled into the shop, a long, dark tunnel of a workspace, where the tools include a 5-ft. chainsaw and hatchets. Piles of bark and damp shavings avalanche across the coarse concrete floor. Stuart Boudwell, who has shaped more than a half-million bowls in some nine years on the lathe, regularly stops working to politely answer the questions of the 3,000 to 4,000 annual visitors. At the lathe, Boudwell wears a green hard hat and a yellow slicker as he works in a chunky rain of chips and sweet maple sap. With a little tinkering now and again, he manages to keep things running just fine.

Kick starting the business—Granville's three operations include a quartersawn clapboard mill, an over-under sawmill making quartersawn spruce for piano sounding boards and violin tops, and the bowl shop. Although operations are going smoothly today, the business was suffering as it entered the 1980s. Several fires destroyed equipment and parts of the mill. The quality of the bowls had slipped. Big trees had become scarce and expensive; it takes about 175 years to grow a tree big enough to yield a 22-in. bowl. The business had become something of a captive to its own "old-timey" image. A hundred years ago, there was a greater demand for large wooden kitchen bowls for making bread and for mixing and serving food, and a minor market still exists in kosher kitchens. But

From *Fine Woodworking* magazine (January 1990) 80:53-55

Left: With a backhand knife, a worker removes the stub that remains after turning the outside of a bowl, while Boudwell begins the next cut that will form the inside of one bowl and the outside of the next smaller bowl. Above: the curved arm and tip of the cutting knife determine a bowl's size. The rectangular back plate that locks the arm to the lathe is hidden behind the blank.

most of the business shifted away from kitchen and restaurant suppliers to upscale gift shops and Granville hadn't made the transition. Granville Manufacturing needed a kick in the pants.

That swift foot arrived in 1981 when "retiring" business executive Bob Fuller and his family took over Granville. Fuller was formerly with Johnson & Johnson; his wife, Carol, had some experience with marketing in the New York City retail clothing industry. Fuller is a tall, outgoing fellow who is obviously excited about his second career and the opportunities to turn the mill operations around.

The heart of these operations is the bowl making, which begins with a stack of green logs piled outside the mill. Here, Merrill Johnson, 70, cuts 18-in. to 22-in. sections with a 5-ft., deck-mounted electric chain saw. To prevent the logs from drying out, Johnson frequently sprays them with water. After cutting the logs, he then rolls each section over and chalks out two or three straight lines on the endgrain, avoiding the heartwood and imperfections in the wood. A 5-ft. circular saw on a traveling carriage cuts each section longitudinally along these lines into two or three chunks each with an internal flat plane and a round, barked exterior. The flat side of each chunk is mounted on the lathe's screw-centered faceplate and an additional screw is driven into the chunk from the back of the plate.

Roots in the 19th century—The lathe that turns out today's bowls is the same lathe built when the plant was founded sometime in the 1860s by the brothers R. N. and Daniel Hemenway, of nearby Warren, Vt. And it's been reinvented by every Granville Manufacturing maintenance man since then. The lathe used to be hydraulically powered by the White River, which runs just behind the shed. Now an amazingly quiet 10-HP motor does the job. Old babbitt bearings have been replaced by ball bearings, and except for the shaft, all other mechanisms are pneumatically powered. These are the only significant changes the machine has undergone in more than 130 years, and as efficient as the lathe is when it runs true, it seldom does for long. The fallibility of this antique rescues the whole turning process from becoming merely another machine-based production setup. Constant human judgment and dexterity are required, and the piece being worked is always at risk.

Woodworkers and bowl makers sometimes speak of the buried shape within a tree, which is slowly revealed by removing all the

wood except the shape itself. This lathe does not entail that kind of gradual hollowing out to discover a contour. It's more like the rapid surgical excision of an imposed form. A sharp cutting edge swings into the workpiece like a squared-off gouge on the end of a massive grapefruit knife, shaping the inside of one bowl and the outside of the next smaller bowl at the same time, as shown in the photos above. This is repeated with a succession of knives of diminishing but concentric radii until only a small and partial sphere remains screwed to the faceplate.

Turning the bowls—Pumping one foot on a clutch like a race-car driver, Boudwell starts the first hooked knife into a fresh chunk of maple in a tentative manner, as shown in the photo on the previous page, well aware from experience that the eccentric edges on the chunk's outer shell could fly off once they are undercut.

The rough tool marks left by the lathe are removed in a series of sanding operations. A worker places bowls on a revolving table, which automatically belt sands the edge of each bowl.

Sometimes he'll stop the lathe completely and chop these hazards away with a hatchet. The clutch controls both the feed rate of the arm and the speed of the spindle. The first knife leaves an outer shell connected to the first bowl by the equivalent of a 1-in. dowel about ⅜ in. long. A smart smack with the palm of a hand separates the shell, and each new bowl from then on.

While Boudwell retracts the first knife, an assistant swings in a backhand knife from the other side and shaves the little nub off the bottom of the bowl. A pneumatic clamp makes changing knives as easy as switching cassettes in a tape deck. Then, Boudwell is ready for the next pass, shown in the left photo on the top of the facing page, that shapes the inside of the first bowl and the outside of the second bowl. When he notices that the wood is ripping or tearing or bowls are coming out thick or thin, Boudwell calls on the shop maintenance specialist, Michael Eramo. There's no factory rep to call when this quirky antique goes awry. Eramo is responsible for all the equipment in each of Granville's shops, but he spends nearly half of each day in the bowl mill, making knives completely from scratch, sharpening cutting edges and truing up the lathe.

Each knife has three parts: a rectangular back plate that is locked into the lathe, a curved arm that represents the contour of the bowl and a cutting edge at the tip that's ⅜ in. to 7/16 in. wide, which has more in common with a saw tooth than a chisel or a gouge (see the top, right photo on the facing page). When Eramo came on the job in 1985, tearing and pulling was a big problem. He reversed the cutting edge, putting the tip up. Perfecting the size and clearance of the ears and the rake of the tooth took him three months of experimentation, but eventually it reduced production losses from 40% to just 17%. A tip might last three weeks, with sharpening maybe twice each day.

Eramo trusts his eye to get the right curve to the arm and the proper elevation to the tip and then lets the first pass of the new arm reveal the accuracy of his setting. Because each knife must be parallel to the preceding knife for the bowls to have a uniform ⅝-in. wall thickness, the slightest eccentricity is immediately apparent. While the larger bowls may run closer to 11/16-in. wall thickness, Eramo has found that too many bowls are lost to checking if the walls are any thicker or thinner.

The bowls are moved in stacks from the lathe to a drying room. Until very recently, all of Granville's bowls were dried outside in unheated sheds. It took some six weeks in the summer and about four months in the winter to get the bowls down to the desired 12% moisture content (MC). Now they are stacked in an upstairs room kept between 60°F and 80°F. A small household humidifier is always pumping away. The more controlled drying conditions reduce losses during drying to about 4% and allow Granville to get the bowls through the drying process in 10 to 14 days year-round.

Yankee ingenuity—The sanding room is another testimony to seat-of-the-pants machine design. A combination of Rube Goldberg-like contraptions sand the edges, the insides and the outsides of the bowls as they are moved from one station to the next, as shown in the bottom photo on the facing page and the two left photos below. Machine operators smooth the spinning, oscillating bowls with 60-grit and 120-grit sanding belts.

Granville puts a finish on only a very small percentage of the bowls it sells, using mineral oil with a 5% paraffin content. The Granville name goes only on those bowls sold in its own store. The rest are wholesaled and wind up with the retailers' imprints. On the balance sheet, the bowl operation doesn't bring in as much as the clapboard mill. Fuller says he loses money on the smaller bowls, breaks even on the 11-in. bowls and makes money on the larger sizes with a 15-in. bowl retailing for $50, a 17 in. for $75 and a 20 in. for $110.

When I visited Granville in May, Bob Fuller was distracted. He couldn't get logs for the clapboard mill and the bowl lathe was shredding bowls like they were classified wooden CIA memos. But when I went back one damp, cold day in September, I found him expansive and voluble. The yard was piled high with logs. A second bowl lathe was on the production line and a third was being built. A "producing crafts village" was being planned, along with a video for visitors. A glass viewing wall was going up next to the bowl lathes. Michael Eramo had slowed the feed rate on the oldest lathe, and good bowls were coming off in the kind of quantities that make a chief executive officer smile. He took the afternoon off to play golf and to dwell for a while on cups, not bowls. □

Richard Ewald is a freelance writer in Westminster West, Vt.

The operators control the pressure of the belt sanders with various levers and pedals as they sand the inside (above left) and outside (above right) of each bowl.

The bowl lathe at Granville can turn as many as seven bowls from a single block of wood in as little as six minutes. The nested bowls in the foreground were all cut from the same block of birch.

Photos above and below: Stretch Tuemmler

A Boatbuilder's Bowls

Overlapping techniques

by Stu Gillam

My work as a boatbuilder has both grown out of and fostered my appreciation of shape. Lately, I've found my lathe work is similarly motivated by my preoccupation with examining the various objects around me in terms of shape, surface texture and line. So it was, I found myself on the beach one day, a shell in my right hand, a bud in my left, noting the similarities between the two and admiring how their edges seemed to wrap around each other. It occurred to me that I could produce such shapes in wood by combining boatbuilding techniques with turning.

In brief, my method is to turn the shape, cut it open, boil it and roll it up. The turning is fairly straightforward. If I have a large enough blank, I screw it directly to the faceplate and part off the turning beyond the reach of the screws. If the blank is too small for this, I simply glue on an extra pad of wood with five-minute epoxy, then part off the turning at the seam. The pictured vases are butternut, which has proven to be a near-perfect wood for slit turnings. It's very stable, turns well and bends easily when heated.

I turn the outside first between the faceplate and a live center on my Shopsmith, sanding the wood smooth and sealing it temporarily with Butcher's wax to prevent checking. The finished outside surface then serves as a reference for hollowing the inside. Turning the inside of a vase through a small opening creates a couple of problems. For one thing, the lathe needs to be periodically stopped so shavings trapped inside the vase can be blown or vacuumed out. Also, because the cutting edge is as much as 12 in. from the tool rest, tool chatter becomes a major problem, especially on a Shopsmith, which isn't robust enough to support deep faceplate work. To compensate, I've ballasted the machine with a block of granite and railroad iron and rigged up an adjustable steady rest that supports the outboard end of the turning with two pairs of furniture castors.

To further control chatter and to allow undercutting of the vase's abruptly curved shoulders, I've developed my own turning tools. The largest of these, for deep roughing of the inside, is made of an old file 18 in. long and ¾ in. in section. A second tool has its shank bent so the cutting edge is roughly parallel with the axis of the handle, making it possible to pivot the shank on the tool rest to cut around corners. I press the handle against my hip and grasp the tool shank just inside and just outside the pivot

Inspired by shells and buds picked up on the beach, Gillam combined his boatbuilding skills with an avocational interest in turning to produce these slit bowls and vases. They're made of butternut finished with a linseed oil/varnish mixture.

From *Fine Woodworking* magazine (May 1988) 70:64-65

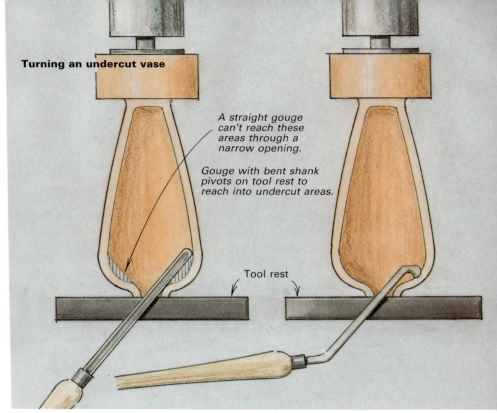

Turning an undercut vase

A straight gouge can't reach these areas through a narrow opening.

Gouge with bent shank pivots on tool rest to reach into undercut areas.

Tool rest

Deep faceplate work isn't the Shopsmith's forte, so Gillam ballasted the machine with granite and iron, then clamped on a steady rest made with furniture castors. Above, he's roughing the bowl's interior with a gouge made from an old file.

After turning, the vase is sawn along its length. The edges are beveled so they can bend past each other more easily. In the center photo, Gillam pares a teardrop-shaped bevel for clearance. Ten minutes of boiling plasticizes the butternut enough for bending.

point on the tool rest. Using this three-point grip with a little body English, light, controlled cuts are possible.

I've found wall thicknesses of about 1/8 in. bend and fold easily after heating, yet are sturdy enough to withstand bending. Because a section through the wall is exposed after bending, its thickness must be uniform and fairly smooth, otherwise tool marks and pits will show as an irregular edge. When the piece has been turned inside and out, I sand the outside with 320 grit and what I can reach of the inside with 400 grit. Then, using stiff paper as a batten, I lay out a line for the sawcut. While the piece is still on the lathe, I cut to the line with a fine-toothed saw. To ease the strain of one edge passing over the other, both edges must have relief cuts. At the base of the sawcut, I chisel or knife a relief cut on the edge I want to pass underneath. This bevel goes from a straight feather-edge at the top of the sawcut to a teardrop shape nearer the bowl's base, as shown in the photos above. The teardrop shape is necessary because the bowl's walls are less flexible near the base and thus can't be bent as easily as the walls nearer the top. At this point, the vase can be parted off the lathe and prepared for bending.

In boatbuilding, planks are steamed or soaked in hot water to plasticize the wood for bending, but my bowls are small enough to simply plop into a washbasin of vigorously boiling water for

five or 10 minutes. To heat the piece evenly, I hold it underwater with a stick. My hands protected with heavy gloves, I fish out the turning and immediately bend it, tucking one edge under the other and rolling it up, just as you would a newspaper. A scrap of cloth wrapped tightly around the bowl holds the shape until the wood cools. I generally shape the exposed edges with carving tools, then sand again with 320-, 400- and 600-grit sandpaper, taking care to get under the overlap. I use a sanding disc mounted on the Shopsmith to true up the vase's bottom, because the bending usually distorts it so badly that the vase won't stand up correctly. I finish my turnings with a mixture of one part turpentine, two parts spar varnish and three parts boiled linseed oil.

A final word about shape: A tall, narrow vase, like the one shown here, will roll easily as one edge can be deflected toward the center. The broader-shape bowl won't surrender so easily. The only way I've managed to fold this kind of shape is to carry the sawcut all the way across the bottom and then pare a triangular clearance notch in one edge halfway up the bowl's side. This allows the two edges to interpenetrate during bending. I make a plug from parted-off scrap to patch the bottom. ☐

Stu Gillam builds boats and turns wood in Hancock, Me.

Turning Large Vessels
Coping with weight and wood movement

by James R. Johnson

A chunk of wood the size of a tree stump rotating on your lathe at more than 100 RPM can be scary indeed. But if your equipment and the techniques are properly matched to the task, you can do large-scale work with no more trepidation than turning a table leg. But before I describe the tools and methods I've developed specifically for turning large, deep vessels, I want to talk about the shapes and materials I like to work with.

Most turners want to develop a form that is recognizable as "theirs," but a persuasive case can be made for the classic shapes, which potters have used for centuries. The classic shapes of the urn and vase are very familiar to all of us and are accepted as "natural." If they weren't friendly shapes, they wouldn't have persisted through the centuries. Besides, they offer several advantages to the woodturner. The double-curve lip can resist distortion by having a portion of the wood oriented perpendicular to any movement. The narrow bottom not only minimizes the amount of wood that has to be removed on the inside, with a tool at its maximum projection over the tool rest, but it also reduces drying stresses and consequent checking.

Along with shape, wall thickness is a primary concern. A large vessel with ⅛-in.-thick walls does not have the stiffness to withstand warping, unless you are turning burl wood, while a wall thickness of ⅜ in. or more is liable to develop longitudinal cracks due to uneven drying through the walls. As a compromise between two undesirable extremes, I generally turn my vessel walls to a thickness of ¼ in.

My favorite wood for big turnings is walnut: It's stable, easy to turn and finish, and my customers love it. Next to walnut, I like mimosa, also a stable, open-grain wood with magnificent figure. Unfortunately, its dust can be toxic. Hackberry, if you can catch it at the proper time in the spalting process, is also very good. Elm is nice. Osage-orange, (known as *bois-d'arc* here in Texas where it's pronounced "bowdark") cuts and works nicely, though to prevent cracking, it requires particular care in drying, as do our native oaks and pecan. My least favorite is cottonwood. It takes a horrendous amount of sanding to get a nice surface, but because the wood is lightweight, large pieces are easy to manage; too, favorable public reaction makes working cottonwood worthwhile.

Standing trees that have been dead for a year or so are best. Often spalted enough to be colorful, they are usually dry enough to turn right away and are more stable than green wood. Green wood needs to be air-dried six to 12 months before turning. Always use a sealer—paint, glue or one of the commercial products—on endgrain to help prevent checking.

A heavyweight faceplate lathe—The first requirement for deep-vessel turning is a lathe that can handle a 100-lb.-plus piece of wood. The lathe I built, which is pictured on the facing page, was inspired by a heavyweight lathe designed by Ed Moulthrop, though my version is different in several ways that make it more versatile. The basic frame is a box made from plywood and exterior solid-core doors. It measures 35 in. high by 48 in. long by 21 in. wide. The top is reinforced with ¼-in.-thick

From *Fine Woodworking* magazine (September 1988) 72:86-89

Using a modified boring bar, the author, left, hollows the inside of a large urn. The bar is tipped with a cutting tool, shown in the drawing on p. 30, that can be adjusted to take an automatically controlled cut, and so it can't catch or hang up. This kind of turning is not for the impatient. A vessel this size can take as long as a week to complete.

The author's faceplate lathe, below, made from scavenged parts, is driven by an electric motor through a riding-lawn-mower transmission, which provides variable speed without the need to move the belt from pulley to pulley. Note that the stock is securely lag-bolted to the faceplate.

2-in. by 2-in. angle iron along the front and back edges. The headstock is machined from a scavenged 2³⁄₁₆-in. shaft and rides in pillow blocks 16 in. apart. Faceplate threads are 1½x8 tpi, so I can use standard accessories.

The tool-rest support is a 6-ft.-long 6x6 oak beam that's clamped to the underside of the lathe top with a toggle system, which also supports the beam when it is being moved to a new position. The tool rest is torch-cut from ½-in. angle iron and supported by a 1x2½x16-in. connector bar. A series of holes bored on 1-in. centers in the top of the tool rest let me position a hardened masonry nail to act as a lateral pivot point, or fulcrum, for the long tools I use. These holes have ¼-in.-dia. holes bored through their bottoms to allow dust and chips to be pushed down and out.

Instead of relying on step pulleys for speed control, as Moulthrop's lathe does, mine is driven through a riding-lawn-mower transmission by a 1½-HP, 1750-RPM electrically reversible motor. The transmission not only acts as a gear reducer but also gives four speeds, from 50 RPM to about 475 RPM, with just a tug on a handle. I made a couple of two-step pulleys from turned discs of 14-ply, ¾-in. plywood to double the range.

A threaded motor-support rod with a handle projecting above the bed of the lathe makes belt changing easy and allows the belt to slip when roughing out a piece, where a catch could result in a sprained wrist, or worse. It also helps prevent wear to the bearings and belt caused by the not-inconsiderable weight of the motor, transmission and mounts.

Turning strategy—I turn almost all my large work pithwise, rather than the more conventional plankwise. Several advantages accrue. The grain is oriented along the major axis of the piece, which means shrinkage is more or less even all the way around, and warpage is minimized. And to my mind, the exposed side grain is more attractive than endgrain.

For pieces that incorporate crotches, knots or contrary grain, and for the occasional pieces I turn plankwise, I first rough them out to a wall thickness of about 10% of the maximum diameter and dry them in paper bags for several months. Then, I turn them to within 5% of the maximum diameter and dry them some more. By turning and drying in stages, the familiar oval shape and the ripples caused by uneven shrinkage of end/side grain conjunctions is eliminated.

My usual procedure is to turn the outside of the vessel first (base excluded), as shown in the top, left photo p. 30, and then to turn just past the curve on the inside. Next I sand, apply a coat of oil and continue hollowing the inside. To prevent the base from being stressed and flexed, I leave the diameter there pretty fat until I have hollowed close to this depth and lightened the piece appreciably. By starting to hollow immediately after the outside contour is established, the rim thickness will be the same all the way around, an important part of a good appearance. If I wait until the next day to begin hollowing, the piece will have warped slightly out of round, and it will be impossible to achieve a uniform thickness around the mouth of the vessel.

Anytime I stop work, I fit a large plastic bag over the piece to

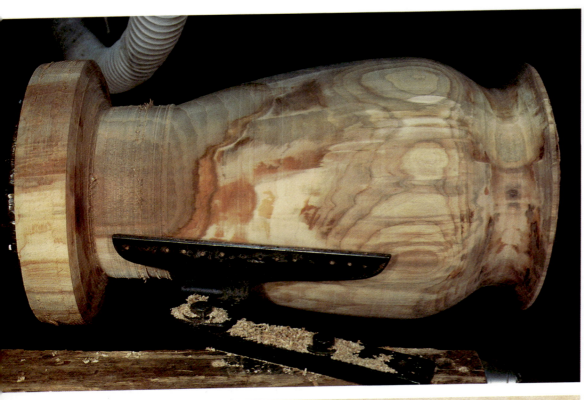

Johnson first rough-turns the outside, left, but waits until he's hollowed the inside to finish turning the base. If he completed the base before lightening the vessel, its weight could cause it to break loose and go flying through the shop. To begin hollowing, Johnson uses a lance, which he levers against a hardened masonry nail inserted in the tool rest, as shown above. Too much pressure will cause a catch, possibly with disastrous results, so he takes his time and doesn't crowd the cut. The 27-in.-tall, 16-in.-dia. elm vessel shown below has what the author calls a "classic shape" and is surprisingly lightweight at 7 lbs.

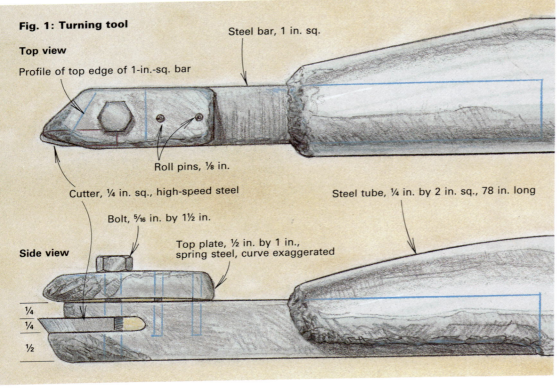

Fig. 1: Turning tool

Top view

Profile of top edge of 1-in.-sq. bar

Steel bar, 1 in. sq.

Roll pins, ⅛ in.

Cutter, ¼ in. sq., high-speed steel

Bolt, ⁵⁄₁₆ in. by 1½ in.

Top plate, ½ in. by 1 in., spring steel, curve exaggerated

Steel tube, ¼ in. by 2 in. sq., 78 in. long

Side view

¼
¼
½

hold in the moisture. This is particularly important for the rim. I have had rims crack, but was able to repair them by wetting them thoroughly, wrapping a long strip of inner-tube rubber around them and gluing the crack with Hot Stuff cyanoacrylate glue when the crack closed. I have to emphasize the importance of keeping the work uniformly moist. Sometimes the wood dries so fast that I have to dampen it with a wet sponge as it turns.

A lance and a pair of boring bars—The tool I use for turning the outside of a large vessel and the first 8 in. to 10 in. of the inside is a lance, patterned after the one Moulthrop uses. It is made from a 30-in. length of ⅞-in.-dia. air-hardening, high-speed tool steel. Generally levered against a concrete nail dropped in holes in the tool rest, the lance can remove palm-size shavings or a minute quantity of wood with equal ease. The nail serves the same purpose as the bevel on a conventional gouge, but gives much more control. After a cut is initiated, the tool's rounded bottom can be used as a bevel and the cut continued, but with care, as the risk of a catch is increased.

For internal turning, I bore to depth with a 1⅜-in.-dia. twist drill held in a T-handle. Next I use the lance as a scraper, with the flat top held horizontally, but again levered against the concrete nail, as shown in the top, right photo on the facing page. Only after the bulk of the wood has been removed is the tool used in a shear-cutting action to trim the wall down to the desired thickness. The lance, although a very efficient tool, is liable to catch after it reaches a depth of about 10 in. So to finish hollowing, I use another tool, which is similar to a boring bar.

The boring bar is made from a slotted 1-in. bar welded to a 6-ft., 6-in.-long piece of 2-in. by 2-in. square tubing. A cutting tip of ¼-in. high-speed steel is clamped in the slot of the 1-in. bar. This thing is so heavy that I have to have an auxiliary support under the back of the tube. I sit between the tool rest and auxiliary support, with the handle under my arm, as seen in the photo on p. 28 and 29. Because I designed this tool so its cutting-edge exposure is limited (see figure 1 on facing page), it cannot hang up. I can make cuts in any direction, but cuts from center out or down the side are fastest. I make finish cuts by withdrawing up the side so the cut is with the grain.

After cutting about 2 in. deep and to about ½-in. wall thickness, I sharpen the cutter and trim to final thickness, then cut another 2 in., sharpen and cut again, until the inside walls are finished. Most of the problems I have in cutting are caused by a dull cutter. The very tip and left side of the cutter is doing all the work, and although made from high-speed steel, it dulls more rapidly than you would think. If there is any one secret to easy turning, it is to keep the tools as sharp as possible at all times.

I control the wall thickness by using a pair of calipers where possible. Where calipers can't reach, I bore a tiny hole with a drill bit made from a sewing needle. To gauge the thickness, I insert a blunted needle through the hole with one hand and push it flush with the inside wall with the other. Pinching the needle and withdrawing it shows the thickness of the wall. A chalk mark around the hole lets me find it again after further trimming.

Refining the shape and finishing—Final shaping on the exterior is done using a 7-in. auto-body sander with 80- or 100-grit paper. The sander is applied while the work turns at a fairly low speed and only long enough to remove tool marks. I locate invisible imperfections in the contour by running my hand up and down the piece. A few seconds with the body sander will fair the hills and valleys. Final sanding is done with the lathe stopped.

Because I hate sanding, I tried foam-backed sanding pads. They did very well, but had a number of disadvantages. First was cost. A 3-in. disc of sandpaper costs 50¢ and lasts about two minutes. Second, the foam is much too hard for the kind of work I do, and finally, the only source for these discs is 2,000 miles away. So, I developed my own.

Easily made from discs of ½-in. plywood, 1-in. foam rubber from computer packing crates and thin leather, these sanding pads are the best I've ever used. I have a couple dozen of them, in diameters from 1½ in. to 5 in., with sandpaper grits from 60 to 600. The foam-and-leather pad softens the edge of the sandpaper, preventing swirl marks and allowing the paper to conform to almost any contour. If you make your own pads, be sure to face the foam with leather: The leather keeps the paper from squirming around on the foam and wrinkling or tearing loose. I stick the sanding disc to the leather with double-sided carpet tape.

For sanding the outside, I like to use a 2,500-RPM drill; faster burns the paper, slower prolongs the sanding. The disc will last a long time, because you never have to sand the entire circumference of the piece to smooth a single spot, as you would if the piece were rotating.

I rough-sand the inside of my pieces with floor-sanding paper backed by foam. If there is sufficient room to get a drill or flexible shaft inside, the soft foam discs are used to finish-sand; otherwise, I sand by hand before applying the finish.

The old traditional oil/wax finish is what I use. Not only can the oil be applied to a damp piece, but also it is relatively unaffected by dust. Just wipe the piece down before quitting for the night. Applying oil also is reasonably fast. Since the bowl must be cured for several weeks anyway, it is almost no trouble to wipe on a few coats of oil while the piece is drying, so the overall time is not lengthened. I use boiled linseed oil because it is available (try to find pure tung oil for example) and affordable (price pure tung oil if you find it), and it works. Other oils, such as walnut oil and some of the lighter cooking oils, do not contain dryers and can become rancid while you sit around waiting for them to set up. Believe me, you can't sell a piece that smells bad.

When thoroughly dry and impregnated with oil, I wet-sand using thinned oil and 400-grit paper on the soft foam pad. This restores the smooth surface the wood had before drying and produces a wood slurry, which I wipe into any open pores. The next day I burnish, using the same 400-grit disc I used to wet-sand, then wax. The major drawback to linseed oil is that it darkens with age, but this can be overcome to a large extent by applying two coats of Armour All—a spray-on protective liquid available at auto-supply stores—before waxing.

Parting off—Special care must be taken when parting off the finished bowl. Due to the weight of the piece, at some point in the parting-off process, the bottom will break around the uncut portion and the bowl will go flying. After losing several bowls this way, I now part 1 in. to 2 in. deep, just enough to form an even rim. Then I saw the bowl free. A ball mill in a die grinder removes the excess wood to recess the bottom within the turned rim. The bottom is then smoothed with a foam-backed sanding disc. If the bottom should warp slightly, the rim keeps the bowl standing straight.

Safety—Any lathe work is inherently dangerous. Turning big pieces is especially so because of the mass involved and the potential for injury if it comes loose from the lathe and goes flying through the shop. This means making for a sure connection between the turning blank and the faceplate.

When I bought the spindle for my lathe at the salvage yard, I also picked up five blind flanges for pipelines. These I had drilled and threaded for faceplates. They are 6½ in. in diameter, ½ in. thick on the flange and have a massive amount of steel around the threaded portion. One of these I subsequently modified by welding on a disc of ¾-in. steel 14 in. in diameter to make a faceplate for pieces over 250 lbs. or so. I fasten the faceplates to the turning blanks with ⅜-in.-dia. lag screws from 2 in. to 5 in. long. I have never had a piece come loose and never intend to have it happen. The thought of a 200-lb. log section ricocheting around my shop is not something I like to contemplate.

Tool design also affects safety. The cutting edge of the boring bar tool I use to hollow is ground and positioned on the bar to limit the amount of cut that can be taken. By reducing the cutting-edge exposure, I can eliminate catches. Of course, the cutting tip projection can be increased, but being able to hog the cut isn't worth the risk of a catch, which could break a jaw, or fracture a skull.

One last thing: Never even try to use a skew chisel on large-diameter turnings—the point is too close to the work and the slightest jiggle will cause a catch. □

James R. Johnson is a computer operator and woodturner. He lives in Bastrop, Tex. Photos by author.

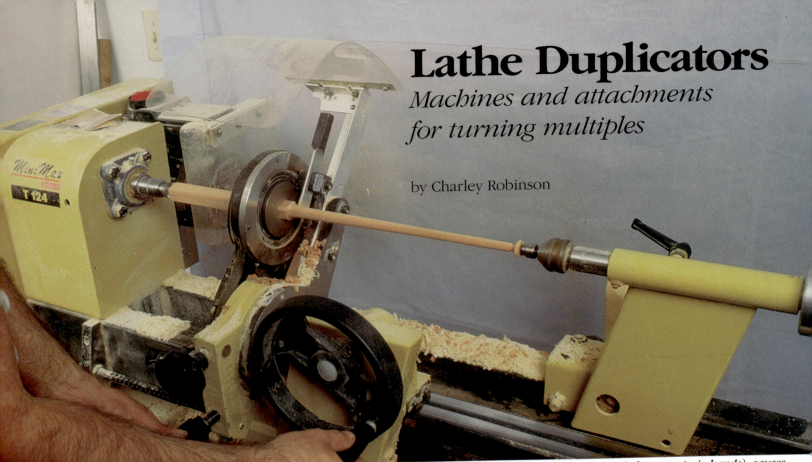

Lathe Duplicators
Machines and attachments for turning multiples

by Charley Robinson

Duplicating lathes can mass-produce spindles more quickly than hand-turning. A hand wheel and gear moves the carriage of this Minimax along the lathe bed via a stationary chain, while a stylus following a template (hidden behind the operator's hands) causes the V-shaped cutter, mounted on a cantilevered arm, to mirror the image in the spinning blank.

Working on the lathe is a lot of fun because it's quick and easy to turn out a bowl or spindle. But drudgery and complications set in when you have to produce duplicates, say four identical table legs or a series of turned balusters for a porch railing. Skilled production turners can hand-turn fairly uniform spindles with amazing rapidity by simply mounting a reference spindle behind the blank mounted on the lathe and then turning the required copies, judging the curves and dimensions by eye or gauging them with calipers. But I bet many less accomplished turners react as I did when faced with a big job: start thumbing through catalogs looking for a duplicator attachment to bolt to my lathe or for a copy lathe that includes the necessary hardware to simplify all that fussy repetitive work.

I was surprised to find more than 30 manufacturers selling duplicating lathes and/or attachments, with prices ranging from under $200 to more than $60,000. There were too many machines for me to try, and so I prepared the chart, shown on pp. 34-35, to compare the various models. I focused on those machines normally marketed to the home craftsman. These machines are generally less expensive than industrial-grade equipment, but shouldn't necessarily be considered cheap: some cost up to $3,600 and are adequate for even small production shops. In this article I'll discuss what I learned about how these machines operate and the things they can and can't do.

I was most concerned with duplicating spindles mounted between the lathe's headstock and tailstock, but some machines can also do faceplate work to copy bowls, as indicated in the chart. For ease of comparison, I divided them into two categories: manual models and semi-automatic devices, depending on whether the cutter is supported and controlled by a hand-guided unit, as shown in the bottom photo on the facing page, or in a carriage that runs along rails parallel to the lathe bed, as shown in the

photo above. Basically each type produces copies the same way. A stylus, which is designed to bear against and follow the contours of a sample part or pattern, is connected to a cutter assembly in such a way that any movement by the stylus is mirrored exactly by the cutter, which runs against the spinning blank mounted on the lathe. Because the cutter ultimately determines the accuracy and the finish of the copy, I'll discuss it first.

The cutting edge – Duplicator lathes come with a variety of cutters (see the bottom photo on p. 37); some are designed to make a scraping cut, but I found I obtained smoother surfaces from those that made a shearing cut. Although some lathes had mild-steel cutters, which wouldn't hold an edge well and had to be sharpened frequently, most featured high-speed steel (HSS) cutters. HSS takes a keen edge that can yield clean, smooth cuts requiring a minimum of sanding. Carbide tools are rare because they are difficult to sharpen and because carbide doesn't take as sharp an edge. Different cutters will need to be sharpened differently; the reversible shear cutter shown in the bottom photo on p. 37 can be honed on a stone, but there is very little metal for grinding and so it will need replacing more frequently than other types. Most scraper-type cutters can be sharpened on a regular grinding wheel. In some instances, it will be necessary to reshape your wheel to match the shape of your cutter.

While there are a variety of cutters, almost all are V-shaped and sharpened to about a 30° included angle, as shown in the bottom photo on p. 37, which influences the cuts they can make. For the manual duplicators, the cutter shape is not a factor because you can control the angle at which the cutter is presented to the blank, enabling you to copy square shoulders and even some undercut details. The carriage of semi-automatic duplicators, however, travels parallel to the axis of the lathe and the cutter is restricted to moving

From *Fine Woodworking* magazine (January 1991) 86:68-73

n and out perpendicular to the axis. Because of the linear track of the carriage and the shape of the cutter, any angle on the original that is greater than about 75° cannot be copied. This limitation leaves you with two options. You can design spindles without square shoulders and other fine detailing, or you can copy the spindle as best as the duplicator can and then touch up the details by hand.

Some of the duplicator attachments can be secured to and operated from the back of the lathe. In addition to throwing the chips down and out of the way, this leaves the front of the lathe free for using hand tools with the regular lathe tool rest for adding details before removing the turning from the lathe. A possible problem with this arrangement is that the lathe must be accessible from both sides, requiring a great deal more shop space. One turner's approach to detailing spindles was to design an auxiliary tool rest that clamps to his duplicator's carriage, as shown in the top photo on p. 37. After copying a spindle, he simply cranks the carriage into position and uses a skew or parting tool to square up shoulders and refine details. Another approach is to copy the full number of spindles that are required and then remove the duplicator mechanism, rechuck each spindle and add the details. This makes sense for a production shop where less-skilled workers could use a duplicator to turn out basic spindles, which could then be finished by a skilled turner.

There are other cutter factors that can affect the quality of cut. As the cutter extends farther from the carriage, vibration and, in turn, the amount of carriage movement increase, which can obliterate details and leave rough surfaces. Also, the stylus should be the same shape and/or size as the cutter. While you can use a larger cutter for roughing out stock, once you get into actual pattern work, differences between the cutter and stylus will be evident because the template shape will not be transferred to the stock accurately.

Making templates – All of the machines on the chart can make duplicates from either an original spindle, or a flat pattern or template. If you have just a few copies to make, you can clamp the original on the duplicator and crank out your copies. But every time you run the stylus over your original, you create a flat strip down the length of the spindle that gets wider with each pass, steadily deteriorating the details. Also, the original spindle may bend under the pressure of the stylus unless the spindle is supported in the middle, as well as at both ends.

If you are doing more than just a few reproductions, a template is recommended. Although some manufacturers recommend ¼-in.-thick plywood for templates, I found that after just a few copies, details were lost due to stylus pressure wearing down the high points. Tempered hardboard performed only slightly better. Aluminum and steel sheet stock, ³⁄₁₆ in. or ¼ in. thick, will last almost indefinitely, but these materials are harder to obtain and work. Acrylic, like Plexiglas, or polycarbonate sheets, such as Lexan, make excellent, long-wearing templates, and these materials are readily obtainable and easily worked.

Take the time necessary to make your pattern accurate; any mistakes will be duplicated with each spindle. To make a template, you can bandsaw the original down the middle and simply trace the outline onto the template material. Or, if you can't afford to sacrifice the original, you can transfer the key transition points from the original to the template material and then, using calipers, lay out the diameters of the points (see the drawing on pp. 36-37). Complete the template, connecting the points with a variety of straightedges, French curves, a compass and freehand drawing. To get the most accurate templates, bandsaw to the waste side of the layout line, and then file and finish-sand precisely to this line. This also leaves a nice smooth edge that is easy for the stylus to follow.

You can include features in your patterns to overcome some of the duplicators' shortcomings. For example, if your duplicator doesn't have stops to keep the carriage from running off the end of the track, add ramps at each end of the template. Also, for duplicators that require you to bolt through the pattern to fasten it to the machine, make slots rather than holes, so you can fine-tune the pattern's position. When using long blanks, a slight notch in each end of the template will accurately mark the cut-off points for later bandsawing the spindle to length. And if you want to leave a square portion at the end of the spindle, as on many table legs, don't forget to measure the diagonal of the square that you want when laying out that part of the template, or else you'll wonder why that section you thought was going to be square is suddenly round.

How duplicators work – The manual models listed in the chart have the cutter and stylus mounted in a hand-held unit that is supported by the lathe's flat bed (see the bottom photo below) or by an auxiliary table bolted to the lathe. The operator guides the cutter into the blank by sliding the hand unit along the table and making progressively deeper cuts until the stylus fully contacts the

(continued on p. 36)

The spring-operated plunger mechanism of this semi-automatic duplicator pulls the stylus to the template and the cutter into the blank at the same time. Slots in the template for mounting screws allow adjustments; ramps at the end of the template act as carriage stops.

Manual duplicators have a hand-guided cutter-and-stylus holder that slides either on the lathe bed or a special table bolted to the lathe. The stylus is moved along the template, near the lathe bed, as the cutter shapes the blank to create duplicates. This freedom of cutter movement is a real advantage when copying undercuts and square shoulders on small-detailed work.

Woodturning Duplication Systems

	Company	Model	Duplicating Method	Carriage Drive	Carriage Stops	Universal Mount or Manufacturer Only	Number of Cutters	Cutter Action	Cutter Material	Cutter Feed
Duplicator Attachments for Lathes	Delta (Taiwan)	46-408	Semi-automatic	Rack & gear	0	Manufacturer	1	Shear	High-speed steel	Spring plunger
	Elektra-Beckum (Germany)	HDM-071	Manual	Patterned tool rest	NA	Manufacturer	1	Scrape	Carbide tip	Manual
	Garrett Wade (Taiwan)	03BO1.02	Semi-automatic	Cable & pulley	2	Manufacturer	1	Scrape	High-speed steel	Manual
	General (Canada)	2660	Semi-automatic	Rail guided, hand pushed	2	Manufacturer	1	Scrape	High-speed steel	Screw plunger
	Hapfo (Germany)	KA-90	Semi-automatic	Chain & sprocket	0	Universal	1	Shear	High-speed steel	Spring plunger
	Hegner (Germany)	LKH-1200	Semi-automatic	Chain & sprocket	2	Manufacturer	1	Shear	High-speed steel	Cantilevered arm
		LQ-400	Semi-automatic	Threaded shaft	0	Manufacturer	1	Shear	High-speed steel	Spring plunger
	Killinger (Germany)	KM-100	Semi-automatic	Threaded shaft	2	Manufacturer	1	Shear	High-speed steel	Hand-cranked threaded shaft
		KM-300	Semi-automatic	Rack & gear	2	Manufacturer	2	Shear	High-speed steel	Cantilevered arm
	Kity (France)	2660	Semi-automatic	Rack & gear	2	Universal	1	Shear	High-speed steel	Spring plunger
	Konig (Germany)	K1368	Semi-automatic	Rubber friction wheels	2	Manufacturer	1	Shear	High-speed steel	Cantilevered arm
	Sears/Craftsman (United States)	9-24917	Manual	Tool post on platform	NA	Manufacturer	1	Scrape	High-speed steel	Manual
		9-24907	Manual	Tool post on platform	NA	Manufacturer	1	Scrape	High-speed steel	Manual
	Shopsmith (United States)	555209	Manual	Tool post on platform	NA	Manufacturer	1	Scrape	Solid carbide	Manual
	Toolmark (United States)	520B	Manual	Tool post on platform	NA	Universal	1	Scrape	High-speed steel	Manual
		3010	Semi-automatic	Rail guided, hand pushed	0	Universal	1	Scrape	High-speed steel	Screw plunger
	Turn-O-Carve Tool (United States)	Offset System	Manual	Tool post on platform	NA	Universal	1	Scrape	High-speed steel	Manual
	Vega Enterprises (United States)	D-36	Semi-automatic	Chain & sprocket	1	Universal	1	Shear	High-speed steel	Spring plunger
	Wilke/Bridgewood (Taiwan)	BW-439	Semi-automatic	Cable & pulley	2	Manufacturer	1	Scrape	Carbide tip	Spring plunger
Copy Lathes #	Enco (Taiwan)	199-9060	Semi-automatic	Rack & gear	0	NA	1	Scrape	Mild steel	Rack & gear
	Grizzly † (Taiwan)	G1174	Semi-automatic	Rack & gear	0	NA	1	Scrape	Mild steel	Rack & gear
	Minimax (Italy)	T-124	Semi-automatic	Stationary chain	1	NA	2	Shear	High-speed steel	Cantilevered arm
	Symtec (Australia)	1500	Manual	Tool post on flat lathe bed	NA	NA	1	Scrape	Special alloy	Manual

NA = Not Applicable
* = Dealer selling prices are typically 5% to 25% lower.

Final Depth Stop	Duplicating Capacities			Net Weight (lbs.)	Comments	List Price*	Manufacturer (if U.S. office) or U.S. Distributor
	Spindle Dia. (max/in.)	Spindle Length (max/in.)	Faceplate Capability				
Yes	6	36	No	57	Multiple depth stops and micro-adjustment knob on cutter feed; optional steady rest; fits lathes with channel beds	$595	Delta International Machinery Corp.—(800) 438-2486, (412) 963-2400
NA	15	40	No	12	Optional templates	$160	Elektra-Beckum U.S.A. Corp.— (609) 784-8600
Yes	10	40	Yes	83	Optional steady rest and longer tool rest	$395	Garrett Wade Co. Inc.— (800) 221-2942, (212) 807-1155
Yes	12	36	No	48	Also available with 96-in.-long spindle capacity; optional hardware to fit other lathes	$660	Sisco Supply Inc.—(802) 863-9036 Wilke Machinery Co.— (717) 764-5000
Yes	12	37½	Yes	75	Several high-volume production lathes also available	$2,043	E. & R. Supply Co. Inc.— (516) 435-0811
Yes	7	54	No	120	Also available with 37⅜-in.-long spindle capacity; optional hardware to fit other lathes	$1,795	Advanced Machinery Imports Ltd.— (800) 648-4264, (302) 322-2226
No	6¼	15¾	Yes	40	Adjustable for longer spindles; reversible cutters	$845	
Yes	7⅞	39⅜	No	52	Optional hardware to fit other lathes; optional faceplate copying; high-volume production lathes also available	$2,250	Willow Pond Tools Inc.— (603) 485-2321
Yes	7⅞	39⅜	Yes	176	Optional hardware to fit other lathes	$3,600	
Yes	2¾	40	Yes	49	Reversible cutters; clear chip shield on carriage; optional steady rest	$892	Farris Machinery/Kity-U.S.A. Corp.— (800) 872-5489
Yes	6	28	No	80	Optional steady rest, longer tool rest and spiraling attachment	$975	Garrett Wade Co. Inc.— (800) 221-2942, (212) 807-1155
NA	6	33	Yes	25	Only fits Sears lathe model 9-22836	$90	Sears, Roebuck and Co.— (800) 366-3000, (312) 875-2500
NA	6	36	Yes	40	Only fits Sears lathe model 9-22816	$150	
NA	8	34	Yes	36½	Optional steady rest; diamond, round, square cutters available	$379	Shopsmith Inc.— (800) 762-7555, (513) 898-6070
NA	4	Depends on lathe	Yes	19	Shield on hand grip; optional shear cutter	$210	Toolmark Co.—(612) 561-4210
Yes	8½	27	No	50	Adjustable bushings; optional shear cutter; optional accessories for longer spindles	$498	
NA	Depends on lathe	Depends on lathe	Yes	12	Optional steady rest; optional accessories required to copy from spindle	$178	Turn-O-Carve Tool Inc.— (813) 933-2730
Yes	2½	36	No	103	Also available with 16-in.-, 48-in.-, 96-in.-long spindle capacity; optional steady rest and faceplate copying; adjustable bushings; can be rear mounted	$575	Vega Enterprises Inc.— (800) 222-8342, (217) 963-2232
No	4¾	39⅜	Yes	96	Optional steady rest; clear chip shield on carriage	$499	Wilke Machinery Co.— (717) 764-5000
No	7	31	Yes	183	Includes drive center and tool rest; does not include floor stand	$375	Enco Manufacturing Co.— (800) 621-4145, (312) 745-1500
No	7	40	Yes	210	Includes outboard disc sander, pneumatic drum sander, flap sander, tool rest, five cutters	$375	Grizzly Imports Inc.— (800) 541-5537, (800) 523-4777
Yes	7	43	No	375	Includes drive center, tool rest, micro-depth adjustment and traveling steady rest with steady rest precutter; optional fixed steady rest	$2,300	SCMI Corp.—(404) 448-1120
NA	11	37	Yes	285	Built-in grind stone, tool rest and headstock indexer; optional fluting and beading accessories; custom-builds longer beds	$2,495	Symtec America—(902) 893-1915 (Canada)

† = Grizzly also sells three components to duplicate on its G1495 heavy-duty wood lathe.
\# = All integrated copy lathes include bed, motor, duplicator and stand unless otherwise noted.

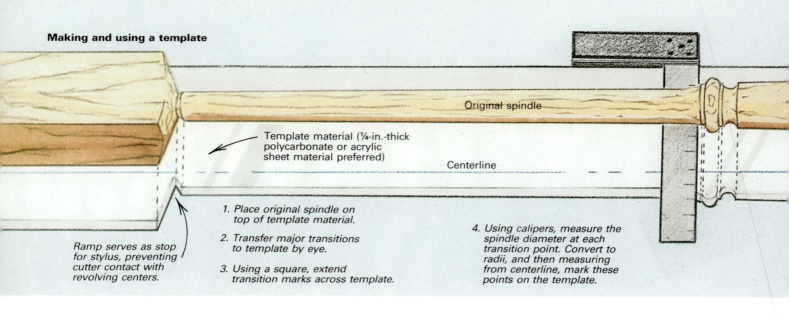

Original spindle

Template material (¼-in.-thick
polycarbonate or acrylic
sheet material preferred)

Centerline

Ramp serves as stop
for stylus, preventing
cutter contact with
revolving centers.

1. Place original spindle on
   top of template material.

2. Transfer major transitions
   to template by eye.

3. Using a square, extend
   transition marks across template.

4. Using calipers, measure the
   spindle diameter at each
   transition point. Convert to
   radii, and then measuring
   from centerline, mark these
   points on the template.

entire length of the pattern. I liked this type of duplicator for reproducing small, highly detailed spindles, but I found it somewhat tedious, and I had trouble getting a smooth surface when working on larger production runs of longer spindles, such as for a porch railing.

The semi-automatic duplicators have the cutter and stylus mounted in a carriage that is moved parallel to the duplicator bed, usually by some type of handwheel/drive mechanism, which I'll discuss later. The cutter and stylus are held against the work and the template by the mechanical force of a spring in a plunger or a cantilevered arm. The more common spring mechanism is a plunger that holds the cutter, as shown in the top photo on p. 33. Some plunger units have an internal spring, while others direct the spring tension through a lever. The plunger system is most often found on copier attachments, and in many cases the spring lacks sufficient force and so a little extra push on the mechanism is required. The cantilevered system consists of a pivoting arm with the cutter at one end and the stylus at the other (see the photo on p. 32). This arrangement provides greater cutting pressure without proportionally increasing stylus pressure, and makes it easier to move the carriage along its bed, which yields a smoother cut.

Some of the plunger and cantilevered systems are available with a special traveling steady rest that attaches to and moves along with the carriage, supporting the spindle right next to the cutter, as shown in the photo on p. 32, allowing heavier cuts and helping to control whip. Unlike a standard, non-moving, adjustable steady rest, these special steadies require separate ring inserts to accommodate various-diameter spindles, and the blank must be accurately dimensioned so that its diagonal is the same as the diameter of the ring insert opening. Some manufacturers suggest making your own wooden inserts, but the friction between the blank and the insert generates a great deal of heat and the inserts fall apart after 30 or 40 spindles. Most of the traveling steady rests can be fitted with a precutter, a lead cutting knife that makes a rough first cut in front of the steady rest as the regular knife makes the finishing cut just behind it. The combination of two knives and a steady rest makes it possible to easily turn out thin spindles, such as those for a Windsor chair, which are difficult to hand-turn because they whip and vibrate (see the photo on p. 32). And this system works best on simple designs because it must complete the entire turning in just a single pass.

Operating a semi-automatic model – Operating most of the semi-automatic duplicators is a two-hand operation. One hand

controls the cutter, pulling it out as you approach high spots on the pattern or pushing it in to help the spring exert cutting force. The other hand moves the carriage up and down the length of the spindle. These lathes employ a variety of mechanisms to advance the carriage, including rack-and-pinion gears, stationary chains with movable sprockets, and stationary sprockets with moving chains or cables. Chain- and cable-drive systems will need periodic adjustments to maintain proper chain or cable tension, and you should avoid getting oil on cable-drive mechanisms, to prevent slippage. In operation, I didn't notice a particular difference between systems, although the cable drives tended to slip when the cutting depth approached ⅛ in. Some of the machines had an open chain mechanism and I was afraid these might clog or jam with chips during the cutting operation, but these fears turned out to be unfounded.

To get the smoothest cut, you must move the carriage down the length of the spindle at a slow, steady feed rate. It will take some practice to get the knack of it. Each machine has its own little idiosyncrasies; if possible, try out the duplicator you are considering or get references from the manufacturer so you can discuss performance with an experienced user. Smoothness of carriage operation is affected not only by the feed mechanism, but also by the fit of the carriage to the bed of the duplicator, which should move back and forth easily, with no play between carriage and bed. Any slop here is amplified at the point of the cutter and affects the quality of the reproduction. Carriages should have some means of adjustment, because even if the duplicator is set up perfectly at the factory, you will still need to adjust it to compensate for wear.

Manufacturers of duplicator lathes and attachments must feel that operating these tools is an intuitive process because the owner's manuals are generally very poor. In working with most of these duplicators, I found the first few attempts produced some pretty exotic firewood. Eventually I worked out a system of cutting my square blanks just slightly oversize and then roughing them out on the duplicators. You might prefer to rough the blanks out by hand first. For most of the duplicators, once the stock was roughed out, I found it easiest to watch the relationship of the stylus to the template instead of the more natural tendency to watch the cutter on the stock. Success of this approach depends on whether the template is visible while operating the machine. Working on one detail at a time, I hogged out the waste with multiple passes by running the carriage back and forth, stopping just shy of the template on each pass, as shown in the drawing. I then

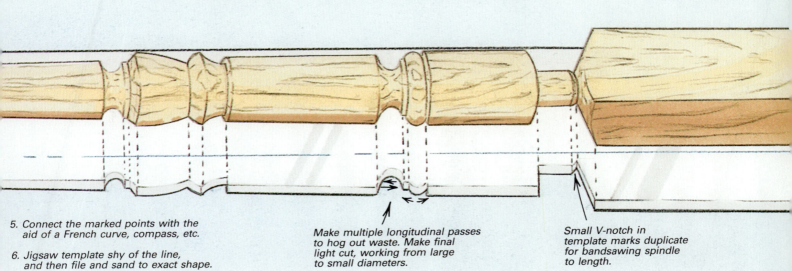

5. Connect the marked points with the aid of a French curve, compass, etc.

6. Jigsaw template shy of the line, and then file and sand to exact shape.

Make multiple longitudinal passes to hog out waste. Make final light cut, working from large to small diameters.

Small V-notch in template marks duplicate for bandsawing spindle to length.

cleaned up each section with a slow, steady final pass, starting the cutter on the larger diameters of the pattern and working in both directions toward smaller diameters. A little additional hand pressure on the carriage ensures the stylus stays in contact with the template, producing a more accurate copy. I found that cutting from small to larger diameters produced more tearout and that if the stylus got hung up on the template, it could distort the carriage, which in turn gouged the stock.

Taking very deep cuts can cause vibration and result in a rough surface. If you are having a problem, try taking lighter cuts and increasing lathe speed, especially on finishing cuts. I also found that steadying the spindle with my free hand helped control whip. A light grip and a glove will keep your hand from getting too hot.

Duplicating devices don't automatically reproduce exact copies of the original. The relationship between the stylus and the cutter determines if the copy will be a one-to-one reproduction of the template. On some of these machines, adjusting the cutter for a deeper pass changes this relationship, and so you must use calipers to check your turning as it progresses, to know when to stop. The more convenient and easier-to-use duplicators offer a locking final-depth stop that ensures all copies will be the same size. Some also have a micro-adjustment knob that allows setting the stop lock slightly full and then making a very light cleanup pass. Another convenience feature is adjustable carriage stops at each end of the duplicator bed to prevent the cutter from contacting the revolving drive center or tail center, or to prevent the stylus from dropping off the end of the pattern. Hitting the centers will dull the sharpest cutter, but there is the potential for a great deal more damage: If the stylus drops off the end of the pattern, the cutter can dig into the stock, jamming the lathe and possibly damaging either the lathe or the duplicator.

Many of the turners I talked to while researching this article indicated there is a break-even point at which they would consider using a duplicator. This break-even point will vary depending on the operator's skill and the degree of accuracy required in the reproduction. One turner, Tom Fantaccione, of Tom's River, N.J., who does a lot of reproduction work for house restorations, felt it wasn't worth the effort to develop a pattern and set up the duplicator unless he was turning more than 10 spindles. When you've reached your break-even point, you'll find that one of the machines listed in the chart will get you rolling again. □

Charley Robinson is an assistant editor of FWW.

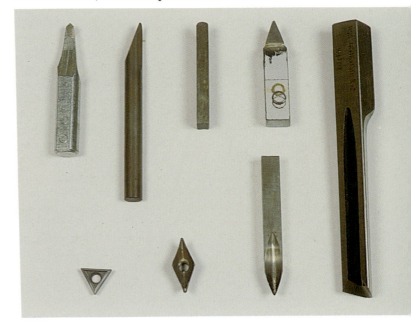

Above: *This lathe was modified with a tool rest so the operator could easily crank the carriage into position to add hand-turned details, such as square shoulders and undercuts, which aren't possible with most semi-automatic duplicators.* **Below:** *Cutters come in a variety of shapes and materials; top row, left to right: mild-steel scraper, two HSS scrapers, carbide-tip scraper. Bottom row, left to right: tri-pointed HSS shear cutter, HSS reversible shear cutter, HSS shear cutter, and V-shaped HSS shear cutter.*

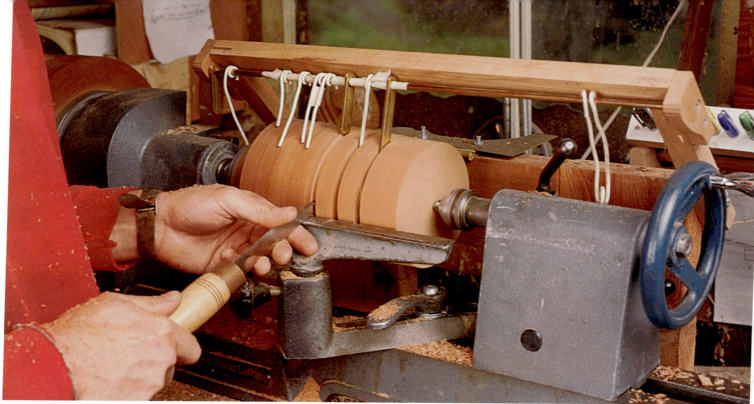

For fast and consistent multiples, the author uses a special jig, consisting of a series of dangling brass and wire fingers supported by a hinged frame. Fingers of varying lengths are set to *ride on specific places on the turning. When a finger falls through a groove that's been cut with a parting tool, Gellman knows he has reached the desired depth.*

Efficient Spindle Turning
Tricks for speed and consistency

by Steve Gellman

I began woodturning nine years ago on a light-duty Walker Turner lathe set up in the mudroom of our home. I turned firewood into mallets, rolling pins and spindles, although my tool techniques were unsophisticated and I used more sandpaper than I care to remember. As I progressed, I kept coming up against the difficulty of making identical copies of objects. With no formal training in woodturning, I had to rely on a laborious mishmash of techniques to get the job done. It was only after hundreds of hours working at the lathe that a process, an efficiency, began to emerge from it all.

Nowadays, I do a lot of architectural work, and specialize in building stairways for which I make all the parts, including balusters, finials and newel posts. I also manufacture several turned items, including wooden tops, turned boxes and a line of falconry accessories. All these products require good production spindle-turning skills. In this article, I'd like to share some of the tricks I've discovered during my trial-and-error learning process. Whichever ones you adopt, I think you'll find that they'll not only speed up your turning, but make it more consistent and enjoyable as well.

Improving your lathe—Whatever turning you do, it's important to work on a well-tuned lathe. Even if you have an inexpensive lathe, you can make several easy modifications to improve its performance. The simplest is to add weight to the lathe stand, which increases the tool's ability to absorb vibration and prevents the lathe from waltzing around the room when you turn a heavy, out-of-round blank. To increase the weight of my lathe, I built a ¾-in. plywood box to straddle the legs and filled the box with 750 lbs. of sand.

A couple of little lathe annoyances that can slow down production are also easy to fix. One is a nicked and dented tool rest, which can lead to a bumpy surface on the workpiece because it prevents you from making a sweeping cut with a smooth, continuous motion. First, you can avoid denting your rest by grinding off the sharp corners of your lathe tools. To clean up dents and nicks, I either file the surface of the rest smooth or epoxy an old hacksaw blade (with the teeth filed off) to the top of the rest. The blade provides a new rest surface, and the hard steel of the blade is very difficult to dent. Another annoyance I lived with for years was the lightweight little plastic handwheel on the tailstock. I finally bought a new 6-in. cast-iron wheel and handle (available from

A shopmade lathe clutch, shown here fitted to Gellman's Rockwell lathe, can speed up many spindle-turning jobs because it makes it possible to disengage the motor without switching it off. The clutch also allows turning speed to be decreased during a cut.

The author's shopmade steady rest consists of two wedge-shape pieces fit between the ways, one with a notch that bears against the spindle, preventing it from whipping. As the spindle diameter decreases, Gellman taps the rear wedge to advance the friction steady rest, which is made from naturally oily teak.

MSC, 151 Sunnyside Blvd., Plainview, N.Y. 11803; 800-645-7270, in N.Y. 516-349-7100) and had it machined to fit my tailstock. The heavier wheel tightens or loosens with a flip of the wrist, and makes mounting or unmounting a workpiece lightning fast.

Another time-saving accessory is a foot-operated clutch, shown in the top photo, above. I learned about this device from Del Stubbs, a California turner and teacher who uses the clutch both to save time and to make turning safer for beginning students. The clutch works like this: The lathe's motor is mounted on a hinged plywood plate that allows up-and-down movement. A cable tied to the motor plate goes up to a small pulley underneath the lathe ways and then down to a hinged foot plate near the floor. The operator disengages the clutch by stepping on the foot plate, hence pulling up on the motor plate and releasing the tension on the drive belt. The clutch makes it unnecessary to shut off the motor to install or remove a turning blank, check the progress of the turning or change the position of the tool rest. The clutch also

allows you to start the workpiece spinning slowly. Work carefully if you build a clutch for your lathe. Install lock washers on all the screws and bolts and use a braided steel cable; if the motor plate was to suddenly release, the lathe would unexpectedly and instantly begin spinning, possibly causing serious injury.

Making steady rests—Long, thin spindles tend to whip during turning unless stabilized by a steady rest, a friction device that supports the rotating spindle. In my shop, I often use my fingers to support the spindle during turning because I can feel what's happening between tool and wood. If a piece gets too hot, I use a rub block, a small piece of green wood with a V-notch cut in it.

There are dozens of steady rest designs, and many of those are described in *The Practical Woodturner*, by F. Pian, 1979, part of the Home Craftsman series published by Sterling Publishing Co. Inc., 2 Park Ave., New York, N.Y. 10016. I use three basic types. One commercially available rest has a rigid rim with three adjustable friction contacts. I prefer it for large architectural turnings because it surrounds the workpiece and locks it on the lathe, even if the piece should come loose during turning. The second type, which I made in my shop, has two ball bearings mounted on a post that fits into the tool-rest base. The bearings roll against and support the spindle—it's unbelievably loud, but effective. The third type of rest, and the one I use most often for production turning, is shopmade from two wedge-shape pieces of teak slipped in between the ways of the lathe bed. One wedge has a V-notch cut out that contacts the spindle (see the bottom photo at left). Although the oily teak prevents burning, I usually rub candle wax into the notch. Unlike a fixed rest that has to be moved and reset as the spindle gets thinner, my homemade rest can be quickly tapped down to maintain constant support of the spindle.

Holding the work—Chucking is the process of holding and driving turning blanks; employing an efficient chuck system is the key to profitably turning a large run of spindles. While there are lots of commercially available chucks, don't limit yourself to what's offered in catalogs. A woodturning lathe allows lots of room for creative implementation of homemade chucks and holding devices. Often in production, the workpiece will go through a number of processes and I often turn a special fitting for a specific job; for instance, if the spindle ends are round, I'll make a concave-shape tip. The only real requirement for homemade fixtures is that the headstock drive chuck must center the work and provide enough friction to spin the piece; the tailstock must grip the work so it runs true and provide enough pressure to keep the piece snug against the drive center. Most high-quality lathes have a Morse-taper hole in the headstock to accept the drive center and a similar hole in the tailstock for a live center. By turning a matching Morse taper on one end of a short blank and a cup, cone, sphere or square on the other end, you can customize a chuck to fit the particular spindle you're turning. Further, a custom center allows a turning that's already been cut from the lathe to be remounted for finish-turning or sanding.

Finding spindle centers—Finding the center of a blank quickly and precisely is important, especially when you have a dozen or more spindles to turn. For smaller spindles, I use a shopmade centering jig mounted under my lathe, shown in the photo on p. 40. It's comprised of four small square frames with a screw point protruding in the center of each one. To use it, you simply push the end of the blank into the frame that's just larger than the blank, rotate the blank until all four edges touch the frame and push in— it's much faster than marking diagonal lines.

Often, a spindle is temporarily removed from the lathe during turning; for instance, to drive a ferrule on a turned handle. To recenter properly, the spindle must go back on the drive center in the same position that it came off. Therefore, I notch one prong of my spur-style drive center with a small grinding bit in a Dremmel tool. After I chuck the spindles once, they bear an impression of the spur so I can easily refit them on the drive center.

Choosing lathe tools—Selecting the right tool is as important in turning as it is in any other woodworking task. This is especially important if you're turning multiples because the right tool will do the job faster and leave a better surface on the turning. Although I own many turning tools, I use just a few of them for most of my production work: a ½-in. deep-fluted gouge ground to a lady-finger profile, a 1-in. straight skew, a 2-in. rounded skew, a 1½-in. "peeler bar" (a square-nose scraper-like tool), ¾-in. and 2-in. gouges and an assortment of parting tools. For spindle work, I prefer tools with steep, slightly hollow-ground bevels that are angled between 30° and 32°. In contrast, most bowl gouges come ground to a shallow angle, sometimes only a few degrees. I also like grinding down the shoulders on all my gouges, producing a lady-finger profile, which looks like the blade of a spade shovel. Even though it means more sharpening, the gouge's steep beveled edge and the rounded shoulders allow me to get into tight places on a turning, like narrow coves or between beads, without the corners of the edge catching.

I've grown accustomed to using a ½-in. "long and strong" deep-fluted gouge for turning most of my beads and coves. A 2-in. gouge is a beginner's delight and a workhorse of a tool. This tool can level, hog out or take very fine shavings. The gouge's 1-in.-deep edge has corners high enough above where most cutting takes place that it has very little tendency to catch the spinning work. With the gouge's edge skewed to the work, I get a cut that's a cross between the cut produced by a regular skew and peeler bar.

I have a couple of different-size skews for different jobs. I use a ¾-in. or 1-in. skew for turning pummels, and for most ordinary operations, such as leveling, my 2-in.-wide carbon-steel rounded skew can't be beat. It's just like a regular straight skew, except I grind the diagonal cutting edge to a shallow convex curve with the edge bevel hollow ground and finely honed. The tool produces a very clean cut because the thin, sharp edge slices the wood fibers instead of scrapes them. I use the rounded skew like a regular straight skew for rough leveling, but the rounded blade gives me more edge to work with and is less likely to catch. Also, since the curved blade has less contact with a flat surface, there's less pressure on the workpiece and less likelihood of breaking a thin spindle.

One of my favorite lathe tools is the peeler bar because its wide edge allows full contact with the workpiece, so I can remove a lot of wood, fast. The tool is like a square-nose scraper, but is beefier and has a steeper bevel. I made my peeler bar from an old planer blade that's 1½ in. wide and ⅜ in. thick. Viewed from above, the profile of the cutting end is square, except for the left corner that's rounded to about a ½-in. radius. The entire cutting edge is ground to a 45° bevel. The rounded left shoulder of the tool allows long, fast pulling cuts from right to left without the edge digging in. To use the peeler bar for say, rounding a square blank, set the tool rest the thickness of the blade below center and position the tool at the middle of the blank. Now, drop one hand so the heel of the bevel contacts the spinning blank on center, angle the tool 15° to the axis of the blank and take a sweeping cut from the center outward (to avoid splitting). I often use my peeler bar to take long leveling cuts on straight or barrel-bellied spindles.

With any of these tools, the most important point to remember is that unless they're 100% sharp, you'll have to force them through the wood, and this is where most problems with tool

Gellman uses his shopmade center-finding jig, mounted conveniently under his lathe, to quickly mark the center on a spindle. After selecting the correct-size frame, he rotates the turning blank in the frame, automatically centering it, and then he pushes the blank against the screw in the center to mark it.

digging or grain tearing occur. My sharpening method involves grinding the bevel on a 100-grit aluminum oxide grinding wheel, turning at a slow 150 RPM to prevent heat from ruining the tempered edge, and then honing the edge on a fine India stone, using soap and water as a lubricant. My sharpening setup is directly behind where I stand at the lathe so I can quickly turn around to touch up an edge and get right back to work.

Jigs for turning multiples—Repetition and consistency are the keys to good production turning. Short of using a duplication lathe, the trick to efficiently turning identical spindles, like all the balusters for a staircase, depends on quickly establishing the location and depth of elements, such as pummels, coves and beads. There are many ways to do this, but the most common is to use a pattern or marking stick to locate the transitions and calipers to check the diameter of the spindle at various points. First, mark the end pummels and cut these shoulders with a skew or gouge. Then, rough-turn the length round and mark the transitional elements from the pattern or marking stick. Next, a parting tool is plunged in at each mark to reduce that detail to the proper diameter, which is checked with calipers; most production turners have enough calipers to set one to each diameter needed. On a long spindle, you'll need to set a steady rest and you might not want to cut the thinnest portions until the rest of the spindle is turned to avoid whipping problems. Now you can turn the areas between the transitional elements to shape. Some turners like to keep a pattern behind the lathe so they can cut the shape mostly by eye. It's amazing how accurate you can be this way.

In lieu of calipers and a pattern, there's a simple shopmade device that can aid the production of identical spindles. The jig, shown in the photo on p. 38, consists of a wood frame that's hinged off the back of the lathe and designed to swing over the bed. The top of the frame holds a rod from which a number of short lengths of wire and/or brass bar hang. These "fingers" are arranged, according to length, directly over the transition areas to act as both markers and depth indicators. Masking tape is used to keep the fingers in their proper locations on the rod. After the blank is turned into a rough cylinder, the fingers ride on the turning while a parting tool is used to cut the grooves. Each finger shows when the tool has cut deep enough by flipping through the groove to the back side of the turning. These fingers can be repositioned as needed and can be tailored to suit any production turning job. □

Steve Gellman is an architectural woodturner and stair builder in Arcata, Cal.

Chasing is an old technique for cutting any size wooden thread by hand on the lathe using simple shop-made tools.

Chasing Large Wooden Threads

An alternative to tap and die

by Richard Starr

W hen I first read about chasing, an old technique for cutting wooden threads by hand on the lathe, I couldn't believe such a simple method could work. How could anyone move a multi-toothed cutting tool across the spinning wood at just the right speed to cut an accurate thread? Yet, all the old books said it was easy so I tried it. Sure enough, after a few tries I was able to scratch out a recognizable thread. Since then, I've used chasing to make screw-top jars and to fit wooden handles to threaded sockets in pottery. Old-time turners used it to thread together sections of long turnings like canes and ivory candlesticks. You may find other applications.

Chasing tools are not available commercially, but they're easy enough to make yourself. Because the tools cut by scraping, they don't work on soft or crumbly woods. Hard maple is about the softest wood that works well. On the other hand, some hard

woods are too brittle and the threads break off. I've had good results with Osage-orange, ebony, lignum vitae and, especially, boxwood. Once, I even chased a thread in soapstone. Old turners chased threads in ivory and brass and probably would have appreciated some of the modern day plastics.

Making the tools—You'll need to make two chasers—an outside tool and an inside tool—to cut matching male and female threads. You can file the tools to cut any pitch, which is the distance between the crests of a thread expressed in threads per inch (tpi). One set can cut a screw of any diameter, though there is a lower limit that can be overcome by slightly modifying the tools—more on that later.

I make my chasers from ⅛-in. or ³⁄₁₆-in.-thick oil-hardening tool-steel flat stock (available from Manhattan Supply Co., 151 Sunny-

From *Fine Woodworking* magazine (September 1986) 60:53-57

After filing the end to a 60° bevel, lay out the chaser teeth with a screw pitch gauge (photo left and drawing below), then file the notches until the points touch the baseline (above). After striking a clean thread with the outside tool, the thread is deepened, or chased to depth, at a slower speed (right). The right hand pushes the tool from right to left.

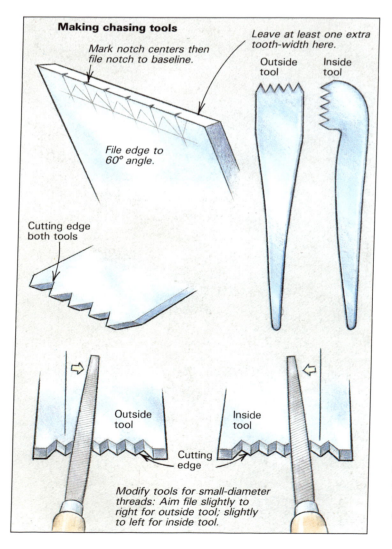

Making chasing tools

Mark notch centers then file notch to baseline.

Leave at least one extra tooth-width here.

File edge to 60° angle.

Outside tool   Inside tool

Cutting edge both tools

Cutting edge

Outside tool   Inside tool

Modify tools for small-diameter threads: Aim file slightly to right for outside tool; slightly to left for inside tool.

side Blvd., Plainview, N.Y. 11803). You can also make chasers from an old plane iron or a file, but you'll have to soften the metal first so it can be filed. This process, called annealing, is accomplished by heating the metal red hot, then letting it cool very slowly. I just drop the piece in the hot coals of my wood stove and leave it overnight with the cooling cinders.

Paint the steel with machinists' layout fluid or a magic marker and scribe the outline of the tool as shown in the drawing at left. Chasers should have four or five teeth, so the width of the tool will depend on the pitch you choose. Leave enough metal for at least an extra half-tooth on either side of the chasing tool.

Because all the filing is done at a 60° angle to the face of the metal, I made the jig shown in the photo (above, center). Hold the file level to the floor and you're at the correct angle. First, file a bevel on the end of the stock to establish the rake (undercut) of the tool. Now scribe the positions of each groove on the beveled end of the tool. These mark the gullets of the teeth, not the points, so the first and last marks should be located at the outer ends of the tool, as shown in the drawing. A five-pointed tool requires six marks. I use a thread gauge to help lay out the teeth since inch-rules aren't calibrated for odd fractions. Scribe a baseline that is slightly farther from the edge than the threads are deep. This ensures that when you file the notches they'll intersect to create sharp points at the cutting edge. For 60° threads the thread depth is about ⅞ of the distance between points.

Use a small triangular file to cut the grooves. First make a shallow notch at each scribe mark to locate the cut. File all the notches simultaneously, a few strokes in each one, rather than cutting one at a time to full depth. Be sure to hold the file level and at right angles to the jaws of the vise (unless you are filing a chaser for small-diameter screws, as explained below). Stop filing when the notch just touches the baseline. If one notch goes too deep, establish a new baseline and deepen all the notches.

Once the teeth are finished, rough out the shape of the tool

determine at what diameter this becomes necessary. You can extend the use of square-filed tools to somewhat smaller diameters by slightly lifting the right edge of the outside tool or the end of the handle of the inside tool as you cut the threads.

Most lathes were foot powered when thread chasing was in its heyday, but most of today's lathes run too fast to use these tools comfortably. I prefer to make the first cuts (called striking the thread) at about 400 RPM and subsequent cuts at much slower speeds. Try out the technique on your lathe as it is, but for frequent work you will want to modify it for lower RPMs. One way is to replace the belt pulleys with a larger one on the spindle shaft or a smaller one on the motor, or both. A better way is to add a jackshaft between the motor and the lathe. For my lathe, I bought a DC motor and an electronic control set originally made for a potters' wheel. The pedal control gives me a broad range of speeds.

Striking a thread—I've developed a style of using these tools that works well for me, but you'll want to find your own way. Turning is an individual's art.

For practice cutting outside threads, chuck a piece of maple or harder wood between centers and round off a cylinder. At the right end, turn a surface a bit smaller in diameter than the main cylinder. Chamfer the right edge to allow the chasing tool to enter easily, as shown in the photo on p. 44. Set the tool rest close to the wood at, or slightly above, the centerline. It helps to file the edge of your tool rest smooth so the chasing tools can slide without catching.

Hold the outside tool in your left hand, palm up, with your forefinger bearing against the tool rest to control depth of cut. Hold the tool level, or with the point slightly downward. The first two fingers of your right hand are used to push the tool to the left, supported by anchoring the other two fingers on the tool rest.

The teeth of the tool should enter the wood in an arc so that the first tooth touches first, then the others descend to the surface. To do this, your left hand pulls the handle slightly to the left, swinging it perpendicular to the lathe as your right fingers push the tool toward the left. Run the lathe at about 400 RPM while you practice this motion without actually touching the wood. Even experienced turners take a few swipes in the air to get the rhythm smooth and even. Feel ready? OK, go ahead and try gently striking your first thread.

Consider this: as the multi-toothed tool moves across the wood, each point is cutting its own groove. But when the tool is moving at just the right rate, the second tooth falls into the furrow plowed by the first, as do all the following points in their turn. When this is happening, the tool is removing much less wood and it moves more easily. This is a tactile cue that tells you you've hit it right. The correct cut tends to be deeper and, therefore, a bit more visible than wrong cuts. I find that if I unfocus my eyes and let them drift over the wood I get a strong visual cue. You'll be surprised how easy all this is, almost magical.

Of course, striking a thread is trial-and-error work and if you've left a rough surface of bad cuts, turn the surface clean for a fresh start. There are two problems that can occur even if you have managed to strike a clear thread. One is "drunkenness," where the thread appears to wiggle as it rotates. This is visible in the top left photo on the next page. You get a drunk thread when you push the tool with an uneven motion or just slightly too fast or slow. You can't correct this problem, so turn it clean and try striking again with a smoother motion and, perhaps, at a higher RPM.

The other error is striking a double thread, wherein the third

with a hacksaw, then file it to final shape. File right to the bottom of the outer notches to leave a complete tooth on either side of the tool. Ease all the edges so the tool will feel comfortable in your hand and slide easily on the tool rest.

Next, harden the teeth. Use a propane torch to heat the top surface of the teeth red hot. Quench the tool immediately in a can of motor oil and stir it around so it cools quickly. In most toolmaking the next step would be tempering, to reduce the brittleness of the steel. With chasers I've found, however, that the teeth are so short that there's no danger of breakage, so the extra hardness is a bonus. But be sure only the teeth get red hot or the tool will be too brittle and may break.

Turn a comfortable handle and make a ferrule from a piece of copper pipe. Drill a pilot hole for the tang of the tool. Heat the tang red hot and force the handle down on the tang, which will burn into the handle amid billows of smoke.

Sharpen the tool by rubbing its top face flat on a fine oilstone until you have a bright and polished surface. A brief touch on the stone during a job can result in a surprising improvement in the tool's cut.

Small-diameter threads—Large-diameter threads look like rings when viewed from the side, but small-diameter threads of the same pitch will look much more like a spiral—you can actually see the threads lean over. This lean is called the helix angle. The smaller the diameter, the more the threads lean. If chasing tools were thin enough, they would be able to cut threads on any size cylinder but, because of their thickness, the underside of the tool may interfere with the leaning threads on small-diameter screws. This results in rough cuts and breakouts. You can avoid this by filing a special set of tools with the grooves slightly skewed to accommodate the helix angle. When filing the outside tool, point the file slightly to the right; point the file slightly to the left on the inside tool. You'll have to experiment to

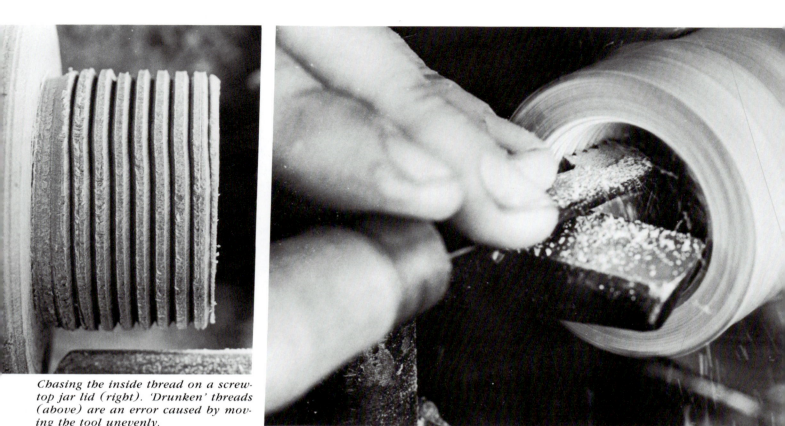

Chasing the inside thread on a screw-top jar lid (right). 'Drunken' threads (above) are an error caused by moving the tool unevenly.

tooth of the tool falls into the groove cut by the first tooth and the second and fourth teeth are cutting their own separate groove. You have pushed the tool exactly twice too fast. You can recognize multiple threads by the large helix angle—they seem to lean over more than they should. You can also check for them by counting the thread starts at the edge of the screw. Triple and quadruple threads are also possible. Turn it clean and try again.

Once you've struck a decent thread, you'll want to chase it to depth. I like to do this at a very low lathe speed, about 200 RPM, sometimes slower. Use the same motion as when striking to introduce the tool, but this time, take care to catch the first tooth of the tool in the original cut. This becomes easier as the cut gets deeper. When chasing, I usually lower the handle slightly, pointing the cutting edge upward. On very hard woods, I get the best cut with the bevel rubbing on the wood as though I was cutting with a gouge.

Never try to cut the threads so deeply that they have sharp crests. The chasing tool will cause breakouts before you get there and besides, sharp threads in wood are fragile.

Inside threads are much less prone to breaking out and are, therefore, easier to chase. Turn a cylinder of scrap between centers, then chuck it in a 3-jaw or screw chuck. Bore or turn a cylindrical opening in the end somewhat smaller in diameter than the outside thread you intend to fit it to. Chamfer the edge of the opening to ease entry of the tool. Set the tool rest near the wood and slightly above center.

The inside chasing tool must slide on its back edge along the tool rest to keep the teeth from snagging on the rest. Hold the tool in your right hand and pivot the tool slightly on its back edge to lift the teeth slightly off the rest. The cutting action will try to pull the tool down flat again, and you must resist this with your right wrist. Your left hand presses the back edge downward on the rest to keep it from chattering.

The inside tool is introduced to the wood in an arc, just like the outside tool. Push the end of the handle away from your body just a bit, and bring it toward you as you push the tool in. Toward the end of the cut, just before the tool hits bottom, twist the handle away from you, raising the teeth out of the cut. So, the motion of your right hand is a combination of pushing toward the headstock while twisting your wrist away from you. It's a smooth, swooping motion and easier than it sounds. Practice the motion a few times with the lathe running, then boldly, but gently, strike the thread. The inside tool practically strikes by itself, but it's easy to start multiple threads.

When chasing the thread to depth, try to disengage the tool before hitting the bottom of the hole. Actually though, the inside threads are so sturdy that they practically eject the tool if it bottoms out.

When fitting outside and inside threads, you trim one or the other, or both, whichever is appropriate for your project. Inside threads can be increased in diameter by trimming the crests with a scraping tool. Outside threads are easily reduced using a skew chisel or a square-end scraper. Then chase the threads to full depth again and try the fit.

Wooden threads should fit quite loosely to accommodate seasonal changes in dimension. I listen for a pleasant click as I wiggle the mating pairs axially. The firmness of the joint comes from the tension between the snugged-up shoulders, not from tight-fitting threads. While fitting, you may have trouble unscrewing a very tight thread. A little candle wax on the threads before testing will prevent this. I keep a monkey wrench nearby just in case. Once you have a good fit, sand the crests of the threads lightly with 220-grit paper. □

Richard Starr teaches woodworking at Richmond Middle School in Hanover, N.H., and is the author of the book, Woodworking with Kids *(The Taunton Press, 1982). Photos by author.*

Turning a screwtop jar

Chasing threads takes practice, but once you feel confident, try making a screwtop jar. I messed up my first four or five, but the rest were easy. The jar shown here is about 1¾ in. in diameter and made of Osage-orange, which is very hard. Like all of my jars, it has an 8-tpi thread.

Turn a cylinder between centers, face off the right end with a skew or small gouge and chuck that end in a 3-jaw or a screw chuck. Part off the stock as shown in photo **1**, leaving enough in the chuck for the lid. Hollow the lid with a ¼-in. gouge and finish with a scraper. I use a ½-in. roundnose scraper sharpened to cut on both the end and the left side. The inside flange of the lid should be a straight-sided cylinder for about ½ in., and be roughly ¼ in. thick.

Now strike and chase threads on the inside of the lid (**2**) as explained on p. 43. You can sand and finish the inside now to avoid having to rechuck it later.

Chuck up the bottom of the jar with the end from which you cut the lid facing inboard and, with a ½-in. skew (or a square-end scraper), turn down the flange that fits inside the lid. Turn the flange about ⅛ in. larger in diameter than the opening in the top. If you're just learning how to chase threads, turn it a lot larger so you can clean up bad threads several times before the diameter gets too small. Square off the shoulder and cut a groove at the shoulder about the width and depth of a thread, to allow the top to screw all the way to the shoulder. With a skew, chamfer both ends of the flange (**3**).

Strike and chase the threads (photo p. 41) and test the fit of the top. You'll probably need to trim the threads on the jar with the skew or scraper to get the lid to fit. After trimming, chase the threads to depth again and re-test the fit. Repeat the trimming, chasing and testing until you get a good fit.

When the lid fits, hollow the jar. I chuck a Forstner or multispur bit in a tailstock chuck, bore out the inside and finish with a scraper. You could also hollow the inside with a small gouge and finish up with a scraper. After hollowing, trim the rim of the flange with a scraper and sandpaper. If you can reverse your lathe, work on the far edge of the rim to avoid chipping the entrance of the thread.

Measure the depth of the jar and mark the bottom on the outside. Now screw on the lid and turn the jar to shape. Remove the lid frequently, to check the wall thickness. Sand and finish the jar on the lathe, then part it off.

In the waste piece left in the chuck, bore and thread a socket to fit the threads on the jar. Now you can turn and finish the bottom of the jar. Save the threaded socket for future jars. —*R.S.*

The threads on the screwtop jar (top) were cut on the lathe with 8-tpi chasing tools. The jar body is parted off (center) leaving the lid in the chuck. A ½-in. skew (above) turns the flange ⅛ in. larger than the opening in the top.

Alabaster on the Lathe

Turning stones into translucent vessels

by Max Krimmel

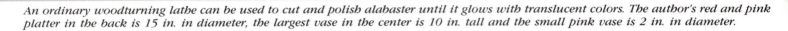

An ordinary woodturning lathe can be used to cut and polish alabaster until it glows with translucent colors. The author's red and pink platter in the back is 15 in. in diameter, the largest vase in the center is 10 in. tall and the small pink vase is 2 in. in diameter.

Turning rocks is tricky, but that just adds to the fun. And delicately colored stones like alabaster, when turned, develop a pleasant translucent glow. I conduct turning workshops across the country and have been impressed at the popularity of alabaster work. I suppose that's not too surprising considering turners are such an adventurous lot, eager to chuck on anything from a worm-eaten tree trunk to a variety of fruits and vegetables. In addition, you don't need any special equipment for alabaster, nor any special techniques. The process is just like scraping out a wood bowl, only slower, although alabaster does have a couple of personality quirks. It's not so much that the material is contrary as that it is different and takes a little getting used to.

Alabaster is a crystalline form of gypsum (calcium sulfate), which is the main ingredient in Sheetrock. Gypsum rates a #2 on one commonly used hardness scale (talc being #1 and diamond #10). You might notice some variation in hardness from piece to piece, but even though it's rock, all alabaster is soft. Impurities are responsible for its subtle colors, which can range from translucent whites through pinks, to browns, grays and greens. The turned pieces are a bit like crystal wine glasses—lovely, but if you drop one, that's that.

You can rough out the alabaster blanks with any variable-speed reciprocating saw and a large-tooth or bimetal blade. A bandsaw running bimetal skip-tooth blades at slow speeds will cut alabaster. The low-tech chisel-and-mallet approach also works fine. Currently, I'm mounting the rock on the lathe and using an air chisel to knock off enough material to balance the piece, then using a narrow scraper known as a Stewart Slicer (available from Dennis Stewart, 2502 N.W. 4th Ave., Hillsboro, Oreg. 97124; 503-640-3089).

For the actual turning, I use carbide-tipped scrapers. Commercially available woodturning tools are fine, but I made my scrapers by unbrazing carbide tips from old router bits, then rebrazing them onto square-stock steel (available from KBC Tools, 6300 18-Mile Road, Sterling Heights, Mich. 48078; 800-521-1740, or 800-482-1047 in Michigan). You can also order tools specially made for alabaster from Jerry Glaser, 8341 Delgamy Ave., Playa del Rey, Calif. 90293. I sharpen my carbide tips with a 120-grit silicon carbide (greenstone) wheel.

High-speed steel scrapers are best for the finishing cuts (see top, right photo on the facing page). The steel edges aren't as durable as carbide, but they produce a cleaner cut, probably because they can be sharpened to a finer edge. I grind the ends square with no bevel. This way I can use one side until it is dull, then flip it over and use the other side. These high-speed steel scrapers are available from Craft Supplies USA, 1287 E. 1120 S., Provo, Utah 84601; (801) 373-0917. Craft Supplies also sells double-faced tape, the type of pin chuck I use (the version included with combination or six-in-one chucks) and Hot Stuff cyanoacrylate glue, which is invaluable for holding the work together.

Alabaster can be crumbly because of fractures and stresses within the stone, so it can break easily on the lathe. I turn each bowl as thin as I dare, usually about ⅛ in. to 3/16 in. My current success rate is about 80% and would be even lower if it were not for the cyanoacrylate glue. Once the outside is roughed to shape, use thin "original" Hot Stuff on anything that even looks like a fracture in the stone. If the glue soaks into the crack, I go over it with the thicker "Super T" Hot Stuff and then spray on the Hot Stuff accelerator, which speeds glue hardening. If the glue doesn't seem to flow into the crack at all, I assume the crack just looks like a fracture. I repeat this procedure whenever I get nervous about things breaking, usually on the inside when the piece is about ¼ in. thick and always just before the final thickness.

Safety hazards—Be aware: There is *always* a chance the block will shatter. Even if everything is going well, dust is a problem. Alabaster dust is similar to Sheetrock dust, so wear a dust mask or a respirator,

From *Fine Woodworking* magazine (January 1989) 74:55-57

A pin chuck, fit into a center hole drilled in the rim side, holds the blank.

The blank can be rough-cut round with a reciprocating saw.

Initial scraping with carbide-tipped tools brings the stone to rough shape. Here, the bottom of the bowl is being trimmed flat with a high-speed steel scraper.

Above: To center and clamp the preturned wood base to the piece, the author uses a stub with the proper Morse taper for the tailstock on one end and threads for a faceplate on the other. The base is then glued to the stone using the tailstock as a centering clamp. Wooden rim segments are applied with cyanoacrylate glue. Below: Turning procedures are much the same as for scraping cuts in wood.

use a dust collector, and if possible, work outside. I use a Makita 410 dust collector, with its intake nozzle mounted near the tool rest. This clears the air and helps keep the dust out of the headstock bearings. In addition to breathing problems, the dust can dry out your skin severely, so I wear latex gloves. Of course, wear a face shield: These are rocks, not wood chips, that will be flying off the lathe. I recommend steel-toe shoes, because the rocks are quite a bit heavier than wood, and if you turn enough of them, you will inevitably drop one off the lathe. The last time this happened to me, the 105-lb. piece hit the floor and rolled off through the wall.

Attaching alabaster to the lathe—I usually start with a pin chuck from the rim side, then proceed as shown in the photos on the previous page. The only unusual gadget I use is a device to center and clamp the preturned wood base to the piece. It is simply a stub with the proper Morse taper for the tailstock on one end and threads for a faceplate on the other end. With the bowl on the headstock and the base on the faceplate, I screw the base/faceplate assembly onto the stub, insert the stub into the tailstock, then wind the tailstock out until the base and bowl connect. This avoids turning a mortise and tenon to center the bowl on the base.

You can also adapt other chucking systems to alabaster. You can grind a flat on what will be the base of the piece with a belt sander, glue on a preturned wood base, glue or, for small pieces, double-tape a waste block to this base and screw a faceplate to the waste block. Or, you can grind a flat on the rim side, tape it to a faceplate, turn the outside, then glue on a base and waste block as before. Use whichever method seems most comfortable to you.

Turning techniques—You must rely on a fairly gentle touch as you turn, because alabaster isn't flexible. The rotational energy of the lathe must be absorbed by the tool, the tool rest and your hands, or by the scraping away of the stone's surface. Too much pressure or a slip with the scraper either stops the lathe, knocks the piece off the faceplate or breaks the stone.

You will likely find two additional crystals in alabaster: quartz and selenite. Quartz crystals are very hard and may be as large as a pencil eraser or as small as a grain of sand. You will feel them and hear them; they will take the edge right off your tool, sometimes making sparks as they do so. If you run into quartz, stop and dig it out. My "quartz digger" is simply a concrete nail with a piece of wood for a handle. Selenite is another crystalline form of gypsum. It usually is found on the outside of the rocks and looks similar to mica. You can cut selenite, and if it runs deep into the rock, it can yield spectacular results. But, selenite crystals usually separate from the rest of the piece, so keep filling with Hot Stuff as you turn, as this will sometimes keep the crystals in place.

If you decide to permanently attach a wood base or rim to the alabaster, the Hot Stuff glue makes a good permanent bond. Whenever one of my joints has failed, there has always been a layer of alabaster left attached to the wood, indicating the stone, not the glue, as the weak link. Just remember: The wood will move as its moisture content changes; the stone will not. With wood pieces as small as the rims on these bowls, wood movement doesn't seem a problem; with the larger bases, it can be. After the piece is turned, finish all surfaces of the base with a moisture-sealing finish.

Finishing alabaster—I first sand the surface with 36 grit for rougher shaping, working up through 15-micron sandpaper (available from The Luthier's Mercantile, Box 774, 412 Moore Lane, Healdsburg, Calif. 95448; 707-433-1823) for that final glow. I use all the sandpaper dry. My favorite finish is paste wax, but you might prefer lacquer or the traditional oil finishes commonly applied to wood turnings.

Finding alabaster

I get most of my stone from Colorado Alabaster Supply, 1507 N. College, Fort Collins, Colo. 80524; (303) 221-0723. Stan Jones, the owner, says that the company deals mostly by the ton, and small pieces suitable for turning are, in effect, waste that may or may not be available at any given time. You may have to wait six weeks to two months for delivery of a small order. Typical cost is as low as 30¢ to 35¢ per pound, with a nominal handling charge.

I suggest you start with a 20-lb. to 30-lb. block, which in my experience, would be large enough for a 6-in. by 2-in. bowl. Drill cores of 2 in. to 3½ in. in diameter are sometimes available, too. Here again, if you want 500 lbs. of cores, Jones will be happy to core out as many rocks as necessary; if you want 10 lbs. and he is out, the order might take a while.

A speedier yet more expensive route is to order from a specialty supplier. Sculpture House (30 E. 30th St., New York, N.Y. 10016; 212-679-7474) has alabaster (mostly imported Italian) for immediate shipment and will help you figure out what to order over the phone. Cost is $1.50 per pound, and the minimum order is $50.

You might be able to obtain the rock from local sculptors or sculpture-supply houses as well: Alabaster is a very popular carving stone. Here in the West, you can often find alabaster at rock shops along the highway. If they don't have it, they probably know who does.

Another approach is to become a prospector, which gets you the best prices of all, usually free. Look for places on the map with names like Alabaster, Gypsum or Plasterville. Gypsum, the main component of Sheetrock, is fairly common, and where there is gypsum, there will be alabaster. By asking around, you can usually get permission to dig it. The question is whether or not it will be solid enough and large enough to be useful. Here's how to test: You want a piece that gives off a good ring when struck. Pick the piece up and give it a sharp tap. (My favorite tapper is a wooden-handle rigging axe, which is a framing hammer that combines a typical hammerhead with a hatchet face instead of a claw.) A solid piece will have a clear clink or a ring. If you get the sound of an indistinct "thud," look for fractures and break off anything that looks loose, or try holding the piece differently, then tap again. This is pretty easy for a 20-lb. rock. With a 150-lb. rock, however, it is more of a problem; still, you can usually balance it on a corner and get a ring. With a 500-lb. rock, good luck!   —M.K.

One final caution about finishes: Your bowls must be purely decorative or at least reserved for the storage of dry goods, because alabaster dissolves in water. How quickly? Well, a few drops of water on a waxed alabaster surface probably won't make marks, but I once filled a bowl with water, and the liquid noticeably etched the surface in half an hour. Obviously, if there is a fracture in the piece where water can seep through, things will only get worse. To avoid this kind of damage, I sometimes lacquer the inside surface, especially on enclosed shapes. I don't especially like the look or feel of the lacquer, but it is hard to see inside these enclosed vessels anyway. I also think that with enclosed shapes it is more likely that someone down the line will put water in them. In those cases, lacquering should work fine, unless a possible natural fracture in the stone eventually causes the lacquer to check.

One of the best rules when beginning to work with alabaster is that if at first you don't succeed, keep trying. As I mentioned earlier, about 20% of my starts are failures, but in the beginning, they were more like 40%. Half of these are due to excessive concentrations of quartz or structural problems with the stone, and half are just my mistakes. Have fun: After all, that's the ultimate point of it all.   □

Max Krimmel is a guitarmaker, illustrator and turner. He lives in Boulder, Colo. All photos are by the author.

Tagua: The Vegetable Ivory Substitute

Clead Christiansen turns palm nuts into translucent vessels

by Fred J. Hunger

Tagua, a vegetable material from the nut of a South American palm tree, looks, feels and works like animal ivory. It has been used for decades to make small functional and decorative items.

Clead Christiansen is one woodworker who turns tagua on the wood lathe to make tiny translucent bowls, boxes, vases, rings and vessels, like the ones shown here.

Animal ivory has been crafted into functional and decorative objects for millennia. But the potential extinction of the animals that provide that precious material has made the question of whether or not to use ivory a serious ethical issue. Those in favor of using ivory say it's a shame to waste the tusks of elephants or walrus that have died naturally; those against it say that even using "antique" ivory, which has been around longer than these issues have been argued, creates a public desire for animal ivory—and a market for the poachers who will wantonly slaughter ivory-bearing beasts into extinction.

Fortunately, there is an ivory substitute available that may resolve the ethical dilemma for many craftsmen who want to use small pieces of ivory. It's a natural material that has most of animal ivory's working and aesthetic qualities, and it literally grows on trees: The tagua nut is the seed of a South American palm tree. One craftsman who has used tagua extensively is Clead Christiansen, a woodturner in Ogden, Utah. Christiansen first became aware of the tagua nut when he saw a scrimshaw artist engraving the material at a Maryland craft show in 1982. He believed that if tagua could be engraved, then it probably could be turned as well. Since then, Christiansen has turned hundreds of tagua nuts into beautiful miniature vases, boxes, bowls, rings and vessels, like those shown above. In this article, I'll describe the tools and methods Christiansen uses for turning a tagua vessel on a regular woodturning lathe. But first, a little more background on the amazing tagua nut.

All about tagua—Sometimes called ivory nuts, tagua nuts come from the ivory palm tree *(Phytelephas macrocarpa),* where they grow in clusters weighing up to 25 lbs. The ivory palm is native to the equatorial regions of Central and South America, and flour-

ishes along the banks of the Rio Magdalena, in Columbia. After the tagua (pronounced tah-wah by Andean natives) nuts are harvested, they become dry and hard, protected by a crusty, shell-like covering. A medium-size tagua nut is approximately 1½ in. long by 1¼ in. in diameter. It is rounded with four slightly flat sides, a pointed end, and a stem end that is slightly concave, much like the indentation on the stem end of an apple. The tagua nut is completely non-toxic, composed of mannose sugar; in fact, when the nut is first harvested, it is soft, edible and sweet.

Tagua ivory, according to Shirl Schabilion's booklet, *All in a Nutshell,* has been used as a crafting and commercial raw material for more than 160 years. The Japanese have been using it for 100 years or more for carved netsukes and, since Victorian times, tagua has been fashioned into jewelry. It was also used extensively in button manufacturing until plastics became popular in the mid-1900s. In past decades, craftsmen have found tagua nut ivory quite suitable for turned and carved needle boxes, dice, cane handles, scrimshaw, and other applications for durable, attractive items. There are even stories that one man used tagua to construct replacement dentures for himself (an indication that the dried, carved nut is moisture resistant). Today, tagua nuts are available from several mail-order sources, including: Woodcraft Supply, 210 Wood County Industrial Park, Parkersburg, W.V. 26102-1686; (800) 225-1153, (304) 428-4866; The Turning Post, 225 23rd St., Ogden, Utah 84401; (801) 393-2320; Mississippi Petrified Forest, Box 37, Flora, Miss. 39071; (601) 879-8189; or Lee Valley Tools Ltd., 1080 Morrison Drive, Ottawa, Ont., Canada K2H 8K7; (613) 596-0350.

Mounting the nut for turning—To prepare the ivory nut for turning, a portion of its outer covering is sanded away, usually at

Left: Before turning, the tagua nut is sanded flat on one end and glued to the end of a dowel to be held in the lathe by a spigot-type chuck. Christiansen checks the nut-to-dowel fit before bonding. Right: Turning small vessels from tagua is much like turning miniatures from dense hardwood. Christiansen uses a ³⁄₈-in. bowl gouge, with the tip reground to a lady-finger profile, to rough-turn the outside of the vessel. Below: Producing shavings that look like coconut, Christiansen starts hollowing the inside of the vessel using a ¹⁄₈-in.-deep fluted gouge, cutting from the edge toward the center.

Left: By positioning a lamp above the spinning tagua vessel, Christiansen can judge its wall thickness by watching the shadow of the tool and the light color of the translucent tagua. He uses a modified dental tool with a reground tip to contour the inside. Above: After sanding all the way down to 600-grit, the tagua vessel is polished to a high shine with a small cloth buffing wheel chucked in an electric hand drill.

the more pointy end, creating a flat surface. The nut is then glued to a short (approximately 2 in. long), 1-in.-dia. hardwood dowel using cyanoacrylate adhesive, which can be purchased at a hobby or hardware store as Super Glue, Hot Stuff or Flex Zap. While gluing, Christiansen uses a spray-on accelerator called Hot Shot to speed the curing time of the glue. I asked Christiansen about using a five-minute epoxy instead of the cyanoacrylate, but he said epoxy didn't seem to work well for gluing tagua.

After the glue is set, the dowel is inserted into the lathe's headstock collet, a spigot chuck or a self-centering three-jaw chuck, so that the dowel extends about ¾ in. beyond the chuck. (Using the three-jaw chuck is a hazard to fingers and hands, and great care needs to be taken.) Christiansen uses an old Oliver lathe, set to rotate at approximately 2,000 RPM.

The method Christiansen developed for turning tagua nuts into tiny translucent products is fairly simple. Actually, turning tagua is very similar to turning regular hardwoods; Christiansen uses the same tools, techniques and about the same amount of tool pressure against the turning tagua. Good lighting is provided by an adjustable lamp set very close to the turning workpiece, shining from the back side of the lathe. Christiansen wears a face shield and follows the same safety practices he would for any woodturning.

Turning the outside—Before turning begins, the tool rest is positioned just below the centerline of the lathe and is set as close as possible to the tagua nut so that it just clears the rough nut. The initial angle of the tool rest in relationship to the lathe's centerline is between 7° and 10°, with the tool rest closer at the chuck end (see the top, right photo on the facing page). This setting allows the bottom of the turned vessel to be shaped first. Then, Christiansen rough-turns the vessel on the outside, using ⅛-in.- and ⅜-in.-dia. fluted gouges. (He uses Henry Taylor brand gouges that are available from Craft Supplies USA, 1287 E. 1120 South, Provo, Utah 84601; 801-373-0917.) The gouge's cutting edges are sharpened to a "fingernail" profile so that they cut with a shear-scraping action, as described in Steve Gellman's article on pp. 38-40. The actual cutting takes place just about the centerline of the spinning tagua nut. Instead of dust, the shear-scraping produces thin shavings that look just like finely shredded coconut. The tool rest should be adjusted frequently to remain very close to the work during roughing out, to prevent chatter problems; however, these nuts have very good dimensional stability and rarely crack or break apart during turning.

The final shape of a turned tagua vessel is affected by several things: the original size and shape of the raw nut, as well as by the nut's internal structure. Each nut has a natural cavity inside and a small hole, connecting the cavity to the outside, covered by a small kernel. You must cut around these features so you don't end up with a void in the finished object, unless it's desired; Christiansen sometimes accentuates a hole in a vessel, such as the small vase in the photo on p. 49. If you're turning a small bowl, vase or other vessel that's open at the top, it's best to glue the nut to the dowel with the navel pointing away from the dowel. Still, the shape of the turning might have to change as you discover the extent of the void inside.

Hollowing—To hollow the inside of a vessel, the tool rest is repositioned perpendicular to the centerline at the free end of the nut. The lip is formed at the beginning of the hollowing process. While cutting the lip, Christiansen stops the lathe often to verify lip thickness, because the dark color of the natural edge looks deceptively wide when seen with the vessel spinning. Christiansen often leaves the natural brown edge of the tagua's crusty outer shell intact on the lip, as a decorative touch.

To start hollowing, an initial entrance hole is made with the ⅛-in. gouge plunged into the nut until it encounters the natural cavity inside the nut. The kernel is removed during the evacuation of the nut's center. Initial cutting into the irregular shape of the nut must be done very carefully to avoid snagging the material. It's best to start the entrance cut at the outer perimeter of the nut and move the tool toward the center. This eliminates chatter, which can result while making the rough surface cuts on the interior of the vessel.

For the major hollowing, Christiansen uses a modified dentist's tooth-filling packing tool. This tool has an approximate 60° elbow near its cutting end, which makes it handy for reaching inside a bulbous vessel. He regrinds the top surface of the tool to create a flat, sharp cutting edge (similar to a round-nose scraper), and then he mounts the tool in a hardwood handle. (Dental tools are available from dental-supply houses for approximately $15 or, if your dental bill is paid, you might ask your dentist for an old one.) As Christiansen hollows the vessel deeper and deeper, the shavings tend to get stuck inside, so he uses a simple soda straw to blow them out.

Christiansen continues hollowing with the modified dental tool until the wall starts getting thin. At this point, he positions the desk lamp above and slightly behind the turning, until he can actually see the shadow of the tool through the translucent tagua nut (see the bottom, left photo on the facing page). By gauging the darkness or lightness of the nut, Christiansen can tell how thin the vessel's wall is getting. Experience with this method tells him when the wall thickness is just right—about 1/16 in.

Trimming, sanding and buffing—After the wall of the vessel is worked to a uniform thickness, Christiansen removes any ridges and smooths out rough areas left from the hollowing-out process. He repositions the tool rest to the outside of the workpiece as before and then shapes the vessel's base and does any final trimming or fairing on the outside.

After all the shaping is done, the tool rest is removed from the lathe to allow unobstructed access to the vessel for sanding and buffing. The nut is then carefully sanded, usually beginning with 220-grit paper. Christiansen sands the vessel's exterior with the lathe running and until all scratches and tool marks are gone. He sands with progressively finer-grit paper, until final-sanding with 600-grit. Next, the nearly finished vessel is buffed using a 4-in.-dia., white-cotton buffing wheel chucked into a hand drill. Christiansen first charges the wheel with brown tripoli buffing compound (available from a jeweler-supply house) and then presses it against the spinning vessel (see the bottom, right photo on the facing page).

After buffing, the tool rest is reinstalled and positioned parallel to the lathe's centerline, to allow the vessel to be parted off the dowel. Most vessels will part-off easily; however, it's prudent to keep a hand around the vessel while parting, just in case. The little ridge or boss that remains on the bottom of the vessel can be sanded away by hand.

In an hour, an experienced tagua-nut turner can produce three or four miniature vessels, which typically sell for about $25 each, although some of the best work sells for hundreds of dollars. Christiansen signs the bottom of the each tagua turning he makes, using a vibrating marker (the kind used to identify tools and other valuables). Hot branding-iron-type markers should be avoided, because the heat may scorch or crack the nut. □

Fred Hunger writes and works in Ogden, Utah.

The Old Schwamb Mill

A place for skilled hands in the Industrial Age

by William Tandy Young

I t's a blistering July afternoon, and the second floor gluing room at the Old Schwamb Mill is a clapboard furnace. Working to assemble a picture frame before the fast drying Titebond sets, I imagine that the beads of dripped hide glue that have built up like coral on the benches and floor of the room since the Civil War will begin to glisten and move if it gets any hotter. Outside, kids with the summer off lounge against the sluice gate and embankments of the stream that runs behind the mill on its way through Arlington, Mass., and into Boston Harbor.

Were it closer to 1864, when the skilled German immigrant brothers Charles and Frederick Schwamb began working wood in

this building, the scene would be somewhat different. The kids might be at a farm or another mill downstream, working for a wage. The stream itself would be powering the mill and other enterprises along the waterway. And I, as one of thirty workers in these cramped quarters, would be furiously brushing that hot glue and clamping work before it gelled, with the room being sealed and heated to a year-round hundred degrees plus to keep the glue workable. Pressure to produce was intense; outside in the yard, where today a few cars dot the parking lot, there used to be stacks of lumber so large that mapmakers drew them as buildings.

The industrialization of woodworking in America was still

From *Fine Woodworking* magazine (May 1986) 58:74-78

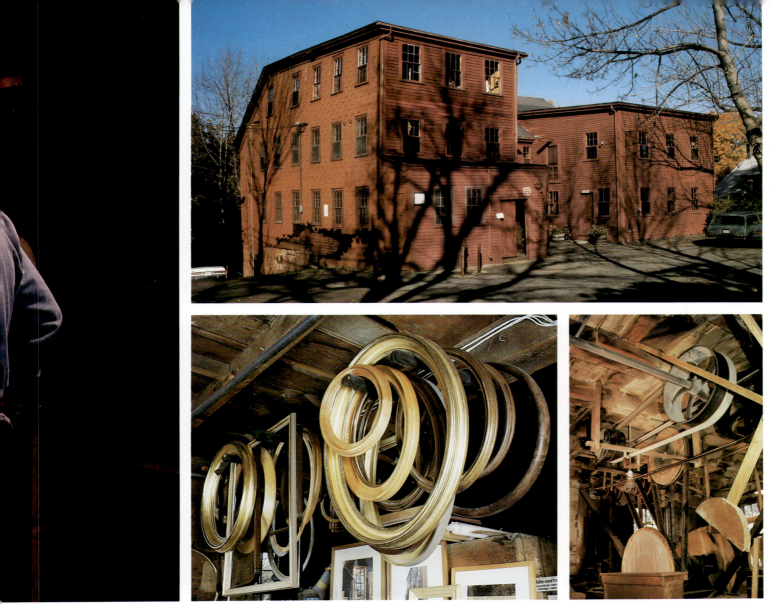

Young demonstrates oval turning on one of the Old Schwamb Mill's eccentric lathes, facing page. In its heyday, up to 30 workers would have made the Mill hum, turning out high-style frames such as the ones shown above. The old system of jackshaft and belts, at lower right, still drives most of the machinery, but two 7-HP electric motors have replaced the waterwheel as the source of power.

gaining momentum when the Schwamb brothers took over the site, which was originally developed in 1650. Saved from demolition in 1969 by mill director Patricia C. Fitzmaurice and other members of the Schwamb Mill Preservation Trust, the mill is now listed in the National Register of Historic Places—a working museum, open to the public. The Mill carries on today as the country's oldest and leading maker of the hand-turned oval and circular portrait and mirror frames that were once essential to high-style interiors. The Mill is an authentic capsule record of the developing Machine Age, one of the few remaining examples of the thousands of small, family-owned mills that once proliferated along moving waterways throughout the land.

While the mainstream demand for handmade oval and circular frames is gone, the Mill continues to produce them for museums and collectors, using the 19th-century machines that dominate the ground floor. There are no toys among these fixed pieces; they include a 24-in. patternmakers' jointer, a 36-in. bandsaw and a double-spindle shaper with a 4-ft. by 6-ft. table. Patterns, jigs, saw blades and cutters abound, and the entire northwest corner of the room is taken over by molding knives, arranged in rows and in pigeonholes with sample cuts, each labeled with a customer's name, not a job or catalog number. It's a system that must only have been fully understood by the molding men themselves.

Two main pulley shafts, one overhead and one below the main floor, drive most of the machinery via metal-laced leather belts that shuttle from idler to drive pulleys to engage individual machines. Where once water, then steam systems powered the pulleys, now two discreet 7-HP electric motors do the job. Babbitt and split-bronze bearings still prevail—during regular maintenance sessions, the machine room can become a forest of oil fills, wicks, dams and catch cups to whoever has to clamber among the machines, squeeze between bracings, or hang from empty girt mortises with one hand on a pump oiler (surely once the job of a twelve-year-old).

The hardest machines to maintain are the elliptical faceplate lathes, in a family of sizes, that were once the heart of the Schwamb operation and that are, today, easily the objects of greatest interest. The faceplate mechanisms are as mechanically other-worldly as the innards of a gyrating carnival ride. At these stout headstocks, the most skillful Schwamb employees stood side by side the day long, scraping profiles and rabbets into glued up oval or circular frame blanks.

The turners worked briskly at daylit work stations—which they could not desert—to earn a workaday wage. Many of the profiles required extensive layout, fancy eyesight, a good sense of proportion and delicate, whole-body movements to execute. To those who are convinced of a wholesale disappearance of elevated hand skills in the burgeoning Machine Age, one can counter that these

How an eccentric lathe works

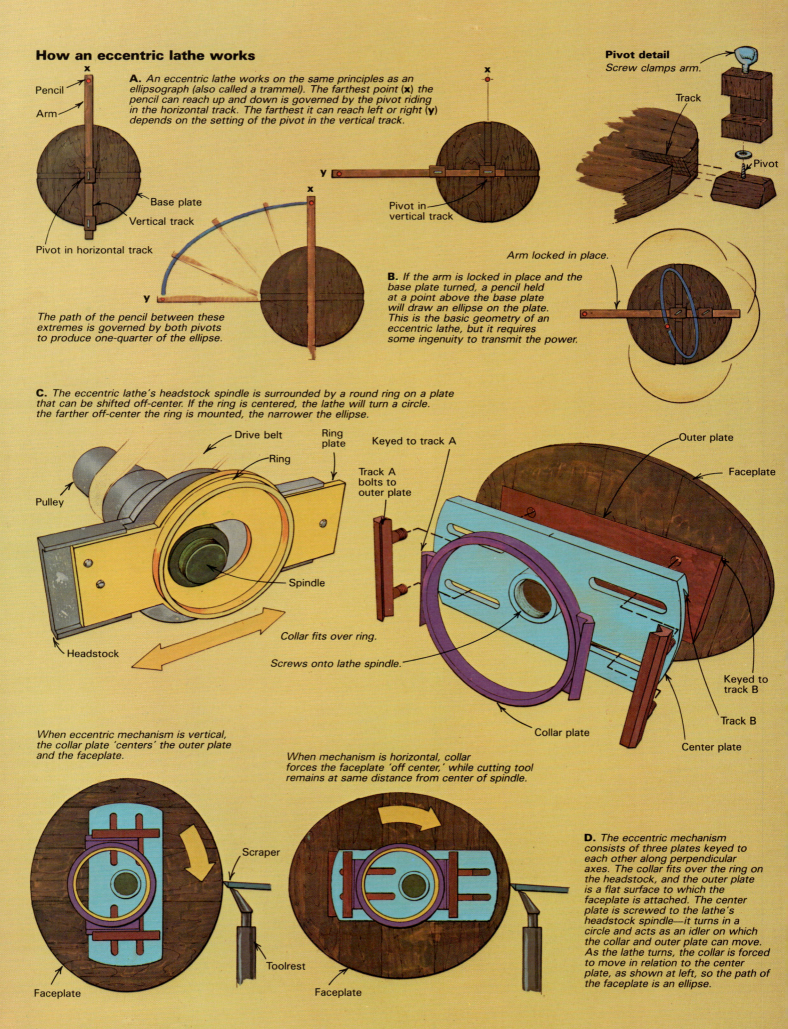

A. An eccentric lathe works on the same principles as an ellipsograph (also called a trammel). The farthest point (**x**) the pencil can reach up and down is governed by the pivot riding in the horizontal track. The farthest it can reach left or right (**y**) depends on the setting of the pivot in the vertical track.

Pencil

Arm

x

Base plate

Vertical track

Pivot in horizontal track

The path of the pencil between these extremes is governed by both pivots to produce one-quarter of the ellipse.

x

y

y

x

Pivot in vertical track

Pivot detail
Screw clamps arm.

Track

Pivot

Arm locked in place.

B. If the arm is locked in place and the base plate turned, a pencil held at a point above the base plate will draw an ellipse on the plate. This is the basic geometry of an eccentric lathe, but it requires some ingenuity to transmit the power.

C. The eccentric lathe's headstock spindle is surrounded by a round ring on a plate that can be shifted off-center. If the ring is centered, the lathe will turn a circle. the farther off-center the ring is mounted, the narrower the ellipse.

Drive belt

Ring plate

Ring

Pulley

Spindle

Headstock

Keyed to track A

Track A bolts to outer plate

Collar fits over ring.

Screws onto lathe spindle.

Outer plate

Faceplate

Collar plate

Keyed to track B

Track B

Center plate

When eccentric mechanism is vertical, the collar plate 'centers' the outer plate and the faceplate.

When mechanism is horizontal, collar forces the faceplate 'off center,' while cutting tool remains at same distance from center of spindle.

Scraper

Toolrest

Faceplate

Faceplate

D. The eccentric mechanism consists of three plates keyed to each other along perpendicular axes. The collar fits over the ring on the headstock, and the outer plate is a flat surface to which the faceplate is attached. The center plate is screwed to the lathe's headstock spindle—it turns in a circle and acts as an idler on which the collar and outer plate can move. As the lathe turns, the collar is forced to move in relation to the center plate, as shown at left, so the path of the faceplate is an ellipse.

Drawing: ATO Studios

people represented a high marriage of artisanry to industry, a refined manual approach to a repetitive specialized task not unlike the job context of a senior journeyman in a pre-industrial shop. Certainly, early industrial America did not develop a sudden independence from hand skill, and within certain workplaces, the uses of machinery added to the skill vocabulary rather than depleted it.

The elliptical lathes have been difficult to document. There are no casting numbers nor maker's stamps, and research into their past has shown only that there is no record of a patent for their design or manufacture in this country. As elliptical turning technology is known to have existed in Europe at the time, the Schwambs or others quite likely brought the knowledge of it with them and re-created the machinery here. Whatever their origin, the lathes are best understood as a means of transforming circular motion into elliptical motion. How this is done is explained in a simplified way on the facing page.

An oval form may be turned from a toolrest just as a circular one would be. While this is a distinct, singular capacity to have at one's disposal, for those imagining the glory of cutting into fine stock on venerable machinery, wonder not. The work is all scraping, lathe speeds are low, work must proceed in a rigidly ordered sequence to be effective or profitable at all, and often the turner is faced with the necessity to simply force the cut.

The lathes, though worn, permit the Old Schwamb Mill to satisfy demands that no production shop could. Orders now come in from around the continental United States, Hawaii, and from abroad, complementing and extending the body of work previously produced, which is included in the collections of The White House, the Vatican, Buckingham Palace, and the Boston Museum of Fine Arts, among others.

A typical order might be: one gold-leafed oval mirror frame, turned with profile number 558 (from the Schwamb production collection) and having a 16-in. by 20-in. inside dimension.

The first task is to develop a template for one quadrant of the ellipse. Schwamb ellipses (and circles) are constructed of regular quadrants of kiln-dried lumber, bandsawn and finger-joined. One template serves for the whole job, and is gotten from the quietest corner of the main floor, where a trammel board rests on an oak cask. The surrounding walls are an orderly fish-scale jam of the cardboard quadrant arcs that the Schwambs cut over the years.

If a pre-made template can't be found in the array, the trammel is set to size and a new template is cut, then traced on the stock. The four sections of the frame are bandsawn, jointed flat, and cut to length on a sliding-table circular saw.

The finger joint is made on a gang saw, a set of blades with teeth protruding through a wooden plate and between two fixed parallel wooden fences. Each quadrant is gripped like a pistol and pushed through the blades.

Frame blanks are taken upstairs to the glue room as soon as the joints are cut. Here, amid the iron heat pipes and old hide-glue pots, quadrants are ganged up face to face, Titebond is brushed on the joints, and the frame is loosely pieced together on a steel-topped assembly table. A steel band clamp at one of several stations is placed around the frame blank and drawn up quickly with a handwheel, which winds in the slack. The quadrants align, the shoulders draw up, and beads of glue bloom at the joints as the strap comes to full tension.

After overnight curing, glue-squeeze is chiseled away from the back of the blank, which is then jointed flat so it can be mounted on the lathe faceplate. Frame blanks are fixed to the lathe with four screws positioned so they will neither come through a finger joint nor be exposed during turning. The lathe differential,

The first step in making an oval is to make a pattern. This old trammel board, above, is adjustable to draw ovals (and circles) from a few inches wide up to 4 ft. long. The four identical segments that make up an oval frame are finger-jointed on the venerable gangsaw shown below, but today's blades are carbide-tipped.

which governs the proportions of the oval, is set by moving the headstock ring plate to the proper calibration. After a liberal oiling of the mechanism bearing surfaces, the blank is rotated, test-marked and the setting checked for accuracy.

The lathes all run considerably under 1,000 RPM. Low speeds are easy on the equipment, but dictate several turning challenges. The action of worn ellipse mechanisms can become exaggerated, tools grab more easily, and scraping smooth surfaces is more difficult than at higher speeds. Nevertheless, turning circles or moderate ovals is usually a pleasant, direct joy, free of the racy hum and tense power delivery of the typical light modern lathe.

Tools for any order are chosen from the Mill's collection. All

The display may be reminiscent of a barn sale, but these tools are in everyday use, turning out oval frames to match patterns that were drawn and cataloged by the Schwambs 150 years ago.

of these were shopmade from tempered bar stock, with plain handles, iron ferrules, and usually with nails banged in around the tang to take up slack caused by generations of turning. Scraping burrs are turned over without fuss at the nearby grinder, and must be touched up constantly.

To dimension the blank accurately, the face is trued flat and to final frame thickness. A slightly dome-shaped scraper is the first tool used. It bangs the glue off the joint shoulders and takes away "fat" areas of the face, caused by the lathe's deflection from vertical as the old mechanism spins. The worn devices often yield frames with pleasing, subtle inconsistencies such as varying thickness or imprecise elliptical orbits.

A spear-point tool is then used to make planing cuts across the face until final thickness is reached. None of these cuts can be heavy, else the drive belt will slip (leather and wood have no easy time driving the lathes). Watching the tool at work has often reminded me of a phonograph needle moving across a record.

After the face is cut, the inside or "sight" edge is made square to it and sized to the ordered dimensions, again with the spear-point tool. Tool position and angle are critical. There is only one small zone in the entire path of the turning blank when the stock is moving straight down in relation to the toolrest. Within this zone, which is as wide as the toolrest and perhaps an inch in height, the work can be cut as if it were a circular turning. Outside the zone the work also moves sideways, which makes cutting impossible. The turner must choose a particular angle to use from the toolrest to the work in penciling layout lines and making cuts. This angle, once chosen, must be maintained throughout the job. If the tool angle is changed, different cuts will have changing relationships to each other, making the molding elements appear to be in slightly different orbits.

Now, with the sight edge having been cut, the final frame

width is marked on the stock and the outside edge is cut the same way, with the same attention being paid to squareness and to the tool angle.

Next, the rabbet is cut with a special right-angle scraping tool. The developing rabbet quickly fills with centrifugally held scrapings, giving the illusion that making the final depth will take but a moment. In reality, the cutter will lose some length to the grinder before the job is done.

With the rabbet cut, the dimensioned oval blank awaits a profile. Full-size section drawings either come to the machine room with each order, or are specified by catalog number from the Schwamb collection. Most profiles are begun as step cuts, which are made square and parallel to the faceplate with the spear-point tool. The final coves, ogees, beads and other shapes are cut into the steps using the full kit of Schwamb tools. (It is a pleasure to turn an obscure molding for the first time and in the process finally discover the true purpose of a particular odd, neglected tool.)

The tools encounter endgrain and glue four times per revolution on an average cut. Some tearout is inevitable, but can be minimized by touching up the burr frequently. A dulling tool will soon begin to bounce around in the cut, and will remove material unevenly, causing the same off-kilter appearance as a change in the tool angle. The goal is to do all shaping with the cut, not with subsequent abrasives. Sanding the work on the lathe is a rocky necessity that one strives to keep to a minimum—in the best of worlds, sanding would not be necessary to make beads round or to fair coves, but some frames require it.

When the frame is done, it is unscrewed from the faceplate and brought upstairs for finishing. The floor is swept, the tools put in their places, then the cycle begins again.

The mill's workday used to begin around dawn, when the first workers arrived to ready the day's supply of glue. In pre-electric times, work hours and shop layout were controlled by the sun. But I find myself working at a time of day when no 19th-century woodworker would have thought of being in the room. On this winter evening, the Schwamb machines seem like darkened props on a stage out of context. Wire-caged lightbulbs hang from their cords over each machine, and are switched on and off as the work proceeds from one station to the next. The sounds of the structure shift as if under sail, conjuring thoughts of the thirty-at-once who filled these buildings, whose hands wore the flatness and edges from every surface. Tidal cold drafts break in through the clapboards and window frames, rattle the quoit-like collection of failed turnings hanging from the beams, flutter the faded girlie poster and help erode the years of milestones and messages chalked on planks and timbers throughout the framework: first snows, machine safety, company policy.

The upper atmosphere of the room is charged with pulley movement as the whole mill becomes the machine. The slapping belts cadence the work; the 60-watt baskets swing. Sweeps and lands of an emerging profile glance in and out of moving shadow as they spin, and oval pencil lines seem to hula into barely confluent duplicates. The deepening chill of the wind from the faceplate has matched that of the drafts. Working at the old machines for any length of time gives a bone-felt glimpse into the age that begat the works. I rebreathe the breath, regrip the tool, engage the blur. □

William Tandy Young makes furniture in Arlington, Mass. The Old Schwamb Mill, open weekdays from 10 A.M. to 4 P.M., is at 17 Mill Lane in Arlington, Mass., near 1215 Massachusetts Avenue. For further information, call (617) 643-0554.

Vermont Turning School

Russ Zimmerman's three principles for clean cuts

by Dick Burrows

Like many woodworkers, I learned turning with a book in one hand and a gouge in the other. Whenever I read about a slick technique, I'd imitate it, seeking those satisfying cascades of shavings and mirror-smooth finishes. Most often I'd catch the tip of the tool and brutally slash the wood. One night, while holding an ice pack to my jaw, pondering how a shattered bowl could hit so hard, I decided to temper my quest for world-class cutting technique. When things got risky, I'd put the skew and gouge away, grind a burr on my ½-in. roundnose and scrape.

My turning gradually improved anyway, largely because I repeatedly practiced what Dale Nish and Peter Child had written. No matter how good the finished pieces looked, though, I didn't like the hit-and-miss combination of cutting and scraping I used to hack them out, or the pieces I broke trying. Something was wrong, but there weren't any good turning teachers nearby to help. Wouldn't it be great, I thought, to attend one of those intensive seminars, like the ones Child conducted at his home in England, and learn a better way?

Unfortunately, Child retired from teaching before I could visit him, but I recently spent a couple of days with one of his students, Russ Zimmerman, who runs a turning workshop in Westminster, Vt. Zimmerman modeled his school after Child's, but has modified many of the methods he saw Child use in the mid-70s, because of his subsequent experience and his contacts with other turners. As Child did, Zimmerman limits each class to two students, who usually move in with his family for 2½ days and spend most of their waking hours turning. My fellow student, Nils Agrell, a New York City stock investor, and I each had our own Myford lathe to work on in Zimmerman's compact and efficient basement shop.

One of the first things I noticed about Zimmerman's turning is that it's much more relaxed than my mish-mash of techniques. Where I would strangle the tool, jam it in and hang on, Zimmerman stresses control more than brute force. Steadying the tool against his leg or hip, he uses his whole body to move the tool, adjusting the cutting edge with light hand and finger pressure, taking full advantage of the tool's bevel and cutting edge.

Zimmerman bases his turning on three general principles—the cutting edge should be about 45° to the direction in which the work is rotating, the tool's bevel should be rubbing on the wood, and finishing cuts should be made across, not against, the wood fibers. These principles are presented as guidelines for developing a feel for tools and an understanding of what they are doing. Zimmerman urges students to build on this understanding, and to ask themselves what he thinks is the

most important question: "Does it feel right?" His only ironclad *must* is sharpening. The grinder, shown on p. 59, is one of the most used tools in the shop.

Zimmerman demonstrated his principles by hollowing a small walnut bowl using a long-handled, ¼-in. deep-fluted gouge. With the bevel riding lightly against the wood, but not cutting, he moved the tool forward and shifted the tool handle slightly until the gouge began to cut, then moved his body to continue the cut across the wood's surface. He steadied the handle with his side and kept the bevel rubbing while manipulating the angle of the cutting edge. Since I manipulated turning tools with just my arms and hands, I initially thought Zimmerman's style of work was more like dancing than turning, but I soon found that by bracing the 15-in. handle against my leg or hip and moving my body and tool together, the tool's cutting edge was much more stable and easier to control.

After stressing the importance of body movement and bevel contact, Zimmerman urges his students to play with the techniques. He convinced me that I needn't worry about the edge digging in, as long as the bevel was in contact with the wood. Being overly cautious, I practiced for a while with the lathe motor off, turning the wood into the tool by hand. Even with the lathe on, I was surprised at how easy it was to adjust the tool angle and cutting edge, as long as I kept the bevel riding on the wood.

The recommended 45° angle of the cutting edge to the work makes sense if you consider that when the edge is at 0°, just about parallel to the direction of rotation, no cutting takes place. Adjusting the handle slightly to a 15° edge angle produces a light cut and a fine finish, because the bevel is able to polish the surface behind the cut. As the angle increases to 90°, as shown on p. 58, more of the edge contacts the wood, and the cut becomes heavier and more likely to tear the endgrain. The 45° angle compromise produces a good surface and a reasonably fast cut without requiring excessive force. Once the position of the cutting edge is set, Zimmerman describes the angle of the gouge's flute in terms of how a clock face would look with a gouge cross section superimposed in the center of the dial. A straight-up flute would be 12 o'clock; one parallel to the tool rest would be 3 or 9 o'clock. As the flute orientation changes, note how a different part of the edge begins cutting.

The hardest thing about manipulating the bevel is developing a light enough touch to skim the bevel across the wood, instead of rubbing it so hard that it burnishes the wood, heating and dulling the tool. It takes time to develop a feel for moving the handle and cutting edge simultaneously at the same rate. If you shift the handle without moving the tool forward to keep the

From *Fine Woodworking* magazine (January 1986) 56:40-42

Fig. 1: Flute angle

Flute angle is described with a clock face. 12 o'clock is good for roughing out; 3 o'clock better for starting a hollow cut.

Fig. 2: Chisel angle

Direction of rotation

Chisel angle regulates size and smoothness of cut.

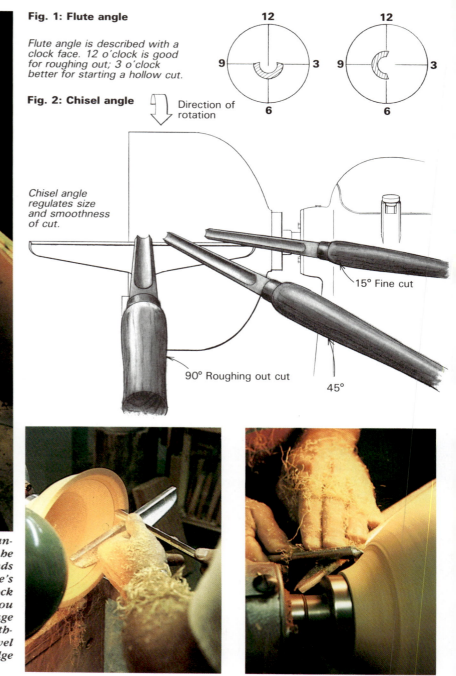

15° Fine cut

90° Roughing out cut

45°

Turning student Nils Agrell, above, braces the tool handle against his hip to steady the cutting edge, while he manipulates the bevel and flute angles with his hands held high on the tool. To hollow a bowl on the lathe's outboard rest, right, adjust the flute to the 9 to 10 o'clock range and skim the tool bevel along the cut surface as you arch the chisel deeper into the blank. A fingernail gouge rides its bevel up the outside of a bowl, far right, smoothly cutting across the wood fibers. Keeping the bevel against the wood at all times prevents the cutting edge from digging into the stock.

bevel skimming the wood, you will either lift the edge off the wood, stopping the cut, or the edge will dig in and the cut will be rough and difficult to control. A rough cut creates a bump, on which the bevel bumps again next time around, cutting another bump, and the bumps will reproduce quickly. Stop, go back to the last smooth area, set the bevel and recut.

Agrell and I had our choice of doing spindle or bowl turning, or both, and each of us elected to spend most of our time on bowls. We began by making a small walnut bowl. We each worked a 4-in.-thick bandsawn blank screwed to a faceplate on the outboard spindle, first turning the outside shape, then flattening the bottom with a ½-in. deep-fluted gouge. Flattening the bottom was a good chance to practice body movements, since the straightness of the bottom depends on the handle moving at the same rate as the cutting edge. Begin the cut with the bevel parallel to the bottom of the bowl and the flute facing 10:30. Then, brace the end of the handle on your leg, set the bevel, and

use your leg to push the tool across to the center.

During each cut, Zimmerman makes his students watch the emerging shape on the bowl in the area opposite the actual cut. If you concentrate on the cutting edge, you'll instinctively try to keep the tool cutting and never notice the character or flow of the shape you are cutting. I found it hard not to focus on the tool, so Zimmerman repeatedly put his hand in front of my bowl, blocking my vision. It's uncomfortable not being able to see the business end of the tool, but he was right—the shape was more flowing and elegant when I didn't just stare at the tool.

Before removing the bowl from the faceplate, we held a second faceplate against the rotating wood, centered it by eye, and held a pencil to the wood at the faceplate's rim. The drawn circle is the guide for remounting the blank. It's a surprisingly accurate method. Instead of screwing the faceplate to the now flat bottom of the blank, we attached it with Permacel double-faced cloth tape. Cover the faceplate with tape, peel off the

Grinding turning tools

Zimmerman insists that a key part of turning is continually sharp tools. He uses a Sears' bench grinder, right, fitted with custom-made tool rests and guides. The two tool rests are 3-in. by 4-in. by ¾-in. pieces of plywood bolted to the grinder's original metal rests. The right-side rest, which is used for skews and parting tools, is angled to produce a 30° to 35° bevel on the tool. Scrapers are ground on the left-hand rest, which Zimmerman sets to produce an 80° bevel.

The third bench-grinder modification is an adjustable tool-handle support for grinding square-edge and fingernail gouges. The ⁹⁄₁₆-in. by 1¼-in. arm slides in a small box mounted to the table under the wheel. A thumbscrew locks the arm in position. The tricky part is setting the height of the rest to fit your tools.

Zimmerman uses a sliding tool support to steady a long-handled gouge as he grinds the cutting edge on a 6-in. aluminum oxide wheel. Note how the tool's cutting edge rides directly on the blade and doesn't touch the grinder's tool rest, which is set for grinding skews and other straight tools.

Clamp an 8-in.-high rest to the arm and put your longest gouge in the support notch. Adjust the rest height and arm length so the wheel contacts the middle of the bevel. Now try your shortest gouge. You may have to compromise on the height to be able to work on both tools satisfactorily. When you have worked out the height, cut the rabbet and assemble the support. Note that when the handle is properly adjusted, the tool rides directly on the wheel and doesn't touch the grinder's tool rest at all. To grind square-edged gouges, first rotate the tool on its bevel. For a fingernail grind, you also have to push the tool up the wheel slightly as you roll the tool onto its side. After grinding, Zimmerman hones the tool with a medium India stone or soft Arkansas stone. —D.B.

backing paper and squeeze the blank to the faceplate for a few minutes with a handscrew.

Most of the hollowing was done with a deep-fluted gouge ground to a fingernail shape (see p. 64). A ⅜-in. fingernail gouge was more maneuverable than a square-edge gouge for the deeply hollowed bowl shape I was working on. On the outside of the bowl, I found I could easily cut across the fibers of the wood and get a smooth surface by cutting from the bowl's small diameter to its large diameter. The flute is held at about 10 o'clock, orientating the cutting edge at 45°. Again, remember to use your body, not your hands, to move the tool. Make a notch to begin the cut, then lower the handle and twist it around, adjusting the flute in the 9 to 12 o'clock range. The swinging motion of your body will arc the cutting edge to follow the curve of the bowl. For deep hollows, you can let the tool's shaft rub against the rim, using it as a fulcrum to cut deeper into the bowl. At first, I expected the edge to catch despite the rubbing bevel, but I kept adjusting the flute orientation and the shavings kept spewing out. I got so carried away that I cut through the bottom.

Zimmerman gets a remarkably clean finishing cut inside the bowl using one side of a ¼-in. deep-fluted, square-edged gouge with the edge held at about a 10° to 20° angle. During this operation, he held one hand lightly on the outside of the bowl to dampen vibration. You can also finish up with a scraper—scrap-

ing isn't a bad word in Zimmerman's shop. He feels it's important to enjoy and to feel comfortable with turning, and some people are just more comfortable with scraping. Zimmerman makes what he calls the slicing scrape with a roundnose scraper, which produces a fine shaving, not sawdust. To avoid the torn endgrain commonly associated with scraping, he cuts with the tool edge held at 45° to the wood's motion, so only one corner of the scraper contacts the tool rest.

Since I hadn't turned much in recent years, I think I went to the seminar with a fairly open mind and unpracticed hands, eager to develop new skills and perhaps to rekindle my interest in turning. Zimmerman's hands-on instruction helped me make sense of many things I had half-learned. Since the seminar I've been turning regularly again, and am finding that I'm cutting much faster and with greater accuracy than before, and producing crisper, more delicate pieces. And it's been fun. I couldn't ask for much more from any teacher. □

Dick Burrows is an associate editor of Fine Woodworking. *Russ Zimmerman's school is in Westminster, Vt., a small community in the southeastern part of the state. His address is RFD #3, Box 242, Putney, Vt. 05346. In addition to Myford lathes, he sells Permacel double-faced tape and Sorby tools, and publishes a chatty technical journal,* The Zimmerman Woodturning Letter.

Arrowmont Turning Conference
New work, new guild

by David Sloan

Last October, I attended the 1985 National Woodturning Conference and Exhibition at the Arrowmont School of Arts and Crafts in Gatlinburg, Tennessee. In the works for over two years, it was the first national-scale woodturning event since the last of Albert LeCoff's Philadelphia turning symposiums back in September 1981.

Stylistically, the work of woodturning's innovators has evolved somewhat since the Turned Objects Exhibition at the 1981 symposium. Current work by many of these innovators was on display at Arrowmont. With technique finally mastered, avant-garde turners are in hot pursuit of form, concentrating on shape and surface without concern for function, or even the illusion of function. Wood, once viewed as the sacred material, has become almost incidental in the work of some turners, like Giles Gilson, whose pearlescent-lacquered forms seem to be made of clay or glass, until you lift one.

The exhibit was juried by turners David Ellsworth and Mark Lindquist, along with Michael Monroe, curator at the Smithsonian Institution's Renwick Gallery. There were a few functional bowls on display, and familiar shapes by a few old-guard notables whose work hasn't changed much lately, but the exhibit leaned toward the novel in an attempt, perhaps, to look away from woodturning's functional past.

I walked alone through the moodily lit gallery-like setting, hefting the pieces I could, and peering at those that were enshrined in little glass cases. Much of the work was outstanding, but something bothered me. The display of these flawless wooden pieces as *objets d'art* seemed inappropriate at a turning conference. I preferred the informality of the display tables downstairs, where you could pick things up and examine them, without feeling as if you should glance over your

From *Fine Woodworking* magazine (January 1986) 56:64-66

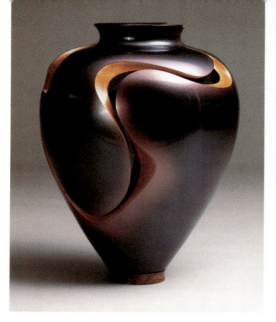

The exhibition at the Arrowmont Woodturning Conference last October showcased the cream of contemporary woodturning, exemplified by the work pictured here. Below, natural-top bowl (dia. 8½ in.) in African blackwood by Ray Key, Worcestershire, England. Clockwise from right, "Black Ribbon Vase" (height: 9 in.) in lacquered birch by Giles Gilson, Schenectady, N.Y.; vessel (dia: 9½ in.) in wormy ash by Dale Nish, Provo, Utah; "Drop Bop Footed Vessel" (dia: 14 in.) in zebrawood, inlaid with plugs of maple, mahogany and purpleheart, by Fletcher Cox of Tougaloo, Miss.

Photos: Nick Cook

shoulder first. Later, when 225 turners crowded into the exhibit, drinking punch, chatting away, rubbing their noses against the glass cases, and popping flash bulbs at everything in sight, the arty aura that had bothered me came down to earth with a delightful crash. Everyone was excited about the work on display, but most people were talking technique, not concept. The rank-and-file turner had come to Arrowmont to learn about turning, not to worship at the shrine of art. I found the irreverence refreshing. It set the tone for the rest of a very lively conference.

For the next three days, there was a contagious energy in the air. Each day, David Ellsworth, Rude Osolnik, Alan Stirt and Del Stubbs turned and explained, and turned some more. Stirt concentrated on bowls, Ellsworth on his trademark hollow forms, and Stubbs on paper-thin bowls and gossamer goblets with long delicate stems. Osolnik, probably the best production turner in the country, ran through the gamut of turning techniques—he even did some metal spinning. People circulated between demonstrators as they wished. Mark Lindquist hauled a huge lathe up from his Florida shop and drew a large crowd as he demonstrated the chainsaw turning techniques he has developed for his sculptural pieces.

In the middle of the conference, a new piece mysteriously appeared in the exhibit. It was sort of an assemblage of rough-turned shapes nestled on a bed of shavings with a sharpened steel pipe driven into the top, and a sensitively applied

"Ceremony" (height: 11 in.) in elm by Michael Hosaluk of Saskatoon, Sask. Hosaluk drilled tiny holes around the opening of the form and stitched down a necklace of porcupine quills with black linen thread. Below, a fluted butternut bowl (dia: 19½ in) by Alan Stirt, Enosburg, Vt.

flesh-colored Band-Aid. As comic relief, it stole the show. The pipe bore a strong resemblance to Del Stubbs's first home-made turning tool. The piece turned out to be the result of a spontaneous, late-night collaboration between Stubbs, Al Stirt and Mick O'Donnell, who'd come all the way from Scotland. As Australian turner Richard Raffan has said, there's something about turning that "gratifies the vandal in us all."

In addition to demonstrations, there were slide shows of work, past and present, a panel discussion on the future of woodturning as a movement, and awards to old-guard turners Mel Lindquist, Dale Nish, Rude Osolnik and Ed Moulthrop, along with Bob Stocksdale and James Prestini, neither of whom showed up. At the big barbecue (complete with bluegrass band) the last night, a special award, a turned disc signed by hundreds of turners, was presented to Albert LeCoff, for his efforts in first organizing turners back in 1976.

Arrowmont was an ideal site for the conference. Gatlinburg is a gaudy tourist mecca on the edge of the Great Smoky Mountains National Park, but the school is set on a pretty park-like campus away from the tourist strip. Credit for the smooth running of the conference goes to the Arrowmont staff, veterans at this sort of thing.

Arrowmont worked because it provided turners, no matter what their level of skill or creativity, with an opportunity to share what they know, and to learn from others. With an eye to the future, Albert LeCoff, David Ellsworth, Dale Nish and a handful of others met to lay the groundwork for a national woodturners' guild. By the end of the conference, a committee was assigned to draw up a charter and elect officers. The guild will organize future turning shows and conferences, keep members posted on turning workshops across the country, and promote woodturning to the general public. If you are interested in becoming a member write to: Robert Rubel, Rt. 2, Box 295, San Marcos, Tex. 78666. □

David Sloan is an associate editor of Fine Woodworking.

Woodturning in Ireland
National guild hosts a seminar

by David Sloan

Once a reform school, the Connemara West Centre in Letterfrack is a training school for crafts. It was the site of last year's Irish Woodturners' Guild conference.

Connemara, in the west of Ireland, is a rugged, lonely land of mist-shrouded mountains, steel-gray lakes and stark, treeless bogs. Here and there the cloud ceiling dips low to blur the line between ocean sky and barren landscape. The narrow road is well traveled by cattle and sheep—less so by cars. There I was last October, banking my little Fiat through the curves, trying hard not to turn sheep into mutton. In this out-of-the-way corner of the country the Irish Woodturners' Guild was hosting a seminar and I was on my way. From all over Ireland, turners were descending upon the village of Letterfrack in County Galway for a weekend of talk and demonstration.

I learned of the Irish Woodturners' Guild last July when I struck up a correspondence with Liam O'Neill, a turner from Shannon. O'Neill started turning in 1968, and for several years he ran the woodturning program at Retos Ltd., a rehabilitation facility for the handicapped in Shannon. He was the driving force behind the first seminar in September 1982 and the Guild's organization in March 1983. From him I learned that there were more than a few talented woodturners in Ireland. Since most of them would be at the Letterfrack seminar, I accepted an invitation to attend.

Turning isn't new to Ireland. Wooden-bowl fragments dating from the 13th century have been unearthed from the peat bogs. But unlike the utilitarian utensils produced by earlier genera-tions of Irish turners, much of today's work is made to be looked at. This difference may seem inconsequential, but it's a major turning point in the development of the craft in Ireland, with particular significance to those who try to earn their living as woodturners. The ramifications of this trend were passionately debated at the seminar.

The conference provided a chance for turners to discuss their work, get inspiration and evaluate the work of their peers. The village of Letterfrack was chosen as the site to take advantage of the facilities at the Connemara West Centre. This cavernous 19th-century building, shown in the photo at left, was once a reformatory, but today operates as a crafts school communally owned by the people of Letterfrack. There, unemployed young people receive full-time training in woodturning, cabinetmaking and woodcarving with the hope that, after they're trained, they'll provide jobs in the area for themselves and others.

For me, the high point of the weekend was the tables where everyone's work was displayed. Here was a sampling of the best turning in Ireland, all in one place. The design sophistication and the level of technical proficiency were consistently high. Judging from the disproportionately large number of delicate green-turned, natural-edge bowls, I guessed that Irish turners as a group were drawing their design inspiration from the same source. This assumption proved close to the mark. Each year, the Guild invites internationally known turners—Richard Raffan from Australia, Ray Key from England and Michael O'Donnell from Scotland—to demonstrate at the seminars. Because these demon-strators were seen by so many Irish turners, their influence has been pervasive.

The guest demonstrators this year were David Ellsworth from the United States and, once again, Michael O'Donnell. Guild members Ciaran Forbes, Liam O'Neill, Niall Fitzduff and spindle turner Jim Foley also demonstrated during the course of the weekend.

O'Donnell, once an engineer with Rolls Royce, now turns full time in the far north of Scotland. He demonstrated his tech-niques for turning large, functional bowls from green wood. O'Donnell impressed me as being a thoughtful, patient teacher. The first thing that caught my eye was the shape of his deep-fluted bowl gouge. Instead of grinding it straight across, he'd extended the bevel well back on either side of the gouge. Several of the Irish turners have adopted the same shape for bowl turn-ing. The box on p. 64 explains how and why.

O'Donnell's own work has taken a unique direction. His wife, Liz O'Donnell, got the idea to saw pieces from a thin-walled bowl that he'd rejected. The result looked, to her, like a bird. Now Liz creates birds from Michael's bowls. After drawing on the

From *Fine Woodworking* magazine (July 1985) 53:74-77

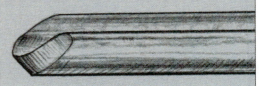

Regrind a gouge

Most turning books suggest a straight-across grind for a deep-fluted bowl gouge and a "fingernail" shape for a shallow-fluted coving gouge for spindle work. But the "fingernail" shape—extending the bevel well back along the sides of the tool—works well on a bowl gouge too, and changes the handling characteristics of the tool. There's more available cutting surface and, since there are no shoulders to catch on the inside of a bowl, the possibility of a catch is greatly reduced. It takes practice to grind this bevel smoothly, and a bit more practice to get used to it, but give it a try. If you don't like it, you can always re-grind straight-across. —D.S.

The guild's seminar drew turners and work from all over Ireland and Great Britain. Michael O'Donnell, top right, shows how to control a deep-fluted bowl gouge. Below, one of his delicate bowls turned into a fanciful bird by his wife, Liz.

David Ellsworth rides again. Irish turners watch as Ellsworth, from the U.S., straddles the lathe to hollow out the inside of a form.

finished bowl and sawing out the shape, the eyes, beak and other details are carved in and painted with oils.

Everyone seemed eager to learn how David Ellsworth turns his hollow decorative forms. Ellsworth works green, and his methods are somewhat unorthodox. He straddles the lathe when he's turning the inside of a form and it's not uncommon for him to stop the lathe and attack a piece with a chainsaw. His 4-ft. long tools resemble harpoons more than lathe tools. My personal favorite features a high-speed steel cutter, similar to a metal-lathe cutter, clamped in a slot at the end of a long steel shaft. This cutter can be turned and clamped at different angles with respect to the shaft. It scrapes rather than cuts and with it, Ellsworth can turn the inside of a piece through a very small opening. Boisterous and outspoken, Ellsworth is as flamboyant as his techniques, but his work is graceful, delicate and devilishly hard to imitate. It will be interesting to see the influence his purely sculptural forms have on Irish turning.

Ciaran Forbes is a Benedictine monk, and the resident wood-turning instructor at Connemara West. Forbes is an accomplished bowl turner with a scathing wit and a penchant for doing imper-

Connemara West's turning instructor, Ciaran Forbes, left, brandishing a heavy scraper which he uses to clean up the gouge marks from the bottom of an 18-in. diameter bowl. Above, a yellow holly bowl by Forbes.

sonations. He introduced me to "bog oak," an Irish oddity which local turners seem to take for granted. Dried peat or "turf," as it's called locally, is burned for heat in many rural homes. Ancient, water-logged oak trees are regularly unearthed from the bogs as a nuisance by-product of the turf-digging industry. Carbon dating shows some of these trees to be 3,000 years old. The wood ranges in color from jet black to a dark brown striped with black. It's wet and stringy and, as it dries, more unstable than any wood I've ever encountered. In a matter of hours, a bowl turned from wet bog oak distorts severely. One jet-black bowl that Forbes turned looked, several days later, as if it had been sat upon. I found this unpredictability intriguing but I never did get a chance to turn any during my visit.

The group-discussion sessions were lively, and marketing was a much-debated topic. A few turners in America and England manage to command high prices for their work by selling it through galleries to wealthy collectors. The best Irish turners are producing work of comparable quality, but the domestic market for high-priced "turnings as art" is very small. There are several reasons for this. Ireland is a small, largely rural country about the size of Maine. Country people just don't buy expensive non-functional turnings. As Michael O'Donnell put it, "People want to justify buying turnings on some practical use." The Irish tax system is another obstacle to sales. Like many European countries, Ireland imposes a value added tax (VAT) on most purchases. VAT rates differ depending on the item. Craft items are considered luxuries, and taxed at 35%—the highest rate. If a turner wholesales a bowl for £40 (about $40) and a shop tacks on another £40, the 35% VAT kicks the price up to £108 (about $108). In a country where, in 1980, the average person earned less than $6,000, that's a prohibitive price. Foreign tourists, on the other hand, are exempt from paying VAT which makes them the best potential customers.

Seven of the 72 people at the seminar were full-time turners, and those few who aspired to make a living from their craft wanted to learn the ropes from O'Donnell, Ellsworth and O'Neill.

They were not exactly encouraging. Ellsworth cautioned, "Don't kid yourself, woodturners don't make a lot of money...It's hard. My wife works, my kids work...." O'Donnell said that he "had to create a market in Scotland," and that he was "only beginning to reap the benefits after 10 years of work." Eventually the hobbyists, who had come to improve their turning—not marketing—skills, grew impatient with the subject and the discussion shifted to design and technique. Ellsworth summed it up: "Don't forget...how nice it is to turn for pleasure."

After the seminar, I drove around the country, visiting craft galleries and the workshops of several turners I'd met at the seminar. First, I dropped in on Nick Adams, an instrument maker in Miltown Malbay. I was fascinated with a magnificent set of Uillean pipes, the Irish bagpipes, that Nick had displayed at the seminar. Turned from African blackwood and ivory, the detail was exquisite as was the tone. Adams makes the entire instrument himself, from the turnings to the brass fittings, reeds and leather bellows.

In Shannon, I hooked up with Liam O'Neill and Michael Dickson, a doctor and woodturner from County Antrim. O'Neill's studio is in a pre-fab structure behind his house. There I spent the day as he turned a few bowls and small boxes from laburnum, holly, walnut and African blackwood. For large functional bowls, O'Neill screws a green blank to a 4-hole faceplate with two opposing holes parallel to the grain. He roughs it out, then air dries the 1⅜-in. thick bowl for several weeks. As the bowl dries and shrinks across the grain it distorts into an oval. When it's remounted on the faceplate for finish turning, the two screw holes that were parallel to the grain will still line up with the faceplate holes and the bowl will be on center.

Several times during the seminar, I'd heard people mention that they finished their turnings with "melamine." They were referring to a thick-bodied, lacquer-based product called Craftlac Melamine (sold by Craft Supplies Ltd., The Mill, Millers Dale, Buxton, Derbys., SK17 8SN, England). As O'Neill demonstrated, it quickly produces an attractive sheen. While the piece was on

Michael Dickson watches Liam O'Neill finish off a large walnut bowl with a ¼-in. gouge. The rim of the bowl is jammed into a groove turned into the pine disc, which is screwed to a faceplate. Above are two bowls by Liam O'Neill and below a large elm bowl by Michael Dickson.

Photo: Norman Wadell

the lathe, he brushed on the Melamine, waited a few minutes for it to dry, then polished with fine steel wool.

Michael Dickson took me to see Ray Cornu who runs a production-turning shop and retail store in the Bally Casey Craft Workshops outside Shannon. His 800-sq. ft. workshop includes an Ebac drying kiln in which he drys all his wood—mostly local elm, ash and sycamore. Cornu and his employee, 20-year-old Martini Currams, produce functional items: bowls, towel holders, barometer plaques, salad & cheese servers, etc. After hours, Currams, who has been turning for only three years, works on her own designs. I predict that she'll develop into one of Ireland's most innovative turners.

Irish bowl turners seem to prefer the short-bed Union Graduate lathe made by T.J. Harrison & Sons Ltd. in England (available in the U.S. from Craft Supplies U.S.A., 1644 S. State St., Provo, Utah 84601). It has four speeds, weighs nearly 400 lb. and can handle bowls up to 19½ in. dia. I heard the same complaint from every Graduate owner that I spoke with: The headstock pulley is fastened to its shaft with a setscrew. This screw works loose and when it does, the pulley spins ineffectually on the shaft since there's no keyway to prevent it from slipping.

Ireland's woodturners are in a unique position. Their's is the only national woodturning guild in the world. Trends in the craft that take years to spread across the U.S. sweep across Ireland in months because of the regular communication among turners. Michael O'Donnell commented that the "work had changed enormously" since his last visit. Right now, Irish woodturners as a group are learning and borrowing techniques and styles developed in America and the United Kingdom. Don't be surprised when the new ideas start flowing the other way instead. □

David Sloan is an associate editor of Fine Woodworking.

Beer-box lathe

by Tim Hanson

I don't do enough turning to justify having a lathe take up valuable space in my small shop, so I designed a portable model that fits in a beer case. When I want to turn, I clamp the components to a sturdy bench, as shown in the photo below, and go to work. The lathe has a 12-in.-dia. swing. Turning distance between centers is limited by the bench size, but 36 in. is a more practical limit for this lightweight tool. When I'm through working, I disassemble the lathe and put it back into the beer box. The box is small enough to fit under my bench or in an out-of-the-way corner.

For the past eight years I've used this "beer-box" lathe to turn table legs, chair rungs, tool handles, Shaker pegs and other small items. You can build it for under $60 (not including the motor). The headstock and tailstock components are readily available; the other necessities are some miscellaneous hardware and a few board feet of a hardwood, such as maple. With everything you need, building the lathe won't take you more than a day or so.

The headstock, tailstock and tool rest are made from 1-in.-thick stock. Maple is tough enough to stand up well to the rigors of turning and its tight grain means the lathe's few critical dimensions can be machined accurately without chipping. The tailstock and headstock are U-shape; each has two vertical endpieces that support the spindles and a bottom spacer block that connects the endpieces. I used a glued tongue-and-rabbet joint, but you can use any strong corner joint. The vertical endpieces are 7½ in. high by 4⅛ in. deep. The overall width of the headstock is 6½ in.; the tailstock, 5½ in. The centerlines of the tailstock and headstock spindles are located 6 in. from the bottom edge of the end-

pieces, making a 12-in.-swing diameter. Before assembling the headstock and tailstock, and while the pieces were still square, I clamped the endpieces together and drilled holes in them for the spindles.

I first drilled ¾-in.-dia. holes in the tailstock endpieces to accept the commercial spindle parts. The spindle, handwheel and tapered cup center (live) are from a Duracraft lathe (model #50537) and are identical to those used on the Bridgewood and Sears lathes. The parts are available from Gateway Resources, 419 N. Main St., St. Charles, Mo. 63031; (800) 431-5937.

Alternatively, you can use a ⅝-in.-dia. bolt to make your own spindle-and-handwheel assembly. If you decide to do this, drill ⅝-in.-dia. holes, instead of ¾-in.-dia. holes, in the tailstock endpieces. To make the spindle, hacksaw off the head of an 8-in.-long by ⅝-in.-dia. bolt. File a 2½-in.-long flat (⅛ in. deep) starting 1¼ in. from the bolt's unthreaded end to provide a bearing surface for the spindle-locking screws discussed below. A tailstock cup center (#4216) for the ⅝-in.-dia. spindle is available from Gilliom Manufacturing Inc., 1700 Scherer Parkway, St. Charles, Mo. 63301; (314) 724-1812.

The handwheel used to adjust the tailstock center is a 3-in.-dia., 3-in.-thick maple disc cut with a fly-cutter on a drill press. Drill a hole in the center of the disc and use a vise to press-fit a ⅝-in. nut into the hole.

To lock the spindle I used ¼-in.-dia. by 2-in.-long thumb screws through the back edge of each tailstock endpiece. I cut threads by drilling ³⁄₁₆-in.-dia. holes and screwing in a ¼-in.-dia. bolt. I filed and tapered the end of the bolt so I could get the

thread started easily. If you work the bolt in and out a few times, you'll have threads adequate for holding the thumbscrew. To prevent the wood from splitting, I clamped the endpiece tightly in a vise.

The headstock endpieces require ⅝-in.-dia. holes for the spindle. In addition, recessed holes for spindle bearings are needed on the inside face of the left endpiece and on the outside face of the right endpiece. The bearings are press-fit into the wood, so size the hole for your bearings. I used McGill #ER10, ⅝-in.-ID x 1.8504-in.-OD bearings, available from Bearings Inc., 930 N. Illinois St., Indianapolis, Ind. 46204; (317) 634-4393. The spindle is a ⅝-in.-dia. by 8-in.-long steel shaft from the hardware store. Tighten the set screws in the bearing case onto the flats filed on the spindle to hold it. A headstock spur center (#4218) and faceplate (#4219) for the ⅝-in.-dia. spindle are also available from Gilliom Manufacturing Inc.

After cutting the spindle and bearing holes, I rounded the top edges and tapered the sides of the tailstock and headstock endpieces on a bandsaw and smoothed the edges with a file. Three, 3-in.-long sheet-rock screws through each endpiece into the spacer blocks reinforce tongue-and-rabbet joints on the spacer blocks and endpieces. To be sure the clamped endpieces are snug on the benchtop and don't rock, the spacer block is offset ³⁄₃₂ in. from the bottom edge of the endpieces.

The tool rest is also made from maple. To set its angle or distance from the blank, place the tool rest in the desired position and tighten a C-clamp to secure it to the benchtop. The fixed height of the tool rest is 6⅛ in., just above the centerline of the blank. The 8-in.-long, tool-bearing edge is angled at 45°. I shaped the sides and cut a slot for the C-clamp on a bandsaw. The base of the rest is made from 10-in.-long x ¾-in.-thick x 3½-in.-wide stock. A wide, ³⁄₃₂-in.-deep groove along the bottom of the base ensures that the outer edges of the base bear on the benchtop when the tool rest is clamped in position. The bottom butts to the vertical piece and is secured with four, 2½-in.-long sheetrock screws.

I use a 1,725-RPM, ½-HP motor, bolted to a piece of ¾-in.-thick plywood, to power the lathe. To tension the belt or change speeds I adjust the position of the motor and clamp the plywood base to the bench top. Belt length, therefore, depends on the width of the bench being used (45 in. on my 28-in.-wide top). The three-step motor pulley (2, 3 and 4 in. dia.) in combination with the two spindle pulleys (2½ in. and 3½ in. in diameter) provide six speed options, from 985 RPM to 2,760 RPM. □

Tim Hanson is an amateur woodworker and lives in Indianapolis, Ind.

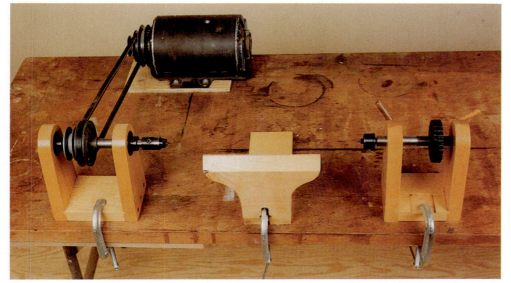

Hanson's shop-built lathe is made from maple and uses readily available hardware. In use, its components are aligned to the edge of a sturdy bench and held in position with C-clamps as shown above. It is stored conveniently out of the way in a beer case when not in use.

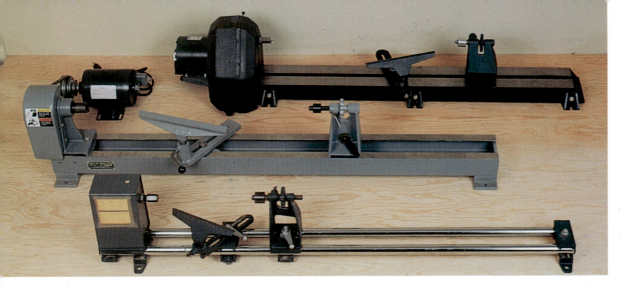

The AMT 4370 (top) and the Williams & Hussey L-82 (middle) lathes are the only economy lathes constructed with heavy castings throughout. The lighter construction in the AMT 373 (bottom), shown without motor, is more typical.

The Grizzly G1025 (top) and Enco 199-9055 (bottom) look-alike lathes are Taiwan imports. The motors for these, and the smallest Sears lathe (bottom), are mounted compactly in the headstock housing.

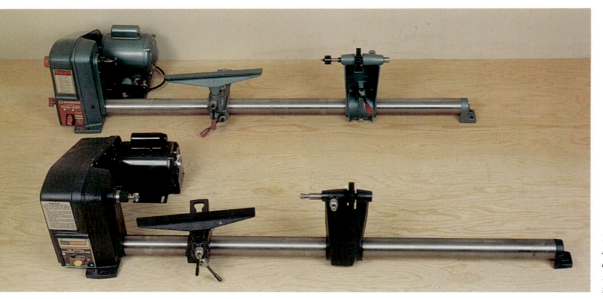

The differences between the Bridgewood BW-1240 (top) and Sears' largest lathe, catalog #9BT22816N, (bottom) are mostly cosmetic.

Economy Lathes

Turning on the light side

by Alan Platt

If you have a yen to try turning, or if you're a furnituremaker with only a limited need for a lathe, you can get started in the craft for less than $500. For years I've had a small, $85 AMT lathe and have been surprised at how many drawer pulls, cabinet knobs, chair spindles, small bowls and candlesticks I've been able to turn. These light tasks don't require the rugged lathes, speed controls or quick-change adjustments demanded by full-time turners, who specialize in production runs of ballusters and other spindles or who turn giant bowls from wood burls or other recalcitrant materials. Stability and vibration-free operation are critical for the professional, and this requires a heavy-duty lathe, precision-machined parts, high-quality bearings and an arsenal of chucks and other accessories. These features, while great for someone needing to turn out a paycheck, push the cost of a lathe to more than $1,500, a price that's difficult for an amateur furnituremaker to justify.

In researching this article, I evaluated several benchtop lathes by turning a series of small spindles and bowls. The benchtop lathes have few frills, but that doesn't mean they are shoddily constructed. And even though they cost less than $500, these lathes are not toys: Many professional woodturners developed and honed their skills on similar lathes before moving up to a heftier machine. If you really like turning, you may want to invest in a larger lathe right away, but I found the benchtop lathes adequate for light work and for developing basic turning skills.

Benchtop lathe characteristics—All lathes, economy models or not, are basically the same: A rigid bed, supports a fixed-positioned headstock and a tailstock that can be moved to accommodate blanks of various lengths. Spindles in the headstock and tailstock allow the wood to rotate. The headstock spindle center is connected to the motor and actually rotates the stock, via a spur center that penetrates the wood or a faceplate that is screwed to the stock. If you're turning a spindle such as a candlestick or a table leg, the tailstock is brought up to support the non-driven end of the stock, which allows it to rotate freely. A faceplate attached to the headstock is all that is needed for bowl turning, although some turners snug up the tailstock to provide extra support when roughing out. The headstock spindle is threaded and is either solid or hollow. The solid spindles can accept only threaded drive centers and faceplates; the hollow spindles accept screw-on faceplates and tapered drive centers that friction-fit into the hollow spindle. On small lathes, turning speeds are controlled by a belt-driven step-pulley system. The motor itself is either directly attached to the bed assembly, or bolted to the bench, or a shop-built stand supporting the bed. A T-shape tool rest, which supports turning tools as they cut the wood, slides along the bed and can be adjusted to different heights and angles. The distance between headstock and tailstock centers indicates the lathe's maximum spindle length; the diameter of the piece being turned is limited by the swing, the distance between the headstock spindle and the lathe bed.

To reduce costs, manufacturers have made lathes lightweight, about 100 lbs.; some are manufactured in Taiwan. The biggest savings are in the bed, which is usually cast iron in more expensive lathes for maximum stability and low vibration. Most economy-lathe manufacturers rely on less-expensive, well-engineered, hollow-steel tubing for beds. (Williams & Hussey and AMT's top-of-the-line models are exceptions.) Cast iron is used for the headstock, tailstock and tool rest, but expensive machining of the surfaces, mostly, is missing.

The Enco and Grizzly lathes come preassembled; the others require an hour or so to assemble and align, which is an easy job: It requires no special tools and the directions are clearly written. If you don't already have a solid bench to support the lathe, you'll have to construct one. Don't skimp here: A rigid bench is essential because it absorbs and dampens vibration and contributes to work stability. Mine, assembled with 2x4s and ¾-in. plywood, is stable enough for light turning, but I installed a bottom shelf so I could add concrete blocks for additional stability.

The lathes I evaluated are shown in the top and middle photos on the facing page; the chart on page 71 provides their vital statistics for comparison. Accessories available for each lathe are also listed.

Evaluating the lathes—To see how well each lathe performed, I turned some 20-in.-sq. maple spindles, up to 30-in. long, and some 8-in.-dia. maple bowl blanks (1¾ in. thick). Each of the lathes I checked can handle up to 12-in.-dia. blanks. All of the lathes worked well for the turnings I tried, and I didn't see dramatic differences in their performance. The headstock and tailstock were adequately rigid on all the models, and didn't flex or move on the bed when the blank revolved or when a cutting tool contacted the wood. The beds also were stiff and rigid, once firmly attached to a sturdy bench. When turning long spindles, all of the lathes were prone to some vibration and whip, making it necessary to take lighter cuts. One or two steady rests, properly positioned to support the workpiece, would help here. Apart from these considerations, your choice boils down to cost and personal preference of each lathe's available accessories and features, such as tool rest setups and speed-changing systems. Power wasn't generally a problem with any of the lathes, but I do note where I felt some of the lathes could benefit from additional punch. Finally, if you're really on a tight budget or don't have much room in your shop, you may want to build the "beer-box" lathe discussed in the article on page 67.

American Machine Tool—AMT's basic lathe (model #2731) uses twin 1¼-in.-dia. steel tubes for the bed. The tubes are aligned in V-slotted castings, which, in turn, bolt to the benchtop. The headstock, tool rest and tailstock are light castings and bolt directly to the bed cylinders. Because the castings are not machined smooth, the sliding surfaces of the tool rest and tailstock tend to jam, making adjustments annoyingly awkward. If you are handy with a file, the castings' rough surfaces can be smoothed to minimize the problem. Also, the lock bolt, used to anchor the tool rest's horizontal position, easily tilts out of position, making tool rest adjustment cumbersome.

Two other AMT models (#2731B and #373) are built the same as the basic model but have some added features. The basic model (#2731) comes with a ¾-in.-dia. headstock spindle and a ball-bearing (live) cup center in the tailstock. Ball-bearing centers rotate with the spindle and are less likely to burn the wood than dead centers, which are stationary tapered posts. The headstock in #2731B is equipped with a ¾-in. double-sealed, ball-bearing spindle—a step up. Model #373 also has the double-sealed ball bearings for the headstock spindle, in addition to a live tailstock center and longer bed cylinders, which increase the spindle capacity from 36 in. to 41 in. The recommended ½-HP motor, three-step motor pulley, mounting brackets and faceplate are sold separately for all three models.

The headstock spindle is belt-driven, providing four speed options (860 RPM to 3,850 RPM); the weight of the motor on its pivoting mount tensions the belt. I found it quick and easy to change speeds by simply lifting the motor to release belt tension, then repositioning the belt onto the appropriate pulley. When making medium to heavy cuts, I found that even light tool pressure would slow, and sometimes stop, rotation because the weight of the motor alone provides insufficient belt tension. Hanging a 25-lb. sandbag from the motor solved the problem. Even with short spindles (20 in.), vibration was often a problem, which meant I had to take lighter cuts and invest some time to achieve a smooth finish, particularly on endgrain.

AMT's top-of-the-line lathe, #4370, and the Williams & Hussey model I'll discuss later, are the heftiest and most-expensive lathes I evaluated. All of the 4370's components, including the bed, are quality, machined castings. The headstock bolts to the cast-iron bed, and additional bolts facilitate aligning the headstock spindle parallel to the bed. A bracket and locking nut under the tailstock can also be adjusted to align the live center with the spur center in the headstock—a feature missing on most of the lathes. For most turning jobs, perfect alignment isn't important; but when turning very short spindles or bowls, in which the tailstock is snugged up to the blank for additional support, misaligned centers can cause the bearings to wear faster. I like the solid feel of this lathe and found that its machined surfaces made movement and adjustment of the tool rest and tailstock, which function similarly to those on AMT's less-expensive lathes, smooth and trouble free.

The #4370 model is equipped with a three-step pulley-drive system that provides six easy-to-select speed options (275 RPM to 3,065 RPM). It is powered by a ½-HP, 1,725-RPM General Electric motor, but I think this ruggedly constructed lathe could benefit from the additional power of a larger motor for heavier cuts and larger workpieces. The additional power would also come in handy if you installed the optional gap bed that extends the swing from 12 in. to 16 in.

The 4370 has an indexing feature that divides the circumference of the workpiece into 24 equal parts. This allows you to precisely orient and lock the workpiece in position for cutting decorative flutes or notches on turned stock. A screw through the headstock engages slots in the rim of the indexing spindle pulley and is secured with a locking nut. When I wasn't using the indexing feature, I had to lock the screw to prevent vibration from "walking" it into the spinning pulley. For ordering information, contact American Machine & Tool Co. of Pa., Fourth and Spring streets, Box 70, Royersford, Pa. 19468; (215) 948-0400.

Bridgewood BW-1240—The Bridgewood BW-1240 from Wilke Machinery Co. (120 Derry Court, York, Pa. 17402; 717-846-2800) is an economy lathe that looks very much like one of the Sears models I tried. Its 2-in.-dia., machined-steel bed is two hollow cylinders held together end to end with a ⅜-in.-dia., 20-in.-long bolt. The same bolt secures a cast-iron foot at the tailstock end and, in turn, is bolted to the benchtop. The bed fits to a bored hole in the headstock and is secured with a setscrew. The tailstock and tool rest ride smoothly on the bed. The tailstock is aligned with the headstock by means of a keyway along the bottom of the bed. To make the alignment, the setscrew and bolt that hold the bed sections together are loosened and the bed is rotated in place along with the headstock and tailstock until their centers align. I found this clever arrangement easy to assemble and align, and it worked well.

The adjusting levers on the tool rest and tailstock also work effectively, but I found them a bit small for comfortable handling. The belt guard is hinged to swing open for changing speeds; unfortunately, it's made from flimsy sheet metal and didn't fit well on the lathe I had. A useful chart on the belt guard shows the belt settings required for the five available spindle speeds (575 RPM to 3,580 RPM) as well as recommended speeds for roughing out and finish-turning soft and hard woods. There's no way to reduce the belt tension; changing speeds requires both hands to wrestle the belt onto the desired pulley. This lathe performed well for both spindle and faceplate turning. I liked the reserve power its ¾-HP motor provided, permitting heavy cuts without stalling.

Wilke's Bridgewood lathe offers two standard features that are sometimes unavailable with other economy lathes. The first feature

is that its hollow drive spindle and tailstock spindle accept #1 Morse tapers, making for quick and easy spindle-mounting. I prefer tapered drive centers because I can quickly tap them into the end of a blank then slide the center into its spindle without having to screw the whole assembly onto the headstock, as is common with threaded drive centers. The second feature is the lathe's outboard turning capability, although the lowest-speed, 575 RPM, seems too high for safely turning large-diameter work in which the surface speed at the rim of the workpiece can be dangerously high. The headstock also has a 36-position indexing mechanism, handy for simple fluting operations and for locking the headstock when removing the faceplate.

Enco 199-9055—This lathe and the Grizzly discussed later are both made in Taiwan and look very much alike. The Enco (Enco Manufacturing Co., 5000 W. Bloomingdale Ave., Chicago, Ill. 60639; 312-745-1500) comes preassembled, ready to be secured to your benchtop. At first I was concerned about its lightweight, steel construction: Two square cross-sectional steel tubes form the bed and are welded to the steel-plate headstock at one end and a steel-plate foot at the other. The lathe did, however, run smoothly when I turned spindles and bowls; I was surprised that vibration and whip were no more bothersome with this lathe than the others I reviewed.

The long tool rest and tailstock are well-made solid castings and slide smoothly on the bed. Both are inconvenient to adjust because tightening or loosening them requires you to blindly feel for the locknut located underneath the lathe's bed rails. All the adjustments are made with a wrench, rather than an attached adjuster; I find the wrenches are liable to be misplaced or lost under piles of shavings. To snug up the tailstock, most economy lathes have a handwheel, which is generally located in the center of the tailstock casting, making it awkward to turn. The large handwheel on this lathe, however, is conveniently located on the far end of the spindle and is easy to operate.

The ½-HP motor provides sufficient power, but changing speeds is time consuming (the owner's manual recommends loosening the two motor-mount bolts each time). I found I could get around this by rotating the pulley shaft while coaxing the round drive belt onto the desired pulley with my fingers.

The Enco comes with a sanding table that attaches to the lathe bed and has a 9-in.-dia. sanding disc to fit the headstock spindle.

Grizzly G1025—Only small differences distinguish this lathe from the Enco: The bed is bolted, rather than welded, to the headstock and foot plate, and the round drive belt and step pulleys are visible through a window in the headstock, so it's easy to see the lathe's speed setting at a glance. The lathe performed about the same as the Enco model. For more information, contact Grizzly Imports PA Inc., 2406 Reach Road, Williamsport, Pa. 17701; (717) 326-3806.

Sears models—Sears offers two lightweight lathes. The bed on the least-expensive lathe (catalog #9BT24907C) is a sturdy, machined ¼-in.-thick steel T bar. It comes in two sections and is bolted together with two 5/16-in.-dia. bolts. Castings at each end of the bed have holes for bolting the lathe to your benchtop. The cast-iron headstock is grooved on the underside to slide onto the bed and is held in place with a single setscrew. In addition, the tool rest and tailstock are also castings and are grooved to slide freely on the bed; the bolt that locks them in position on the bed has an attached, pivoting handle to make adjustments convenient and quick. The tool rest surface has been machined smooth and is 12 in. long; adjustments to its height, angle and proximity to the blank

ECONOMY LATHES

Company and model	List price	Motor	Motor speeds (RPM)	Distance between cutters	Swing	Bed	Standard equipment (see footnote #1 below)	Available accessories
AMT 4370	$340	½ HP**	275, 515, 920, 970, 1725, 3065	36 in.	12 in., 16 in. with gap bed	Cast iron	Indexing attachment	Gap bed, 3- and 4-jaw chucks, 8-in. faceplate, live center.
AMT 2731 and 2731B	$73 $85	½ HP**	860, 1150, 1725, 2600, 3450	36 in.	12 in.	Two steel cylinders, 1¾ in. dia.		Heavy-duty tool rest, 4- and 8-in. faceplates, live center, long bed conversion to 55 in.
AMT 373	$104	½ HP**	860, 1150, 1725, 2600, 3450	41 in.	12 in.	Two steel cylinders, 1¾ in. dia.		12-in. tool rest, 4-in. faceplate.
Bridgewood BW-1240	$99	¾ HP	575, 980, 1560, 2520, 3580	37 in.	12 in.	1 steel cylinder, 2 in. dia.	6- and 12-in. tool rests, indexing attachment, outboard turning	3- and 4-jaw chucks, 9-in. sanding disk, sanding tube, 6-in. faceplate, bowl-turning tool rest.
Enco 199-9055	$178	½ HP	875, 1350, 2250, 3450	40 in.	12 in.	Two steel cylinders, 1⅜ in. dia.	Sanding table	
Grizzly G1025	$155	½ HP	850, 1250, 1750, 2570	40 in.	12 in.	Two steel cylinders, 1¾ in. dia.		3- and 4-jaw chucks, 8-in. faceplate.
Sears 9BT24907C	$150	1 HP*	875, 1350, 2250, 3450	36 in.	12 in.	T-bar steel plate		3- to 12-in. faceplates, duplicator attachment, bowl-turning tool rest.
Sears 9BT22816N	$210	½ HP	875, 1350, 2250, 3450	37 in.	12 in.	1 steel cylinder, 2 in. dia.	Indexing attachment, 6- and 12-in. tool rests	Speed reducer, 3- to 12-in. faceplates, sanding table, disc duplicator attachment, bowl-turning tool rest, 3- and 4-jaw chucks.
Williams and Hussey L-82	$498	½ HP**	800, 1200, 2500, 3750	46 in.	12 in.	Two ground steel ways, 3 in. wide	Outboard turning	8-in. faceplate, sanding discs, drill chuck and adapter, live center, indexing attachment.

1. All lathes are supplied with tool rest, headstock (spur center), tailstock center (live or dead) and a faceplate.
* Maximum-developed HP.   ** Motor not included.

are easy to make. Here again, a pivoted handle locks the tool rest.

I like the convenience the #1 Morse-taper centers, used on both the drive and tailstock spindles, afforded in changing blanks. Because of the lathe's light weight, I didn't expect it to perform as well as it did. I did, however, have to take light cuts to prevent the motor from stalling. Sears rates this motor at 1 HP (maximum developed horsepower), but it still seems underpowered.

Sears' top-rated lathe (catalog #9BT22816N) has four available speeds (875 RPM to 3,450 RPM), a 36-position indexing capability and a hollow-steel bed much like the Bridgewood BW-1240 discussed earlier. Unlike the Bridgewood, the Sears' lathe doesn't have outboard turning capability. Other than that, the lathes seem to differ only cosmetically. For example, the belt guard on one is made of plastic and on the other it's made of sheet metal; of course, the labeling is also different. In operation I wasn't able to detect any differences at all. (For your nearest Sears distributor, contact Sears, Roebuck & Co., Chicago, Ill. 60684; 312-875-2500.)

Williams & Hussey No. L-82—The L-82 lathe from Williams & Hussey Machine Co. (Riverview Mill, Souhegan Street, Box 1149, Wilton, N.H. 03086; 800-258-1380, 603-654-6828) has few frills, but it is a ruggedly constructed lathe that's hefty in the right places, runs smoothly and is relatively vibration free. The headstock, tool rest and tailstock

are heavy castings and fit to a pair of machine-surfaced, 3/16-in.-thick steel, U-shape channels that form the lathe bed. Foot castings at each end of the lathe are bolted to the bottom of the bed and have pre-drilled holes for securing the lathe to your benchtop. Even the belt guard, bolted to the headstock, is a heavy casting that is open at the back, making it easy to move the belt to change turning speeds.

A motor mount that permits quick belt changes can be purchased separately, but I found that bolting the ½-HP motor to a piece of plywood and, in turn, clamping the plywood to the benchtop worked well for aligning the motor and spindle pulleys and for tensioning the belt. The four available speed options range from 800 RPM to 3,750 RPM. (The power switch is mounted directly on the motor, which I don't like because it requires reaching over the spinning blank to operate the switch.)

The tool rest and tailstock slide smoothly on the bed, and the adjusting mechanisms for changing the tool rest height and securing the tailstock spindle are attached and easy to use. I wish the locking mechanisms for securing the tool rest and tailstock in place on the lathe bed were also built-in, rather than having to use the separate, small wrench provided. The spur center and cup center used on this lathe are the screw-on variety.   □

Alan Platt is an assistant editor at Fine Woodworking.

Shopmade Lathes

Low-Cost Wooden Longbed

by Carlyle Lynch

I designed and built this lathe to turn everything from chessmen and chair rungs to tall bedposts. The materials cost $179.25 including $30 for a used ½-HP motor, but not including some scraps of plywood and oak left over from other jobs. The spindles are made from machine steel tubing, which I threaded and reamed to a #2 Morse taper so standard Delta lathe accessories will fit.

Sources for heavy timbers are so uncertain that I decided to glue up the 3-in.-thick wooden members from kiln-dried southern yellow pine framing lumber; two 2x10s, four 2x8s, and one 2x6, each 12 ft. long. My local building supply dealer let me flip through his stacks to find pieces with straight grain and few knots. Besides the ready availability of standard "2 by" lumber, laminating had other advantages over heavy timbers. Until final glueup, most of my work was easier because I was hefting just half of each member at a time. The laminated members are also stronger and more dimensionally stable than heavy timbers.

Each of the ways is made from two pieces of 2x8 (1½ in. by

7 in. after dimensioning), as shown in the drawing below. After temporarily screwing the ways together, I clamped the uprights to each way in turn, and made sure that the ways were square to the uprights. I drilled the carriage-bolt holes in the ways with a long electricians' auger bit guided through the dadoed bolt holes in the uprights. Then I glued, screwed and clamped the ways together.

The headstock brace was made a snug fit between the headstock uprights and the ways and fastened to the headstock leg with two ½-in. by 5-in. lag screws and washers.

Each foot is made of two pieces of 2x6 (now 1½ in. by 5½ in.). I outlined blind mortises for the leg tenons, unscrewed the pieces and cut the mortises in each half. The foot halves were then glued, screwed and clamped together, then bandsawn to shape when dry.

The tailstock is made of two uprights joined to a base with dovetails. I cut 10° tails on the base with the bandsaw. I cut the

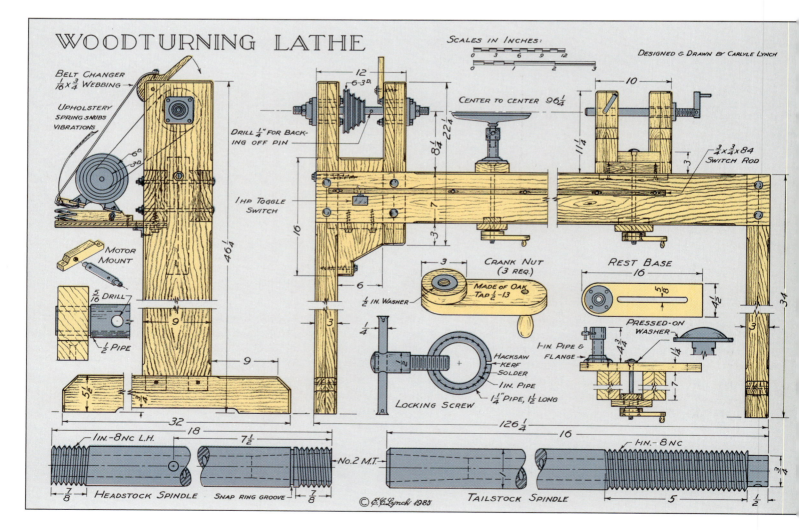

Glued up from yellow pine framing lumber, Lynch's wooden lathe cost less than $200 in materials. With its 10½-ft. bed, it can handle up to 8-ft. work. A strip of wood, screwed to the bed through slotted holes, activates the on/off switch from anywhere on the bed.

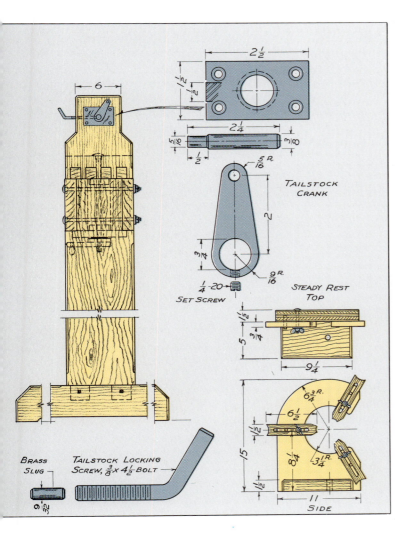

2½

6

1½

2¼

5/16   3/8

1/2

TAILSTOCK CRANK

5/16 R.

2

3/4

9/16 R.

¼-20

SET SCREW

STEADY REST TOP

1/2

3/4

5

9¼

3/64 R.

6½

15

8¼

3¼ R.

1/2

11

SIDE

BRASS SLUG

TAILSTOCK LOCKING SCREW, ⅜ x 4½-BOLT

9/32

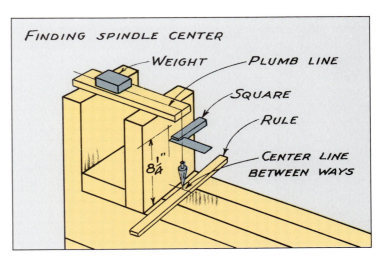

FINDING SPINDLE CENTER

WEIGHT — PLUMB LINE

SQUARE

RULE

CENTER LINE BETWEEN WAYS

8¼"

Hardware specifications:

2—One 1-in. bore, 4-groove cone step pulley, 3, 4, 5, and 6 in. dia., and one to fit motor shaft (Made by Browning Mfg., Emerson Electric Co., P.O. Box 687, Maysville, Ky. 41056)

2—1-in.-bore flange block bearings (Fafnir RCJ, made by Fafnir Bearing Div. of Textron Inc., 37 Booth St., New Britain, CT 06050)

1—12-in. toolrest (Delta part no. 46-692; Delta lathe parts are available from local Delta dealers or may be ordered by phone from Delta International, 1-800-223-7278.)

1—6-in. faceplate, 1-in. -8 thread (Delta part no. 46-937)

1—Spur drive center #2 M.T. (Delta part no. 46-933)

1—Cup center #2 M.T. (Delta part no. 46-439)

1—Headstock spindle; 16 in. by 1-in.-OD machine steel tubing

1—Tailstock spindle; 15 in. by 1-in.-OD machine steel tubing

The headstock spindle turns in flange-block bearings bolted to the head-stock uprights. The weight of the ½-HP motor keeps tension on the belt. Pulling forward on the lever pulls a strip of ¾-in. webbing to lift the motor forward and take the weight off the belt for changing speeds. The upholstery spring under the motor damps vibration. A birch-plywood indexing ring (above) screws on the inside of the inboard headstock upright. With the belt removed from the motor pulley, a pointer fits around the headstock spindle so that an 8d nail can slide through a hole in one of five concentric rows. A bar on the pointer passes through a hole in the spindle.

matching pins on the tablesaw by setting the miter gauge at 80° and standing the board on end. The other three tailstock pieces shown in the drawing are glued to these three parts. On the underside of the base, I screwed an oak guide block exactly as wide as the gap between the ways, so the tailstock moves smoothly on the ways without any side play.

To locate the headstock spindle hole on the inboard headstock upright, I assembled the lathe and leveled the bed in both planes by shimming the feet. I laid a rule across the ways and dropped a plumb line over the upright to the center point between the ways, as shown in the drawing on the previous page, then marked the center. I disassembled the lathe and drilled the spindle holes on the drill press—1⅛ in. dia. on the inboard upright and 1¼ in. dia. on the outboard leg.

To mount the spindle, I clamped one of the flange block bearings to the inboard upright, inserted the spindle, and clamped on the outboard bearing. I stuck a spur center in the inboard end of the spindle, and with plumb line, ruler, and a short spirit level on the spindle, I maneuvered the inboard flange block until the spindle was level and centered in the headstock upright. When it was, I clamped the inboard flange block in place. A strip of wood clamped under the flange block provided additional support while I drilled through one of the four mounting holes in the bearing for a bolt hole. With that corner bolted, I drilled and installed a bolt in the corner diagonally opposite. I moved the spur center to the outboard end and centered and bolted the outboard bearing in place. Once the headstock spindle was in place, I tightened the locking collars (supplied with the bearings) that hold the spindle in the bearings.

To mark the center for the tailstock spindle, I placed a spur center in the headstock spindle and slid the tailstock along the bed until it bumped into the spur center. Using this dent as center, I drilled a 1-in. hole through the inboard tailstock upright and a 1¼-in. hole in the outboard tailstock upright on the drill press. I spun the threaded steel plate onto the tailstock spindle threads and inserted the spindle through the holes in the tailstock. With a center in the tailstock spindle, I slid the tailstock up to the headstock to align the points. When the tailstock spindle was aligned and level, I clamped the steel plate in place and drove two No. 8 screws in diagonally opposite ¹¹⁄₆₄-in. holes in the plate, checked again for alignment and installed the other two screws. Then, two at a time, I removed the screws, drilled out

the holes to ¼ in., and replaced the screws with ¼-in. by 4-in. machine bolts. I made the tailstock spindle handle from a piece of flat steel bar, but a handwheel would be better.

The ½-HP motor rests on a plywood platform held to the back of the lathe bed by a piece of angle iron and a wood brace. The weight of the motor furnishes the belt tension. A piece of ¾-in.-wide webbing and an eccentric lever take the weight off the belt to make changing speeds easy, as shown in the photo, above left. An upholstery spring under the motor acts as a snubber to take out slight motor vibration. A 20-amp, single-pole, single-throw toggle switch is mounted on the front side of the bed. Slots cut in a ¾-in.-square 84-in. pine strip allow control of the switch from anywhere along the bed.

The drawing shows a wooden toolrest base with a pipe flange and short length of pipe that holds standard Delta toolrests. A 30-in.-long wooden rest can also be made for long work.

Tall bedposts and the legs of Sheraton tables are often reeded, fluted or carved, necessitating an indexing ring, not shown in the drawing. The ¾-in. birch-plywood ring is fastened to the left side of the inboard upright, as shown in the photo, above right. With the belt removed from the motor pulley so the lathe can't be accidentally started, a pointer is fastened on the headstock spindle so that an 8d nail can slide through any one of five holes in the pointer to engage one of five concentric circles of holes in the ring. Working in from the outer circle, the number of holes in each circle are: 60, 11, 9, 7, and 8. The circles were scratched by holding the nail against the plywood ring and revolving the spindle. A pair of dividers found the correct spacing by trial and error.

Long spindles must be kept from "whipping" while being turned, so I made a steady rest, as shown in the drawing. I carefully and slowly turn long pieces to a smooth cylinder for a couple of inches in the middle before turning the whole piece. Then, I set the hickory jaws of the steady rest against that smooth surface, turn the lathe on and touch on paraffin to lubricate the friction spot.

I finished the lathe with shellac, about the only finish that will prevent sappy grain and knots bleeding through. The lathe is bolted to the floor with angle irons, to keep vibration down. □

Carlyle Lynch is a retired teacher, cabinetmaker and designer in Broadway, Va.

Heavyweight Lathes

by Jerry Blanchard

About five years ago, I looked around for a lathe that would swing 24 in. over the bed. Big patternmakers' lathes had the capacity I wanted, but they cost a fortune and take up half the shop. Instead of buying one, I designed and built the lathe I had in mind—heavy, versatile, and bull strong.

My lathe is fabricated almost entirely of structural steel members. I machined everything myself on a 10-in. Delta metalcutting lathe. If you aren't up to basic machining, or don't have access to a metal lathe, a local machine shop can probably do the machining for you, working from the drawings.

I designed the lathe in sections that bolt together so I could move it piece by piece; alone, if I had to (three times so far). It would be simpler to weld things together if you don't care about portability. With a little scrounging, you can pick up most of the steel at a low price, as I did. The legs are made from 5-in. by 5-in. H-beams, and the bed is made from two lengths of heavy 6-in. channel iron spaced 1¾ in. apart. My lathe is 6 ft. long, but you could make the bed longer or shorter.

The headstock uprights are made from 3-in. by 6-in. mechanical tubing with a ⅜-in. wall thickness. The flat plates that make up the tailstock assembly, and other parts here and there, are mild steel. I cut the plates to shape with an oxyacetylene cutting torch and a hacksaw, ground the edges clean with a hand-held disc grinder, and arc welded the parts together with low-hydrogen welding rods (E7016 or E7018).

I made the headstock spindle from a 16-in. piece of 2⅜-in.-dia., seamless mechanical tubing with an inside diameter of ⅞ in. The ends are turned down to 2³⁄₁₆-in. diameter, as shown in the drawing on the following page. This massive spindle may seem like overkill compared to store-bought lathes, but I like to overbuild. I reamed a #3 Morse taper in each end to hold centers, and cut the threads on the Delta lathe. I could have mounted a step pulley on the spindle, but I planned to use a variable-speed motor so I didn't need a step pulley to change speeds. I wanted an indexing device so I combined functions and machined a heavy, one-piece pulley/indexing head that slips over the spindle. To drill the twenty-four ¼-in. indexing holes, I scored a centerline around the face of the pulley using the Delta lathe, spaced off the holes, and drilled them on a drill press. The pulley/indexing head is a press fit on the spindle, held in place with a key. As an extra touch, I crowned the surface of the pulley/indexing head slightly, just in case I ever felt like running the lathe with a flat belt off a lineshaft.

The headstock bearings are Fafnir self-aligning 2³⁄₁₆-in. ball-bearing pillow blocks (available from bearing-supply companies in major cities). These compensate automatically for twist or other misalignment of the headstock so precision machining of mounting surfaces isn't needed. Pillow blocks come in various strengths, types, and sizes. Commonly-used sizes are cheaper than others, so it pays to buy pillow blocks that your dealer has in stock and make your spindle to fit. Fafnir pillow blocks come with eccentric locking rings that lock the spindle tightly to the bearings. I supplemented these with threaded rings at each end of the spindle to take heavy thrust loads applied from the ends. One-inch-diameter threaded rods bolt the headstock to the bed.

The tailstock assembly shown in the drawing works just like the tailstock on most store-bought lathes. The thrust bearing is not essential, but it makes it easy to really tighten up the spindle

This scarlet behemoth swings 24 in. over the bed, weighs about 500 lb., and knocks down for portability. The body of the lathe is welded and bolted from stock structural steel shapes. The headstock spindle turns in pillow-block bearings bolted to the headstock and bed. A variable-speed motor eliminates the need for a step pulley. An adapter (shown above on inboard end of spindle) permits use of standard size faceplates and chucks.

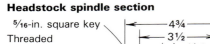

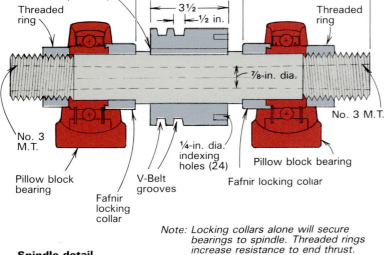

5/16-in. square key
Threaded ring
4¾
3½
½ in.
Threaded ring
7/8-in. dia.
No. 3 M.T.
No. 3 M.T.
Pillow block bearing
Fafnir locking collar
V-Belt grooves
¼-in. dia. indexing holes (24)
Pillow block bearing
Fafnir locking collar
5¾

Note: Locking collars alone will secure bearings to spindle. Threaded rings increase resistance to end thrust.

Spindle detail

2¾
2⅜
2³/₁₆

Tailstock section

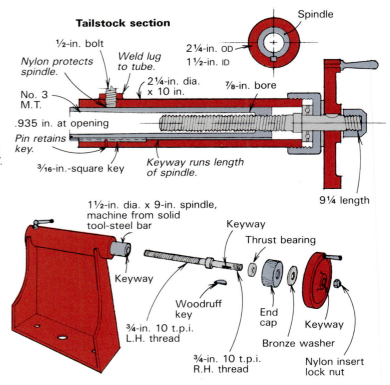

½-in. bolt
Nylon protects spindle.
Weld lug to tube.
Spindle
2¼-in. OD
1½-in. ID
No. 3 M.T.
2¼-in. dia. x 10 in.
7/8-in. bore
.935 in. at opening
Pin retains key.
3/16-in.-square key
Keyway runs length of spindle.
9¼ length

1½-in. dia. x 9-in. spindle, machine from solid tool-steel bar
Keyway
Thrust bearing
Keyway
Woodruff key
¾-in. 10 t.p.i. L.H. thread
End cap
Keyway
Bronze washer
¾-in. 10 t.p.i. R.H. thread
Nylon insert lock nut

Josephus Daniels

Blanchard poses with the super bowl lathe (newly pinstriped) that he made for bowl turner Neil Weston. The lathe swings 8 ft. with the toolrest removed, and 36 in. with the rest in place. The top is a 21 in. square of ¾-in. steel plate welded to 3-in. by 3-in. angle-iron legs. Two non-syncromesh G.M. transmissions from the 1940s—a 4-speed truck and a 3-speed—provide 13 forward speeds from 33 RPM to 856 RPM, and some in reverse for final sanding. Power comes from a 2-HP, 220-volt single-phase Baldor motor, mounted on the floor to isolate vibration. The spindle is a length of 2½-in.-dia. heat-treated shafting. The clamp on the toolrest post is made from Powermatic lathe toolrest clamp parts ordered from the Powermatic parts catalog.

without too much effort on the handwheel. I made a lot of attachments for my lathe: centers, faceplates, steady rest, a sanding disc and a metal-spinning toolrest. Most useful, so far, is an adapter that allows me to mount standard lathe faceplates and chucks on the big spindle.

The motor on my lathe is an ancient G.E. variable-speed reversing model that works by mechanically shifting the brushes with a lever. It's underpowered, but the brushes spark and it smells wonderfully of ozone, and it pleases me to use it.

I spent some time sanding everything smooth and painting it shiny red with gold pinstriping. The lathe was a lot of work, but I enjoyed making it and it does what I wanted it to do.   □

Jerry Blanchard, engraver, machinist, woodworker, and gunsmith, lives in Pebble Beach, Calif., and teaches woodworking at nearby Monterey High School.

Safety warning

A lathe is a dangerous machine. A block of wood that is carelessly secured can fly off and hit you in the face with enough force to maim or even kill. You can't make a lathe completely safe, but you can eliminate this danger by turning large-diameter bowls and out-of-balance blocks at the slowest speed setting on your lathe. Be sure your wood is securely mounted. Double-check your speed setting and rotate the stock by hand to make sure that it clears the toolrest before you turn on the lathe. As you throw the switch, stand to one side, just to be sure.

Before turning, take off ties, loose clothing and jewelry. If your hair is long, tie it back. Long hair can wrap around the spinning wood and pull your face into the lathe with frightening speed and force. Above all, *never turn wood without wearing a Plexiglas face shield.* Safety glasses and goggles don't protect your face.

The Bowl Gouge

Using long-and-strong tools to turn the outside

by Peter Child

Woodturning gouges are of three types: one designed for bowls, one for between-center coving and small rounds, and one for roughing square stock to cylinders and sweeping curves, also between centers.

The blade of a bowl gouge is always "long and strong," meaning heavy duty. A good new one measures 12 in. from cutting edge to tang. It has a deep U-shaped flute with much meatier metal at the bottom, or keel, of the flute than at its two wings. Bevel angle varies with how tall a person the turner is, but it is always less than 45 degrees, although not so small as to make the edge fragile. There is no second bevel as in a bench chisel or plane iron, and there is no point. The edge is shaped square across.

Four sizes of bowl gouges are in current production: 1/4 in., 3/8 in., 1/2 in. and 3/4 in., ranging in weight from 4 to 16 ounces. Each size has a particular function. The 3/4-inch is absolutely the largest that can be used correctly; any bigger gouge is not a bowl gouge, however long and strong it may look. The heavy-duty handles should be about a foot long, and hefty—weight and length are necessary for control. This is why bowls should be turned outboard and should not be attempted between centers, where the lathe bed restricts movement of the gouge.

Coving gouges, for between-center work, are of medium strength and have a longer bevel and a lighter handle than bowl gouges. They also have pointed, "lady fingernail" noses

---

Peter Child, author of The Craftsman Woodturner, *died in 1986. His son, Christopher, continues to work and teach in the family studio in Halstead, England.*

and a much shallower flute. Common sizes range from 1/4 in. up to 3/4 in. The roughing-down gouge serves for larger work.

Roughing-down gouges are of medium strength, deeply throated, semicircular rather than U-shaped in cross section, beveled at 45 degrees, and of even thickness. Their lack of keel makes them unsuitable for bowl work, whatever the size. They range from 3/4 in. up to 1-1/2 in.

Depending on the mood of the factory grinder, the bevel of a new tool can be any angle or length at all, and so the purchaser will have to reshape it. Any point must be removed so the edge is straight across. The bevel should be hollow ground right up to the cutting edge, without a second bevel. A skilled operator can thus provide himself, straight from the grindstone, with an edge that has a fine sawtooth cutting burr. Such an edge would horrify a cabinetmaker or carver, but it is most practical for a turner as it can be resharpened in seconds on the grindstone. An absolutely flat bevel does the same job as one hollow ground, but takes longer to obtain and maintain with a flat stone. Although the final result will be much sharper than the sawtooth edge, it may not last long enough to merit the time and care taken to obtain it. Also, with a stone it is very easy to round the bevel, exactly opposite to hollow ground. The slightest belly is intolerable since it causes the tools to lose most of their usefulness.

When cutting, the whole length of the bevel is in full contact with the wood. Take a piece of wood and hold it in the bench vise. Use the gouge to make a groove in the wood, as though starting a carving. In controlling the cut there

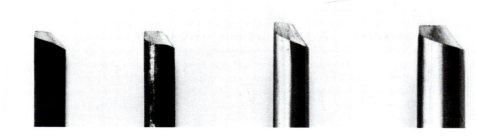

The different sizes of bowl gouges corresponding to cabinetmaker's planes are shown below. From the right, the 3/4-in. gouge is equivalent to a scrub plane, the 1/2-in. and 3/8-in. are jack and smooth planes, the 1/4-in. is a block plane for cleaning up end grain. A turner with a new set should start by grinding all the bevels to the angle of the 1/2-in. tool, second from right. To try your hand without investing in a whole set, choose the 3/8-in. or 1/2-in. gouge. At right, starting from the top, head-on views of the three kinds of turning gouges, all at 3/4 in. Bowl gouge is ground square across; spindle or coving gouge is ground to a pointed nose; roughing-down gouge at bottom is ground square across.

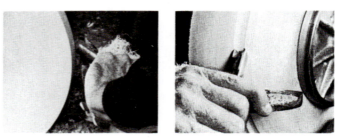

Child slices curls of wood from the rotating disc. Proper gouge work depends upon correct stance, hand position and coordination of eye, hand and leg. With the bevel always rubbing (bottom middle photo) the trick is to roll the tool over in the direction of the cut, while lifting the handle straight up. The cut begins at 12 o'clock high (left) and slices a downward arc to three o'clock (top and middle right). He watches the progress of the cut at the silhouette at the top of the whirling disc. His right hand rolls and slides the

handle up the thigh; his right leg supports and powers the thrust of the tool, his left palm presses firmly on the rest, the thumb pushing the blade and the fingers curled around and controlling it. The shaving is narrow at the start and broad at the end, but its thickness does not change. At bottom right, the gouge digs in. The wing away from the direction of cut, here the left wing, has been allowed to touch the wood. It scores a deepening ring in the bowl, ending in a sharp tear, startling the operator out of his careless stupor.

should be no space between the bevel and the wood. Now try to make a similar groove with the bevel not in contact, holding the handle more or less upright. It will be almost impossible. A gouge can remove wood without the bevel rubbing and without conscious effort, but only because the power of an electric motor is scraping it off. Only with the full bevel rubbing is it possible to take clean cuts.

There are two main methods of turning a bowl. One is to screw the wood to the faceplate and turn the outside and base first, perhaps with a flange or lip, and then remove the wood, reverse it, and somehow reposition it on the faceplate to turn the inside. The other way, my method, is to flatten and sand the bottom of the blank first, then fix the base to the faceplate and turn the outside and inside in one operation. There is a little more cutting against the grain, but the troublesome end grain is the same in either case. And I am saved the tricky problem of getting the bowl back onto the lathe in exactly the right place, since I never take it off.

Let us move to the lathe to cut the outside of a bowl with

the long-and-strong gouge. The blank is sawed to a disc, screwed to a faceplate and mounted outboard. The tool rest is parallel to the axis of rotation, set about center. The height of the rest is adjusted according to the height of the operator, so that the gouge cuts at the center of the disc or slightly above center. (We assume the operator is right-handed and cutting from left to right, from the face of the disc toward the faceplate.)

Every cut has to be fully under control from beginning to end. The operator has to stand centrally behind the gouge, with its handle upright. He cannot see the bevel. With the blade on the rest, the heel of the bevel rubs the revolving wood. The cutting edge is not yet touching the wood.

Keeping the blade on the rest, he gradually lifts the handle straight up until a thin shaving appears at the center of the U-shaped channel. This indicates that the whole bevel is rubbing, without the turner having to move to one side to look. At this stage, the blade will be in contact with the front, not the top of the tool rest.

The left hand holds the blade close to its cutting edge and on the rest, palm over the blade, first and second fingers curled around it, and thumb, if not curled around, then pushing against the side of the blade. This hand does not move for the duration of any one cut—the fingers may move slightly at the end of the cut, but the palm remains where it is. The right hand holds the long handle very close to the bottom in a tennis or hammer grip.

The shearing cut of the gouge starts at the top (12 o'clock high), coming down in an arc to finish at 3 o'clock. The first cut is started about 1/2 in. from the right-hand edge of the disc and removes wood from left to right toward the faceplate.

The shaving is removed first by the center of the blade, then, progressively, by its right-hand edge or wing, so that only half the cutting edge is occupied. To do this the turner rolls the blade over to the right and at the same time lifts the handle straight up. This coordination has to be learned and the way to do it is to start a thin shaving with the center of the gouge and keep the shaving at the same depth for the duration of the cut. If the blade is rolled too much the shaving will finish thicker than it started. If the handle is not lifted, the cut will be straight across and not in a downward shearing arc, which is the best cutting action. Do not attempt to remove too much wood with one cut—a cut that traverses a half inch at a time is ample for practice, and this should be done again and again, keeping the shavings the same thickness throughout.

Sometimes the gouge digs in, a startling and unpleasant jump that leaves an unsightly gash in the wood. All sorts of circumstances can lead up to this shock—bevel not rubbing, gouge out of control due to incorrect holding or wrong position, blade not sharp, or overcutting. What actually happens is that the unwitting operator allows the blade to roll in the wrong direction, from right to left, and the left wing of the blade comes into contact with the wood. This is what digs in.

To avoid this, I emphasize rolling and lifting the gouge and using its center and right wing only. This motion keeps the left half of the blade away from the wood and out of harm's way. This "wrong half" is the only cause of a dig-in.

Time and again I am puzzled at seeing an operator standing in one position, albeit a correct one, and endeavoring to traverse more and more wood with each cut. To keep the blade cutting he has to roll it over more, move his hand along the rest (incorrect), and lift the handle uncomfortably high. This is overcutting, an awkward motion which can easily lead to a disastrous dig-in. I now firmly believe this mistake is a result of training, probably in other crafts. Consider a cabinetmaker hand planing at his bench. He stands still. Likewise a woodcarver and a potter with his clay. But to keep constant control of a gouge, a turner seldom stands still for long.

After a disc has assumed a distinct rounding, say from half of full thickness to almost the faceplate diameter, try the following. Take an even cut from full disc thickness toward the right. The gouge will tend to come off the cut after about 1/2 in. of travel. Do not force it to cut further, but move your feet a little to the right and take up the cut from where you left off. You should find absolute control in cutting, and a comfortable action. Remember that each cut is still from 12 noon to 3 o'clock. The bowl might look a little ridged, but

not much. A practiced turner can do the whole area from middle thickness to faceplate in one or two sweeping cuts, but his feet are continuously moving him sideways to the right. The majority of bowl turning is done by body and legs, not hands alone.

The normal stance of a right-handed operator is left leg in front of right, with the right hand holding and providing thrust to the gouge. To make a smooth and even cut over wood containing end grain, hard and soft areas and perhaps knots can be quite difficult. The blade may skip over a hard area, then plunge too deeply into the soft.

Try this. Stand directly behind the gouge in the correct position, but reverse your legs so that the knee or mid-thigh of the right leg touches the end of the handle. It will feel most peculiar at first. Take a cut, but with the handle not quite in contact with the leg. Next, take a cut with the handle butt touching your leg and either raise your heel to lift the handle, or slide it up your thigh. The handle is always lifted straight up, not sideways, so the leg can support the tool over the full cut. Turners use this leg action to control depth of cut, whatever the terrain, and as a third hand or power source to remove large shavings in minimum time. The 3/4-in. gouge cannot be used to full capacity with the hands alone, unless one has the mighty thews of a blacksmith.

While the left wing of the blade must be kept away from the wood to avoid dig-in, no harm will result if the gouge is rolled so far that the whole right wing is cutting. Try having the bevel rubbing, but not cutting, and rolling the tool to the right over the whole working area. Repeat the exercise, but deliberately look away from the blade—don't watch what you are doing. This should convince you that nothing untoward will happen, and will give confidence to an otherwise apprehensive and tense approach. Now start a cut, looking at the blade, and immediately transfer your gaze to the top of the disc. A suitably placed lamp will help. You will be able to see the effect of the cut without looking at the cutting edge. The coordination of roll and lift, so difficult for beginners, is automatically simplified when the eyes transfer information directly to the hands. If the gouge is rolled over too far, the cut will immediately thicken and you will see it happen at the top of the disc. Your eyes will send a correction directly to your hands. As a bonus, you can govern the shape of the bowl much more easily. By starting each cut just before the finish of the previous one, you can reduce and practically eliminate ridging. The gouge does the work almost alone.

A basic woodturning principle is that all cuts are made from large diameter to small, and never going uphill from small diameter to large. Too deep a practice cut can lead into this, so watch it.

Up to now we have assumed the turner is right-handed, and most technical writing ignores the hapless left-hander, who must mentally reverse all the directions. But when a bowl bellies out in the middle so one has to work both right to left and left to right to keep working toward the smaller diameter, then a right-hander must also learn to switch directions and hands. If he doesn't, the fingers are pulling the blade and it can easily roll back the wrong way and dig in. A gouge blade should always be pushed, never pulled, and the hand that is doing the pushing has the opposite leg supporting the handle. I always tell my right-handed pupils they will be better turners when they learn to do it left-handed and I am nearly always proved right.

Woodturning Chisels
The squarenose, the skew and the woodturner's sway

by Peter Child

I encounter someone almost every week who persists in calling *all* turning tools "chisels"—so let us get this out of the way first. Woodturning tools fall into two main categories: cutting tools and scraping tools. The cutting tools are parting tools, gouges and chisels. Scrapers are not chisels.

There are standard and long-and-strong chisels. L&S is our term for heavy-duty. Chisels 1 in. in width and more should be the heaviest available. Blade weight is important for control. A 1¼-in. blade and tang should be at least 13 in. long, ⁵⁄₁₆ in. thick and weigh over 1 lb. A 2-in. blade and tang should be 15 in. or more long, ⅜ in. thick and weigh over 2 lb. Handles for these chisels should be 10 in. or longer.

Bench tools such as planes, firmer chisels and carving gouges may have two bevels, a grinding bevel and a secondary, very short sharpening bevel, both on the same side of the blade. A woodturning chisel has two bevels, but they are on opposite sides of the blade and are both grinding bevels—no additional sharpening bevels. The chisel should be sharpened, and kept so, in a dead flat plane from heel to cutting edge. Avoid even the slightest rounding or "hill in the middle," as my old master called it.

Grinding and honing — I am fond of hollow grinding because it saves time in honing. I use a clean, dry carborundum wheel 6 in. in diameter by 1 in. wide, spinning 3,000 RPM. The wheel is unguarded because I need access to its top, but I wear safety glasses that supposedly can deflect a .22 bullet from close range. Must test them sometime.

For me, accurate grinding by eye is easy. Most of my pupils, however, make a complete hash of it because they are nervous at the grindstone and tend to grip the tool too firmly, sacri-

ficing fluid, smooth control. Grip the tool only enough to *rest* the bevel on the stone and maintain the same angle while moving it back and forth. The grindstone, kept clean by frequent application of a star-wheel dressing tool, does all the work. Because (for comfort) I grind on the upper part of the wheel I cannot use the grinding rest, so I rely on my hands, elbows tucked in, to maintain the angle. To sidle the tool I move my body—the "woodturner's sway."

For a start, hold the chisel lightly. Note the height at which you first make contact and take one light pass, then look at the result. There should be a faint grinding scar nearer the heel than the edge of the bevel, say just below center. If there is not, try another pass, again noting the height. When you are near enough, put the chisel on the wheel, and with minimum pressure *keep it there*, swaying from the body to move it slowly back and forth over the wheel.

Now take a breather and let the chisel do the same. A pupil of mine, who is a metallurgist, told me that quenching hot steel in cold water weakens the steel. Before starting the wheel again, lay the blade on it with the handle down, tool edge up off the surface. Slowly lift the handle and feel the groove fit itself onto the wheel. Now start the wheel, bring up the handle into the fit position and resume grinding. In a few seconds, with the blade held in place by the groove, slowly lift the handle, spreading the width of the groove toward the chisel edge. When it has extended to within ¹⁄₃₂ in. of the edge, stop.

If you have made the groove too wide by starting too far down the blade, the chisel will still work, though not keenly for long, as the cutting edge will be fragile and need frequent resharpening. This will gradually reduce the length of the bevel, so eventually all will be right again.

Hollow grinding removes metal that would otherwise have to be honed away. Because less steel is in contact with the stone, you can sharpen a hollow-ground blade faster. Honing gradually removes the hollow, and it takes longer, until you decide enough is enough, and regrind the bevel.

To hone the edge I hold the chisel upright, the handle supported on some firm surface, and rub the stone over the chisel. I find honing the other way, rubbing the chisel over a fixed stone, to be tedious and difficult—a rounded bevel almost certainly results. I use a lightly oiled, fine to medium, flat stone that fits my hand. With the stone firmly in contact with heel and edge, I rub until with the ball of my index finger I can feel a distinct "rag." Then I turn the chisel over and hone the other bevel until the rag appears again. I repeat this from side to side until there is only the barest trace of a rag, then remove it by stropping on a length of hide leather glued to a wooden base.

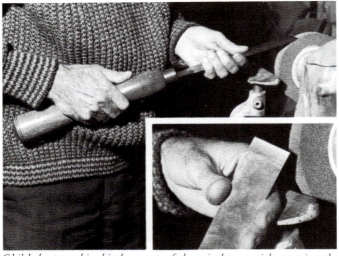

Child sharpens his chisels on top of the grindstone without using the tool rest. He determines the proper angle by eye and maintains it with a light grip, elbows held close to the body. With the 'woodturner's sway,' he moves the chisel back and forth across the stone.

Using the chisel to smooth a cylinder —

There are two chisel shapes, the well-known skew or long-corner, and the not so well-known bullnose or squarenose. They have distinctly different purposes. Most books and articles show the skew being used where the better tool for the job would be the squarenose. However, to illustrate its deficiencies, I will deliberately make the same error and start with the skew.

You need a piece of wood about 2 in. by 2 in. and as long as can be accommodated by the tool rest, say 10 in. It is easier if it is softwood, possibly pine, and easier still if it is green. First hand-plane or machine a shaving or two to see if it takes a good finish from the planer. If not, no amount of dexterity with the chisel will give a good finish. Mount the right piece in the lathe and rough out a cylinder. It is common to see this done with a shallow-fluted pointnose coving gouge, but this leaves a rippled surface. I use a 1¼-in. roughing-down gouge, which has a straight nose and a deep, half-circle flute. Easy to use and impossible to dig in, the roughing-down gouge removes large quantities of wood in a hurry, leaving a fine, clean surface that requires only one or two passes with a chisel to make the job perfect.

The purpose of the chisel is to plane the wood smooth. When we hand-plane in the bench vise, the plane is on top of the wood and easy to control. Try planing with the plane on the side of the wood and see how much control you have. In lathe work, using a chisel with the tool rest in its normal position, just under the centerline of the stock, has the same unsteady effect. Unlike any other tool between centers, use the chisel with the rest high so the blade lies almost on top of the cylinder rather than halfway down its side.

For the following instructions, we need to get our nomenclature straight. The long, acute corner is the *trailing* point; the other, obtuse corner is the *leading* point. The trailing point must not touch the wood or it will cause severe 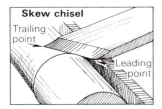 splintering, at the least. The leading point can touch the wood, but it blocks the shavings and is not good turnery.

Place the chisel on the right-hand end of the tool rest, its edge on the wood 1 in. from the tailstock. It is impossible to start the cut from the extreme ends of the cylinder because the blade must have support from the wood before cutting can commense. The trailing point should be safely away from the wood, and the blade tilted slightly so that only the lower left-hand corner of the blade touches the tool rest. The remainder of the under-blade is in the air, except where the edge touches the wood.

With the chisel on the wood and the lathe stopped, first see how far the chisel has to be lifted before the center of the cutting edge enters the wood just under top dead center. You will be surprised at how high the handle can come. Have someone turn the lathe slowly for you. Bring up the handle until the edge center starts to cut and push it along slowly, taking a small curl shaving. Do not push down hard with your left hand, or the corner where the blade touches the tool rest will make smooth travel difficult. Hesitant, jerky movements will result in a ribbed surface, or in a dig-in. Keep your left hand light; control is in the right hand, handle and body.

Start the lathe, spread your legs and make sure that you keep the handle against your right-hand side. Without moving the blade along the rest, lift the handle until the center of the blade wants to cut, then hold the handle tightly into your

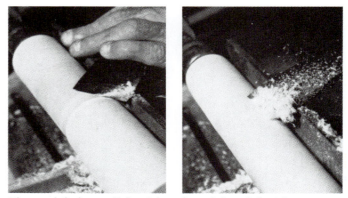

Photo at left shows a light trial cut from right to left with squarenose chisel. Only the center of the blade edge is cutting, slightly below top dead center of the cylinder. At right: a perfect full-cut. All of the edge except the points is cutting. Note that left hand is not necessary to steady the cut; control is in the right hand, chisel handle and body.

side and cut along, swaying from your hips and legs. The handle should not leave your side—your body goes along with it. Cutting tiny chips with the center of the edge is not using the chisel properly, but it will increase the confidence and understanding you need to follow the next instructions.

To get a proper shaving, much more of the edge than just the center must be cutting. You need to angle the chisel so that most of the bottom edge (toward the leading point) and a bit more of the top edge (toward the trailing point) come into action. Here is the problem with the skew. Because of its angle, the skew can be placed naturally on the wood only in the "amateur position," the trailing point well away from the wood. To get more of the blade cutting, with the handle firmly attached to your body, you have to move uncomfortably far to the left. It is not a good position to smooth from. So for this particular purpose the skew is out.

The squarenose chisel is far easier for smoothing a cylinder and much more comfortable. All the same rules apply, of course. If a 1¼-in. is available use it first for practice, cutting small with only the center, then move the handle over a little to the left so that more of the blade cuts, then a little more and the shavings are beautiful. A little too much and oops! Start again. Full-bodied cutting with a chisel means using as much of the edge as possible with neither the trailing nor the leading points touching the wood. As my old friend and master turner Frank Pain said, "Good woodturning runs very close indeed to spoiling the work."

A 1¼-in. squarenose is right for turning up to about 3 in. in diameter. For larger diameters you need a 2-in. and possibly a wooden heightener affixed to the tool rest so it comes up far enough. Actually a 2-in. is fine for smaller turning too: lots of blade so the trailing edge is comfortably away from contact. After practice from right to left, the right-hander can try cutting from left to right and become a leftie. Please remember to sharpen the chisel often.

Using the skew in parting — The skew has the Achilles syndrome in its toe, not its heel. Because of its acute angle, the point is weak and susceptible to damage. If you cut with it incorrectly, the point overheats, and becomes weaker still. Take care in grinding and honing to keep the point angled properly, not rounded over. It must be exceedingly sharp.

Skew chisels are available in sizes from 2 in. to ⅛ in. I use a long-and-strong 1¼-in. for most work, and a lightweight

Cleaning up a rough parting cut with a skew chisel. Begin with handle down and over to the right so the left-hand bevel will be in contact with the cut surface. Slowly raise the handle, arcing the point into the work, to slice a thin section. Do not move the bevel away from the cut surface or end the cut with the handle higher than parallel to the floor; the tool is liable to kick.

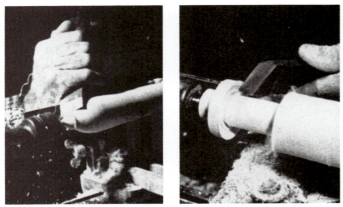

Variations on the right-angle cut: curved taper (planing with square-nose chisel), left, and saucer cut (arcing in with skew chisel), right. In each case the bevel follows in contact with the cut surface.

Traditional parting tool leaves rough surface and splintered corners because the side of the tool scrapes rather than cuts the wood.

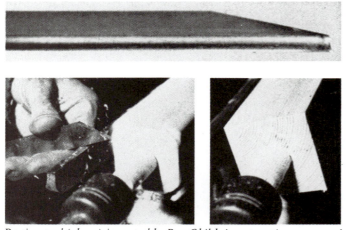

Parting tool (above) invented by Roy Child, incorporating a grooved and pronged cutting edge, parts cleanly, eliminating need for clean-up with skew chisel.

½-in. for parting off because I can manage it with one hand. I also use it to mark off distances between turning features for, say, copy turning. Light nicks along a cylinder are clearer and more precise than pencil lines.

The skew-chisel cutting movement, different from the planing movement used to smooth a cylinder, always begins the same. Hold the chisel with the cutting edge vertical, skewed side up, and arc the long-cornered point (what for smoothing is the trailing point) down into the wood by raising the handle. The skew is like an ax, shearing across the grain. Pushing the point straight in (parallel to the floor) is just asking for trouble. Heat builds up rapidly and you have a bright blue tip. Most of my pupils never have the handle low enough at the start; if they do manage an arcing cut, the handle is too high on completion and the point ends below the center of the cylinder, resulting in a kick like a mule's.

Besides arcing the cut, the bevel must follow the point and stay flat against the cut surface, or you risk another kick. I do not offer the usual suggestion that the bevel *rub* the wood because pressing rigidly against the end grain can lever the point away and cause the blade to buck.

To practice, turn a length of 2x2 softwood to a cylinder and with a common parting tool cut notches ½ in. wide by ¾ in. deep, leaving ½-in. spaces between notches. The end grain will be roughed up because the side of the tool scrapes rather than cuts the wood. With the skew clean up the roughness on the right-hand side of the notches first—handle well down and the skew point up in the air. Start the cut at 11 o'clock and slice down the side of the notch in an arc. The handle is over to the right, the left-hand bevel in contact and only a thin slice of wood separates as you lift the handle. Too thick a slice is inviting trouble. A beginner's tool is guaranteed to kick. Do not attempt to cut the same notch again—move on to the next. Then try the left-hand side of the notches.

These cuts are all at right angles to the cylinder. It is possible to taper or curve the cut, but remember the point always enters first and the bevel is always in contact. You can also "saucer cut" to make inside curves, but not very deep ones.

Another job the skew does well is to form the pummels of furniture legs and the like—squares of wood left in turnings to take the rails in a mortise-and-tenon or dowel joint. The practice wood should be short lengths of 2x2. About 2 in. away from the headstock, make a line all around the wood with a try square and a soft pencil. You will see this line plainly when the lathe is going. Have a light behind the lathe directed toward you, and the corners of the revolving wood will show up in a blur, the darker shadow at the center being the size of the cylinder you have to reach. Make a cut down to this with a common parting tool. However carefully applied, this tool is bound to cause some splintering at the corners. Widen the cut toward the tailstock until there is room to clean up with the skew. Take the unwanted wood down to a cylinder with a ¾-in. squarenose roughing-down gouge.

One way to avoid the roughness of the parting tool is to use the skew alone to part the pummel. With the chisel on the tool rest, its handle over to the right so the left-hand bevel is at right angles to the work, lift the handle to arc the point in along the marked line. Cut no deeper than ⅛ in. Then

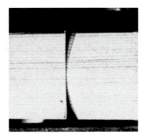

Rounded pummel is cut 'ax' fashion from alternate sides.

shift the handle to the left and cut the waste away, forming a half-*V*-notch. Another cut with the left-hand bevel at right angles deepens the nick, followed by another waste-removing cut. Continue until the cut extends to the face of the square. When you remove the waste with the gouge, the end of the pummel is clean and at right angles to the cylinder.

To make round end pummels, make the first cut arcing in to the left of the line, followed by a cut to the right. This forms a starting *V*-cut which you deepen by alternating from side to side until you have cut the wood down to the surface of the square. The point then smooths the curve, which the bevel follows.

The skew is also useful in the final stages of parting off. When wood is held between centers, you can part completely through only at the headstock. Use the parting tool first to turn down to the smallest safe diameter; depending on the wood I sometimes take it down to as little as 1/16 in. In very hard wood, boxwood, ebony and the like, a shallow, preliminary, diagonal sawcut helps a lot.

You needn't be afraid to bring the diameter down small. If you have had the unnerving experience of the wood suddenly fracturing and being thrown violently from the lathe, it's probably because you applied far too much pressure with the tailstock center when setting up. My drive center is a hardened four-prong, and I much prefer a live tail-center. Before setting up in the lathe I *hammer* the drive center into the wood in order to get a good deep drive from the four prongs. Then with the driving center in the headstock, I bring up the tail only a touch more than is necessary to fully engage the already prepared drive. I test for any slackness by vigorously rocking the wood by hand. I do not agree with those who center-punch each end of the wood, align it between centers and crank the tailstock in until the drive center engages. It's a pernicious practice that does the bearings no good.

Now when I have parted down to a judicious diameter I take the 1/2-in. skew in left hand alone, the right hand hovering over and around the turning but not in contact with it. One or two slicing cuts from the chisel and the finished turning, suddenly deprived of the power of the motor, comes to rest in my right hand. Try putting short lengths of 3/4-in. diameter wood between centers, part down at the headstock end to 1/4 in., then one-hand the chisel to nibble away. When you have recovered from the surprise that it is harmless and easy, you can progress to larger diameters. □

Master turner Peter Child, author of The Craftsman Woodturner, *died in 1986. His son, Christopher, continues to teach woodturning courses in Halstead, England. Child's article on long-and-strong bowl gouges appears on pp. 77-79.*

Turning four footstool legs off-center

This project involves some skew work and yields something close to a true cabriole leg. Begin with 2x2 sawn or planed hardwood, four pieces, 7 in. long. Draw diagonals at the ends, corner to corner, to obtain true centers. Now you need two other centers. The one at the headstock should be a little off true, say 1/4 in., on any diagonal. The one at the tailstock should be on the same diagonal, but on the other side from true center, at a distance from true center equal to half the radius of the largest circle the square will hold. Draw this circle with a compass and be sure to locate the two off centers diagonally across the true centerline *(photo A)*. Two inches from the headstock end, square a heavy line all around with a soft pencil to mark the end of the pummel.

Set up the stock in the lathe between true centers and, with the skew, form the pummel. Then turn the wood between the pummel and the tailstock into a cylinder *(photo B)*.

Now set up the work between the other two centers and revolve by hand to make sure it clears the tool rest. When you start the lathe, you will see a shadow (better with a light behind the lathe), large at the tailstock and sloping down to nothing at the pummel. Within this tapered shadow will be a darker, conical shadow.

One inch from the tailstock, remove the wood making the faint outer shadow by alternating cuts from side to side with a 1/2-in. coving gouge until the bottom of the cove reaches the dark, central cone shadow *(photo C)*. Remove the rest of the outer shadow along the

A

B

C

D

length of the stock up to the pummel with a 3/4-in. roughing down gouge. Stop the lathe and see what you've got *(photo D)*.

Finally, set the leg up once more between true centers and round off the toe with a long-and-strong beading and parting tool *(photo E)*. If the other three legs have been centered like the first, their shadow guidelines will be the same. Longer legs can be turned. The eccentric center at the foot is always half the radius, but the one at the headstock may need slight adjustment so that the conical shadows meet at the pummel. —P. C.

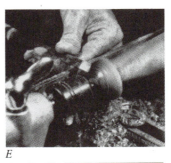

E

Chucks for Woodturning

How many ways can a wood chuck chuck?

by David Sloan

I was taught that you had two choices when mounting work on the lathe—a spur center for long stuff and a faceplate for flat stuff. I can still hear my junior-high shop teacher extolling the virtues of these two implements as he held them aloft. He taught us to glue pretty green felt on the bottoms of our candlesticks and platters to hide the screw holes and spur-center marks. If you wanted another way to mount work on the lathe, you usually had to figure it out and make it yourself. Yes indeed, those were the Dark Ages of woodturning.

Today's turner has other options. There are some clever multifunction chucks being made today that can hold work in ways my shop teacher never dreamed of. Each chuck has limitations of its own, but adding one or two to your collection of faceplates and centers will make your lathe more versatile.

Some of the chucks being made today have features based on old designs that professional turners have been making out of wood for years. Screw chucks, cup chucks and "spigot" chucks (British turners call a round tenon a spigot), for example, are among those described in John Jacob Holtzapffel's 1881 book, *Hand or Simple Turning: Principles and Practice* (reprinted by Dover Publications, Inc., 180 Varick St., New York, N.Y. 10014).

England is the spawning ground for many of today's combination chucks. The first was the Myford 3-in-1. Designed by Edward Barrs in the mid 1950s, it combined faceplate, screw chuck and collar chuck. The Coil Grip Chuck, designed by Roy and Peter Child, expanded on the features of the 3-in-1 by adding a way to grip the work by compression. The 6-in-1 chuck, designed by Nick Davidson, was the first chuck with jaws that expand outward and lock into a recess turned in the bottom of a bowl.

From the ten or so combination chucks in production worldwide, I tried three that met the following criteria: The chuck had to be available from dealers in the U.S. or Canada and come in thread sizes to fit several different lathes. I also tried an inexpensive 3-jaw machinists' chuck. Some interesting chucks that didn't meet my criteria are listed on p. 87.

The chuck you choose depends on the sort of turning you do. If I could have only one chuck, I'd opt for maximum versatility. But, one chuck just doesn't do it all. I like to work with a screw chuck, a 3-jaw and a combination chuck. I've never found a better screw chuck than the Glaser, and I'd choose the Precision or Multistar over the Delta Super Chuck because they're more versatile.

David Sloan is a former associate editor of Fine Woodworking.

Glaser Screw Chuck

The Glaser chuck has the distinction of being the only American-made chuck I could find. It's an efficient, well-made tool and I wonder how I got along without it.

A hardened stainless-steel screw with a special thin thread protrudes from the center of the 1½-in.-dia. anodized aluminum body. The screw has no taper and the thin thread is designed to penetrate the wood with minimum damage. A reversible and removable collar screws over the chuck body to provide extra sup-

port (2½ and 3½ in. dia.) for large stock.

For facework or centerwork, you drill a ¼-in.-dia. hole in the stock and thread it on the chuck. The screw grips tenaciously, even in endgrain—something most screws won't do. Mounting and removing work is fast, which explains the popularity of screw chucks with production turners. Work removed from the lathe can be remounted accurately without much fuss. A screw chuck is also ideal for quick mounting of jam chucks and other homemade wooden chucks and faceplates.

The Glaser Screw Chuck, $69.50, is available from Jerry Glaser, 8341 Delgany Ave., Playa del Rey, Calif. 90293. Please specify type of lathe.

The Glaser Screw Chuck has a stainless steel screw with a thin thread that displaces very little wood, and a removable, reversible collar to support larger stock.

The Precision Combination Chuck comes with the accessories shown above, except for the optional spigot chuck at center right. The dovetail collets expand to grip a recess turned in the bottom of a bowl, top right. The pin chuck fits into a 1-in. hole, center left. When the bowl is rotated, it locks in place. The optional spigot chuck accessory is ideal for turning boxes. The Precision requires two C wrenches to change accessories.

Precision Combination Chuck

Designed by Nick Davidson and made in England, the Precision chuck is the updated version of his earlier 6-in-1 chuck. It is available in both right-hand and left-hand threads for a wide variety of lathes.

The Precision is a complex piece of machining, very nicely executed on computerized machinery. In its basic form it combines five functions. Two for face work: 3½-in.-dia. expanding dovetail collets and a 1-in.-dia. pin chuck, as well as three for center work: a 2⅛-in.-dia. cup chuck, a collar chuck, and a 3-way split ring. Optional accessories include smaller expanding collets, several sizes of screw chuck, a 2-in. spigot chuck, several sizes of collet-chucks and faceplate rings.

Can a chuck that does so many things do them all well? From my experience with the tool I would say yes, although changing from one function to another takes some time. Are all the functions equally useful? There were some that suited my style of working and some that didn't. Other turners I spoke with preferred different functions. I prefer the cup chuck and optional spigot chuck functions for turning end-grain boxes because they require less preliminary stock preparation than the collar chuck and split ring do and they don't waste as much wood. The collar chuck and split ring also impose some restrictions on design because the collar must slide over the stock. It's usually not practical to use them on stock that's more than 2½ in. in diameter.

To use the expanding dovetail collets, you mount the work on a faceplate, screw chuck or pin chuck, mark out a 3½-in. circle and turn a ³⁄₁₆-in.-deep recess with dovetail sides. The cast pot-metal jaws expand inside the recess. They grip well, although I'm not wild about the concept of forcing the wood apart instead of gripping it by com-

pression. Turn away too much of the supporting wood around the jaws and the wood may split when a tool catches.

The dovetail recess left in the bottom of the bowl is preferable to screw holes, and some may choose to leave it, although I prefer to turn away all signs of mounting. A nice feature of the expanding collet is that work can be removed and remounted without loss of center. In my opinion, the expanding collets really come into their own in conjunction with the optional faceplate rings, which screw to the work and have a dovetail recess that fits over the collet jaws. With this system, work can be mounted and removed very quickly, and the rings also cost much less than conventional faceplates.

The pin chuck works well for gripping the uneven bark face of a block to turn a natural edge bowl, where you don't have a flat surface to attach a faceplate or screw chuck. The 1-in.-dia. pin can hold a heavy block of wood securely. With the blank on the pin, you turn the outside and turn a tenon for a spigot chuck or a recess for the expanding collet chuck.

To sum up, the Precision is a chuck that I'll always find a use for, even if there are some functions I don't really use. The nice thing about the Precision is that you can choose from so many optional accessories to suit the type and scale of your work. I haven't tried every accessory, but I find the chuck more useful with the 2-in. spigot chuck for boxes and a smaller 2-in.-dia. set of expanding dovetail collet jaws (the standard 3½-in. jaws are just too big for most of my bowls).

The Precision Combination Chuck is available from Cryder Creek, Box 19, Whitesville, N.Y. 14897, or Craft Supplies USA, 1644 S. State St., Provo, Utah 84601; $99.95.

Delta's Super Chuck Kit comes with two expanding collets, two wing cutters to cut the collet recesses, and a screw chuck. The backing plate doubles as a small faceplate. The split ring expands outward to lock into a recess cut in the bowl bottom.

Delta Super Chuck

Designed by Bruce Leadbeatter of Belmore, Australia, the Super Chuck is manufactured Down Under and imported by Delta.

The Super Chuck comes with two expanding collets (2 in. and 3 in. dia.), a screw chuck and backing plate that doubles as a small faceplate. Two wing cutters are included for drilling the recess into which the collet expands. The instructions recommend clamping the bowl stock to a drill-press table for this operation. A sharp ridge around the collet perimeter bites into the sides of the recess.

The chuck is simple and works well. The machined-aluminium jaws are contained by a spring, so they don't flop around and fall out as you insert them into the recess. As you twist the chuck, a cone-shaped boss draws against the backing plate, spreading the three collet jaws apart—simple and effective. Unlike the Precision, no wrenches are required to expand the jaws.

The collets are designed to keep you from turning away too much of the supporting wood around the jaws. This cuts down on the number of flying bowls, but limits how small you can turn the base with work mounted on the chuck—3¾ in. with the 3-in. collet and 3 in. with the 2-in. collet.

Centerwork can be mounted on the screw chuck, but the short screw doesn't grip as well in endgrain as the carefully machined thread of the Glaser chuck.

Delta Super Chuck is available from Woodworker's Supply of New Mexico, 5604 Alameda N.E., Albuquerque, N. Mex. 87113, and other Delta dealers; $120.

Grizzly 3-jaw chuck

I have always wanted a big 3-jaw chuck but balked at spending $200 to $300 for one. Sorely tempted by the bargain-basement price, I ordered a 6-in., Taiwanese 3-jaw from Grizzly. The Grizzly chuck has reversible self-centering jaws and it works. What more could you want?

Three-jaw chucks are dangerous. They don't grip as securely as the chucks designed specifically for woodturning, so a catch invariably sends the work flying. *Always wear a face shield.* Don't use one until you are so proficient with tools that a catch is a rarity. In addition, you can't see the protruding jaws when the chuck is spinning, and you'll get hurt if you touch them. If you paint the ends of the jaws with Day-Glo orange paint, you can see where they are.

The 3-jaw chuck is available from Grizzly Imports, P.O. Box 2069, Bellingham, Wash. 98227; $55.50.

The Grizzly 6-in., 3-jaw chuck sports reversible, self-centering jaws.

More chucks

Multistar Duplex Chuck System (£63.82, about $90, from Multistar Machine and Tool Ltd., Ashton House, Wheatfield Rd., Stanway, Colchester C03 5YA, England). A versatile combination chuck that grips by expansion or compression. Five jaw sizes available. Optional accessories include pin chuck, screw chuck and indexing device.

Myford 4-in-1 ($75.75 from Frog Tool Co., 700 W. Jackson Blvd., Chicago, Ill. 60606). A 3-in.-dia. faceplate, screw chuck, collet and screw-grip chuck. Available only with 1 in. by 12 right-hand thread for the Myford lathe.

Precision Collet Chuck (£46, about $65, from Craft Supplies Ltd., The Mill, Millers Dale, Buxton, Derbys. SK17 8SN, England). This one combines features of the existing Handy Collet Chuck and the Precision Spigot Chuck. □

Mode's wooden chuck allows him to turn shallow-domed lids or lids with irregular projections. The holes allow him to gauge the lid thickness. A wooden collet chuck can be made with a piece of springy hardwood and a hose clamp (shown below).

Do-it-yourself chucks

Professional turners often need to make special chucks for special jobs. Michael Mode, of Zionsville, Pa., came up with this ungainly-looking chuck, enabling him to turn thin, shallow box lids and lids with irregular projections, that would be awkward to chuck by any other means. The holes in the sides of the chuck allow him to feel both sides of the lid to gauge thickness.

The lid chuck starts as a block with two holes, mounted on a screw chuck and turned into a hollow cylinder with a shoulder at one end, as shown. Mode roughs the exterior of the lid on a faceplate, then trims the chuck to fit. He taps the lid into the wooden chuck to hollow the inside. When he's cut away too much of the shoulder, he glues an insert into the end of the chuck. —D.S.

An Improved Screw Chuck
Good engineering refines a common design

by Richard Starr

The screw chuck is a convenient way to mount work on the lathe for faceplate turning. It requires little preparation of stock, wastes little wood and the work is easy on, easy off. An avid amateur turner, Jerry Glaser of Playa del Rey, Calif. focused his engineer's eye on the screw chuck and came up with a superior device. A perfect replica of Glaser's chuck would require machinist's tools and skills, but some of its features might be used to improve existing chucks.

First, Glaser emphasizes that a faceplate chuck should screw to the spindle of the lathe rather than be secured in the tapered socket. Morse-tapered chucks are fine for work between centers but are not built to resist much radial thrust; a taper-fitted screw chuck not secured by a draw bolt is likely to wear the taper and the spindle socket, eventually resulting in a loose fit.

Next, Glaser examined the contact between the work and the faceplate. Stock is seldom faced off perfectly flat. Work with a hollowed face will sit securely against a flat faceplate, but slightly convex or uneven ends will wobble and soon become loose when held by a single, central screw. Glaser dished out his faceplate, leaving a narrow rim at its edge; this shape is more forgiving of inaccurate facing off of stock. It also gives a tighter fit since all the compression between stock and faceplate is concentrated at a maximum radial distance from the screw.

Glaser's major innovation is a specially designed screw that is cylindrical in shape with a thread whose section is almost knife-thin. A screw's holding power is directly proportional to its diameter. A tapered screw's grip is concentrated where it is thickest, getting progressively weaker toward its tip. But a cylindrical screw maintains its full diameter, and full holding power, along its entire length. For screws of the same nominal diameter, cylindrical screws hold better. Where shallow penetration is desired for delicate work, the tip of a tapered screw is almost useless.

The tapered screw might be preferable in soft woods where work can be threaded right on the screw without predrilling; some production turners, for example, fit stock on a running lathe. But in harder woods a pilot hole is necessary to avoid splitting the stock. Many turners grind a drill bit to a taper matching that of the screw in their chucks, but Glaser has to drill only a cylindrical hole the minor diameter of his screw. The very thin threads cause minimum damage to the fibers when entering the wood and have little tendency to split the work. They grip better than screws with thicker threads because they take up less room, and there is a larger volume of undamaged wood retained within the diameter of the screw. This is especially important when holding in end grain, as screw chucks usually do.

The screw holds so well that it is sometimes difficult to remove work from the chuck. Glaser recommends waxing the threads before mounting the stock. To keep the chuck from turning he inserts an allen key in the setscrew, propping the key against the tool rest. He then unscrews the stubborn work with a strap wrench improvised from some rope and a stick.

Soft metal won't do for a screw with tall, thin threads. Glaser has his cut in a steel called 17-4 P.H., which comes heat treated to 32-35 Rockwell C (the limit of machinability is about 45 RC). He suggests that it could be cut in drill rod that has been hardened and tempered to a medium straw color. It would be risky to try hardening or casehardening this delicate thread after cutting, for fear of burning its edges. A machinist can cut these threads using the same technique used for cutting acme threads. A square-ended cutter is ground with sides shaped to half the included angle of the screw, but narrower than the space between threads. While feeding the cutter at right angles to the work, a helix is cut to full depth, then subsequent cuts are made setting the tool over to the right until the crest of the thread is sharp.

The front end of the thread should have a ¼-in. lead of a diameter tapering to the core of the screw. The end of the thread is tapered with a file while turning in the lathe so the thread seems to rise in height from the core of the screw. This leading edge is sharpened with a jeweler's file. The thread is polished by brushing some lapping compound on it and screwing a block of wood on and off a few dozen times.

The shaft of the screw has a flat ground onto it as a bearing surface for the setscrew that keeps the shaft from rotating in the chuck. The tension of the screw is taken by a pin through the shaft bearing against the inner surface of the faceplate (see drawing). The screw's protrusion is controlled by adding or removing washers between the pin and the chuck. It is an absolutely secure system capable of small increments of adjustment.

One advantage of the chuck, according to its designer, is the almost perfect recentering of rechucked work it affords. This has allowed him to mount specialized wooden chucks or spuds on the lathe, confident that they will always run true. He also uses a pot chuck that is simply a block of wood with a conical socket turned into its end. The outer surface of the block is turned round and kept from splitting by wrapping it with nylon cord glued with epoxy, a quick and easy ferrule. Work is crudely whittled to fit the taper and jammed into the socket for turning.

For Glaser, the joy of using this screw chuck is its easy versatility. He has used it for turning tiny, very thin objects as well as for big jobs, like an olivewood vase 14 in. long and 8 in. in diameter, turned green. Examples of Glaser's work appear on the facing page. □

Richard Starr teaches woodworking at Richmond Middle School in Hanover, N.H., and is the author of Woodworking with Kids *(The Taunton Press, 1982). Starr's article on chasing wooden threads appears on pp. 41-45.*

Fig. 1: Improved screw chuck

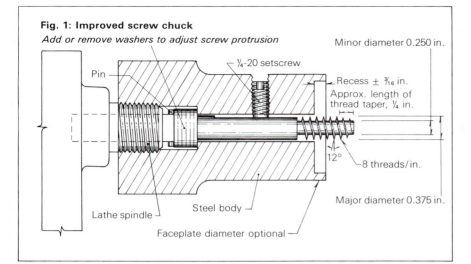

Add or remove washers to adjust screw protrusion

Pin

Lathe spindle

¼-20 setscrew

Steel body

Faceplate diameter optional

Minor diameter 0.250 in.

Recess ± ³/₁₆ in.

Approx. length of thread taper, ¼ in.

12°

8 threads/in.

Major diameter 0.375 in.

Sharp, wide threads of Glaser's adjustable-depth screw chuck secure work with minimal penetration of stock. Optional screw pockets supplement holding power for turning large blanks.

With wooden pot chuck, left, screw chuck can turn the tiniest of goblets. Alone it grips larger stock for vibration-free turning along the full length of mallet, right. Mushroom boxes with putumuju tops, below, evidence more of the versatility and precision possible.

Making a mushroom box

1 Mount blank for top using glueblock

Screw chuck

Bore

Turn

Saw off

2 Mount blank for stem on screw chuck

Bore

Turn; lip should fit top tightly

3 Press top onto stem

Turn and polish

Saw off

Remove top, sand lip for sliding fit to top

4 Turn reusable spud for snug fit in I.D. of stem

Turn and polish

Joe Esposito

Decorative Folk Turning

Ancient techniques survive in East Germany

by R. Steinert and J. Volmer

Over time, isolated peoples develop strong traditions, passed on from one generation to the next. Such has been the case in the Erzgebirge—the "ore mountains"—which form a natural boundary between the Saxony region of the German Democratic Republic and Bohemia, part of Czechoslovakia. Some of the traditional woodturning techniques found in this area are scarcely known elsewhere in the world.

The woodturning tradition flourished in Erzgebirge for several reasons. First, the region was developed for its timber in the middle of the 12th century. Shortly thereafter, mining became an important industry when silver ore was discovered. By the middle of the 14th century, tin was also being mined, and Cistercian monks from Bohemia had opened thriving glass factories, heating the furnaces with spruce from the surrounding forests.

Both the mines and the glassworks demanded a knowledge of woodworking. Miners used wood for tunnel timbering, furniture and housing, as well as for kitchen utensils, vessels and children's toys. In the glassworks, skilled turners provided a variety of wooden molds into which the molten glass was blown.

All things, of course, evolve. As the Erzgebirge mines gave out, the inhabitants found the land too poor and the growing season too short to subsist by agriculture alone. By the 18th century, a few craftsmen were making their living from turning, but it was far more typical for miners and farmers to continue the craft tradition as a hobby that helped supplement the family income, using low-cost materials and equipment. Some lathes were pedal-operated. More often, several woodturners shared a common water-power system, typically one that was left over from the mining days.

Although most of the techniques illustrated on these pages were perfected more than a century ago, the Erzgebirge crafts industry continues to be popular and profitable today. It will be interesting to see how turners in other parts of the world put the techniques shown here to work.

Rolf Steinert is a master turner in Olbernhau, Erzgebirge. He is the author of a textbook for turners and a recently completed encyclopedia, Turning Wood. *Johannes Volmer deals with ancient lathes and tools; he is active in oval turning.*

Hoop turning

The mold turners in the ancient glassworks were expected to produce extremely precise molds with glass-smooth surfaces—anything less would have marred the surface of the glass. Gradually, they developed a series of special slicing tools for their work—tools that, with a little modification, allowed them to devise the unique craft of hoop turning, as shown in the drawings and photos on the facing page.

In this process, the turner creates a ring that has the continuous profile of an object within it. When the ring is split into radial pieces, the hidden shape is revealed. With a little carving and some paint, you have a number of horses, cows, dogs or other farmyard animals. The technique began in simple form, as a means of producing small blocks that could be made into buildings, such as a steepled church. But by the early 19th century, intricate animal shapes had evolved. Today, hoop turning can be used to make a variety of distinctive profiles, including elephants, giraffes and birds.

A hoop turning begins with a length of freshly cut spruce log. If the wood must be stored for some time, the turner usually keeps it underwater; tearout is inevitable with wood that's been allowed to dry. Turners choose trees that have grown in the middle of forests in valleys, so that the growth is regular and the pith is on-center. Areas with knots are discarded, and the rest of the log is sawn into rounds of sufficient size for the shape to be turned.

The lathe itself resembles a bowl-turners' lathe, with heavy bearings to resist vibration, and sturdy bracing to the ceiling and floor. There is no tailstock.

The wood is mounted on a ring chuck, also called a Heureka chuck. As shown in the drawing, above right, it's a ring of sharpened steel with an opening down one side, mounted in a cylinder that screws to the spindle. The hoop turner centers the work over the ring and drives it on with a heavy hammer. Roughing out is done in the usual manner—with a gouge—and the work is faced off square with a chisel.

The specific tools used to turn a ring might vary somewhat from one turner to another. Typically, each turner has between 25 and 30 different tools, but no hoop turner would want to be limited to this number—it's essential to have spare sharpened tools at hand. The full number of tools in the kit is closer to 80, allowing the turner to produce a wide variety of profiles and sizes.

There are two tool rests used on a hoop-turners' lathe. One—a conventional sort, such as those found on spindle lathes—is used to shape profiles on the perimeter of the work. The other, shown in the top left photo on the facing page, is an angled wooden rest across the face of the work. Since much of the cutting is done directly into endgrain, tool handles tend to be

From *Fine Woodworking* magazine (July 1987) 65:70-73

Hoop turning yields a ring of wood with the profile of an animal inside (right). Split-off segments are then carved and painted. Working at a sturdy lathe (above), the hoop turner cuts with a series of special tools, shown below.

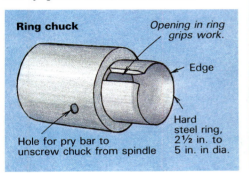

Ring chuck

Opening in ring grips work.

Edge

Hard steel ring, 2½ in. to 5 in. in dia.

Hole for pry bar to unscrew chuck from spindle

Hoop-turning sequence and tools

The numbers below indicate the order of cuts made by a hoop turner in the Erzgebirge. The underside of the animal is shaped first, as shown in the photos above. Then, the ring is parted off and pressed into a jam chuck to complete the figure.

Part off here.

Size gauge

Stick with three notches is held against work as turning proceeds to gauge major dimensions.

Jam chuck

Pfannenstecher

In cuts 1, 2 and 9, an unusual piercing tool, called a Pfannenstecher, is used to slice directly into endgrain.

Hook tool

Various hooks leave clean surfaces at cuts 4, 5, 6, 8, 10, 17 and 18.

Spear-point gouge

The turner uses a conventional gouge for roughing out, but the gouges used in shaping the ring have spear points. They are used in cuts 3, 7, 13 and 19.

Spoon bit

A spoon bit makes cut 11; an ordinary skew chisel is used for cuts 12 and 14.

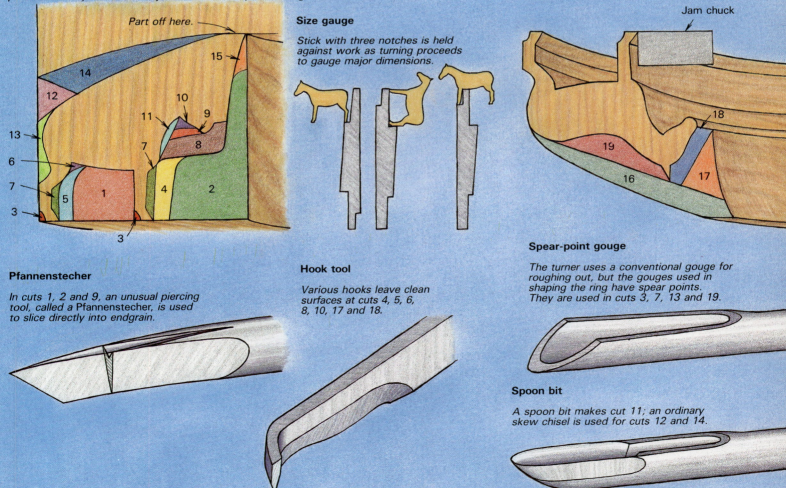

Drawings: Lee Hov. Photos courtesy of the Erzgebirge Toy Museum in Seiffen. Drawings derived from "Das Reifendreherhandwerk im Spielwarengebiet Seiffen" by Hellmut Bilz, Seiffen, 1976.

long—up to 30 in.—allowing extra leverage for control.

The first cuts are made to shape the underside of the animal. When this is done, the work is parted off and fit into a friction chuck, also known as a jam chuck, so the top of the animal form can be turned. Once finished, the ring is pried from the chuck and split with a knife and hammer. The ends are then spread apart to reveal the success of the job.

The uninitiated eye can scarcely discern the shape hidden in a ring. Although the turner has a simple gauge to help control a few major dimensions (see detail, p. 91),

the success of the work depends on skill and experience. If an incorrect cut is discovered when the ring is split, the entire job must be scrapped: the ring can't be returned to the lathe for correction.

The individual shapes are cut off from the hoop, their sharp corners are beveled with a carving knife and additional parts such as horns and tails are glued on. In some cases, these parts are hoop-turned as well, as are many other decorative elements in the traditional Erzgebirge crafts. Spruce is too coarse for the most delicate of these details, so the turners most often make them from native woods such as

basswood, alder and birch. The best animals are carefully painted by hand, but many others are simply dipped in paint, using a seive.

EDITOR'S NOTE: For information on some of the more usual turning tools, see the two articles in this book by Peter Child—"The Bowl Gouge" (pp. 77-79) and "Woodturning Chisels" (pp. 80-83). The hoop turner also employs various piercing tools, called *Pfannenstecher*, as well as some spear-point gouges. The authors are continuing their research, and we plan a future article on these unusual tools. In the meantime, are there any readers who have similar tools in their kits already? If so, we'd like to hear from you.

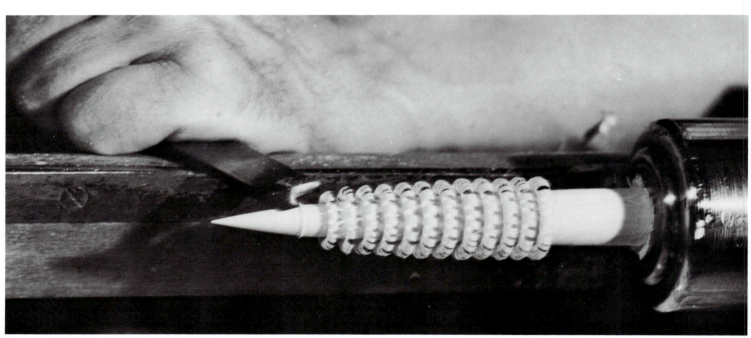

To turn a tree, curls of shavings are raised from the tapered cylinder with a reground skew chisel, as shown in the drawing below.

Shaving curls

This process produces little trees and flowers. It requires basswood that has been split, not sawn, so that the grain is continuous through the workpiece. The other necessity is a reground skew chisel that lifts and curls shavings from the surface of the workpiece without severing them completely.

As shown in the photo above, work begins at the base of the tree and proceeds in bands toward the tip, producing a tapered, conifer-like tree. If spruce is used instead of basswood, the shavings form a more irregular growth, somewhat like an oak tree. As you might imagine, learning this technique requires a lot of practice. But it's not too wasteful—if your first attempt at a tree fails, you can turn it down to a smaller taper and try again.

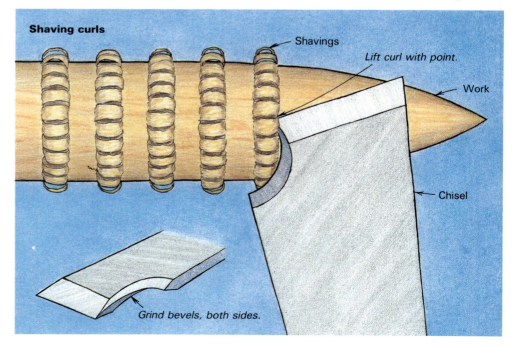

Shaving curls

Shavings

Lift curl with point.

Work

Chisel

Grind bevels, both sides.

Striping and knurling

Turned toys with stripes of tin alloy and knurled decoration.

Most turners are familiar with one type of stripe burning, in which a length of taut wire is held against the turning work to form narrow, decorative rings of burnt wood. Friction is used in two other ways in Erzgebirge turning.

Burnt rings of various shades and widths can be made by pressing one wood—beech or oak, for example—against a softer wood turning in the lathe. If a sharply defined area is desired, the area to be burnt should be marked off by two grooves formed with the heel of a skew (see drawing, below left). The wood used for burning is usually shaped something like a straight chisel, about 1 in. wide and ⅛ in. thick. It is placed edge-down on the tool rest so that its end-grain can be pressed against the work.

Such ornamentation is fast and costs practically nothing. One popular use for it this century has been to mark skittles pins.

Another friction-based banding technique is called tin striping (see photo, right). Instead of endgrain wood, a special tin alloy is pressed against the work. Done just right, the metal leaves a thin, gleaming residue on the turning. The alloy used is 63% tin and 37% lead, although variations of a few percentage points aren't critical.

Best results are obtained on woods without large pores. Red beech and spruce are favorites in the Erzgebirge; maple also accepts metal well. Again, score grooves at the boundaries of the ring to get the best definition. The area to which the metal will adhere should be left slightly rough.

Tin striping requires much practice. With insufficient pressure, the alloy will not melt; too much pressure, and the metal will form lumps and scales. The tech-

nique is best learned by experimenting—by making rings of one width on a uniform cylinder, you will find the correct pressure and lathe speed for the work at hand. Changes in the diameter of the workpiece or in the wood used will require adjustments that can be mastered as your feel for the work improves.

The stripe should be varnished or lacquered to prevent oxidation. It can also be painted, engraved or knurled.

Knurling originated in metal turning. The process embosses a repeating design into the wood by means of a rotating wheel with a pattern on its surface.

Typical wheel sizes range between ⅜ in. and ¾ in., with patterns of notches, fillets, hemispheres and other simple shapes

ground into the circumference. The wheel is held in a metal fork with a handle, as shown in the drawing, below right. One type is hooked over the tool rest, then levered hard against the turning work.

For best results, the pattern should repeat over itself with each revolution of the lathe. This requires that the circumference of the object being knurled be some multiple of the circumference of the wheel. A little experimentation will quickly show which workpiece diameters are suitable—if the diameter is wrong, the pattern will quickly chew itself to pieces.

Knurled designs can be used to good effect on box edges, bowls, candlesticks and the like, and also on the bottoms of plates and other facework. The most suitable woods are fine-pored and dense. □

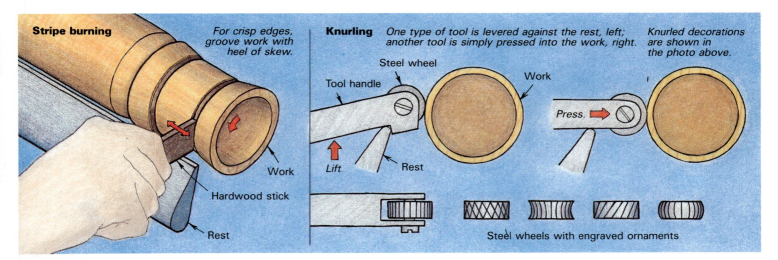

Stripe burning For crisp edges, groove work with heel of skew.
Work
Hardwood stick
Rest

Knurling One type of tool is levered against the rest, left; another tool is simply pressed into the work, right.
Knurled decorations are shown in the photo above.
Steel wheel
Tool handle
Work
Lift
Rest
Press.
Steel wheels with engraved ornaments

Making a Nutcracker

An intrepid trio brings a traditional toy to life

by Fred Sneath

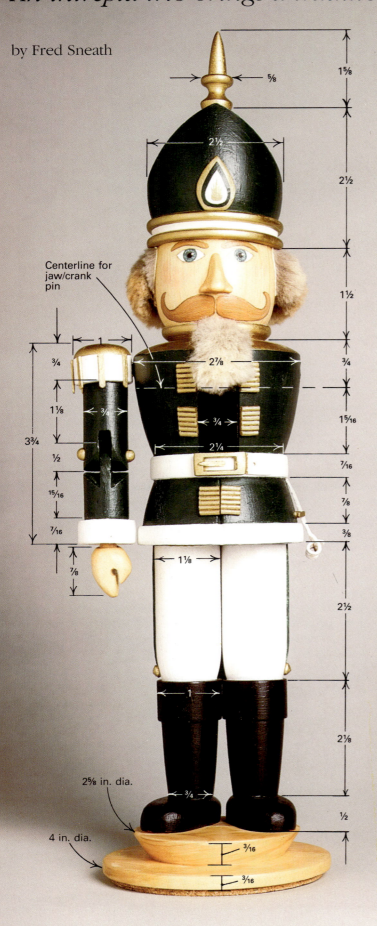

Centerline for
jaw/crank
pin

The idea of making a nutcracker germinated in my mind for years, nurtured by the annual appearance of the brightly painted wooden toys in stores and by seasonal productions of Tchaikovsky's ballet on stage and on television. However, I didn't actually begin turning my first one, a gift for my eight-year-old daughter, until a week before Christmas. The result was the white-haired stalwart in the red tunic, Cornelius Crownheart, shown below. As I recall, the final coat of urethane was still tacky when my wife and I wrapped gifts on Christmas Eve.

Since then I've made two companions: Tobias Trueblue and Reginald Righteous, shown below and at left. The construction of all three is based on the traditional form of wooden figure nutcrackers, such as the hero of the children's tale by Hoffman, *The Nutcracker and the Mouse King,* which is the basis of the popular ballet by Tchaikovsky. Their nominal duties are carried out by manipulating their lower jaws with the crank handles that protrude from their backs. However, there are more efficient ways of crack-

Cornelius Crownheart, right, and Tobias Trueblue face off in a duel. The range of motion of their fully articulating arms makes it easy to imagine them coming to life when the lights go out.

From *Fine Woodworking* magazine (November 1990) 85:76-79

The torso, head and helmet are all turned together. Here the author rounds over the small beads that become the rim of the miter-type hat worn by Reginald, the green-clad nutcracker.

After bandsawing the head, including the helmet, from the torso, Sneath clamps the torso in a hand screw and bandsaws the channel that houses the jaw/crank.

ing nuts, and I designed these fellows to be capable of far greater deeds when spurred on by a child's imagination.

The readily available mass-produced nutcrackers from Asia, and their original European antecedents, are wonderfully suggestive of Christmases past, but they are also fairly static objects. In designing my version, I wanted to increase mobility beyond the working jaw without sacrificing the stiff "wooden soldier" quality. Although Cornelius, Tobias and Reginald stand on their pedestals rigidly at attention, they can brandish their swords and flourish their flags thanks to fully articulated arms that move at the shoulders, elbows and wrists. I added this mobility to capture the magical storybook moment when the lifeless wooden toy becomes the handsome prince.

Making these nutcrackers is quite straightforward. The basic body parts require three separate turnings: The torso, head and helmet are turned as a unit; both arms are turned together as a single spindle and then sawn into shoulder, upper arm and forearm segments; and both legs are turned as a single spindle and then sawn apart. I also turn the pedestal and a finial for the helmet. Feet and hands are carved from wood scraps and the uniform details are fashioned from toothpicks and small dowels. The elbow and wrist joints are the most demanding parts of the job, but even they are not particularly time-consuming.

Turning the torso and head—For the nutcracker described here, I begin by turning the torso, head and helmet from a piece of pine, 3 in. square by 8⅛ in. long. The blank for this turning can be a solid block or laminated from ¾-in.- or 1½-in.-thick stock. I turn the piece with the base of the torso at the headstock and the top of the helmet at the tailstock. The mark left by the headstock center will be covered by the legs, and depending on the helmet style, the mark left by the tailstock center will be sawn or sanded away or will be used to locate the finial, which is turned separately. The only significant details on this turning are the bottom trim of the coat, the belt at the waist, the collar and the brim of the helmet (see the left photo above). Any or all of these details can be varied to give each soldier a unique look. It's a good idea to make the shoulder area of the torso the same diameter as the hem of the coat for two reasons. First, it's easier and safer to get a square cut when bandsawing the head off; and second, it makes it easier to clamp the torso in a hand screw or vise when you need to notch and drill it.

When this turning is complete, the head with helmet is bandsawed from the torso. With the head removed, I clamp the torso in a hand screw and then mark out and bandsaw the ¾-in.-wide channel that houses the jaw/crank. This channel runs from the top of the torso to the top of the belt, as shown in the above photo at right. The channel's sloping extension on the back of the torso (shown in the details on the next page) can be initiated with care on

the bandsaw, but it must be completed with a chisel and file. Next, I bandsaw the jaw/crank from ¾-in. pine (see the drawing), but I leave a little extra at the top where the beard will be attached so I can trim it later to match the profile of the turning. Fit the crank to the channel by either paring the sides with a chisel or sanding the crank.

The jaw/crank pivots on a ³⁄₁₆-in.-dia. mild steel rod. To ensure that the rod runs squarely through the upper part of the torso, I remove the crank, clamp the torso in a hand screw again, and use a drill press to bore a ³⁄₁₆-in.-dia. hole that's 90° to the channel and ⅝ in. below the shoulder line. I remove the torso from the hand screw and insert the jaw/crank into the channel, flush with the top of the torso section. Then, I clamp the torso in a vise and drill through the jaw/crank with a portable electric drill using the hole through the torso as a guide. Now you can insert the steel pin and work the jaw/crank up and down to make sure it moves easily. With the jaw in the closed position, draw along the profile at the top, front of the turning, and then remove the crank and trim the "chin" to this line on the bandsaw.

Turning and fitting the arms and legs—The two legs can be turned from a single 10¼-in.-long spindle, with the thigh tops at the headstock and tailstock and the ankles meeting at the center. Turn the middle 1 in. of the spindle to ¼ in. dia. so that when the legs are sawn apart you'll have a ½-in.-long tenon at both ankles for joining them to the feet. The feet are ½-in.-thick rectangular blocks rounded at the heel, toe and upper edges with a disc sander. The thighs are joined to the torso with a short length of ¼-in.-dia. dowel. I also join the feet to the pedestal with ¼-in.-dia. dowels, and this is as good a time as any to turn the pedestal (using a faceplate). But don't glue anything together until all the parts have been painted.

The arms are turned in the same manner as the legs, with the shoulders at either end of a single spindle and the cuffs meeting in the middle, as shown in the top photo on p. 97. The arm spindle should be 10¾ in. long, which includes an additional ½ in. for each arm to accommodate the overlap in the completed elbow joints and ½ in. of waste at each end of the spindle. After this spindle has been cut in half at the cuffs, bandsaw each arm at the shoulders and elbows before working on the articulated joints.

The drawing illustrates how the arm segments are joined. Of the three joints, the shoulder pin joint is the simplest. The domed shoulder cylinders, which have been cut from the arm spindle, are fitted with two ¼-in.-dia. dowels; one connects the shoulder to the torso and the other links the shoulder to the upper arm. The dowels should be glued into holes drilled in the shoulder cylinder, but be able to rotate freely in the holes in the torso and upper arm.

The elbow joint employs a mortise in the upper arm and a tenon in the forearm pinned with a ¼-in.-dia. dowel. The mortise and tenon may be roughed out on the bandsaw, but additional carving with a knife and file is necessary to open up the joint so the forearm moves forward through 90°.

The ball-and-socket joint, which allows full rotation of the wrist, is the most interesting technical feature of this project. The joint is constructed as a separate unit before being mounted in the hand and forearm. The ball can either be turned or carved on the end of a 1-in.-long by ⅜-in.-dia. dowel that will be inserted in the cuff. The socket, into which the ball must fit snugly, is formed on the end of another short length of ⅜-in.-dia. dowel with a hand-held rotary tool fitted with a round-head carving bit, as shown in the bottom photo on the facing page.

After the socket has been hollowed out, its dowel is cut to ⅜ in. long. This short dowel will eventually be inserted into the hand, but first the ball and socket are drilled so they can be tied together with an elastic cord I scrounged from an airline baggage tag. The elastic cord provides enough tension so the wrist will hold whatever position it is moved into. I drill the holes for the elastic with a ¹⁄₁₆-in.-dia. drill bit in the rotary tool. The joint details show how the elastic is laced through the joint and tied at the end of the ball dowel. Shims made from bits of toothpick are inserted beneath the knot to increase tension on the joint if necessary. The mechanics of the joint are now complete, but this construction won't really come to life until you add the hand.

I use small scraps of pine to carve the mitten-like hands. I leave the fingers undifferentiated to retain some of the simplicity of traditional nutcrackers. A ⅛-in.-dia. hole, bored at the juncture of thumb and fingers, allows the hand to "grip" a sword handle or flag staff. A ⅜-in.-dia. hole is bored into the wrist end of the hand to receive the socket dowel, which is then glued into the hand. To allow freer movement of the hand, I hollow out the end of the cuff a little, and then I drill a ⅜-in.-dia. hole in the center of the cuff to receive the hand-and-wrist assembly. Don't glue the ball dowel into the cuff because you may want to remove it later and add shims beneath the knot in the elastic cord to increase the wrist's tension.

Detailing—Now you can temporarily assemble all the major components and stand back and check out your work. The helmet may require some additional shaping and you still need to make the small details, such as the belt buckle, buttons and sword. Make all the details before attaching any of them and then paint all the small parts before gluing them because you will get a better paint job.

I reattach the disembodied head to the torso by inserting ⅛-in.-dia. dowels on either side of the jaw/crank channel. But first I decide whether or not to tilt the head and helmet back slightly. The type of helmet usually plays a role in this decision. For Cornelius' black bell-shaped helmet, I opted for a stiff-back, chin-in look with the brim parallel to the floor. But I wanted Tobias' flared white

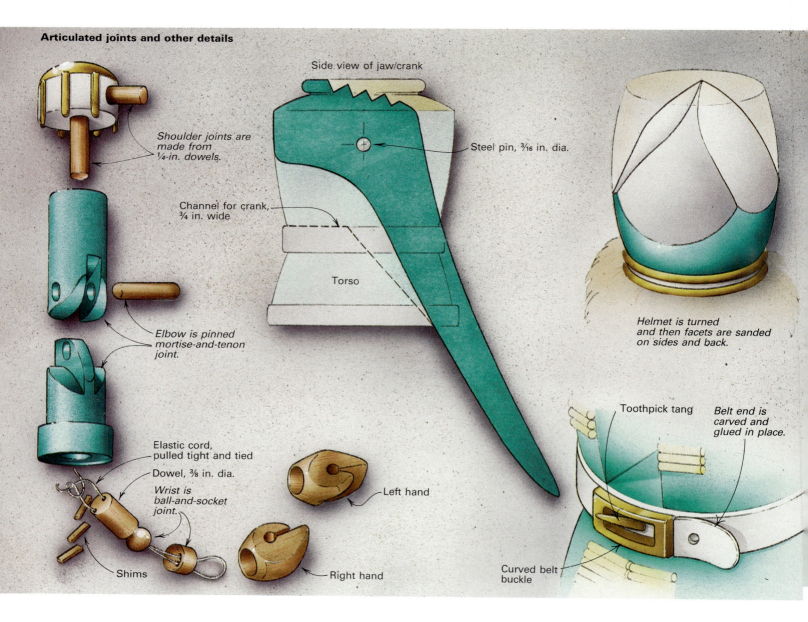

Articulated joints and other details

Shoulder joints are made from ¼-in. dowels.

Side view of jaw/crank

Steel pin, ³⁄₁₆ in. dia.

Channel for crank, ¾ in. wide

Torso

Elbow is pinned mortise-and-tenon joint.

Elastic cord, pulled tight and tied

Dowel, ⅜ in. dia.

Wrist is ball-and-socket joint.

Shims

Left hand

Right hand

Helmet is turned and then facets are sanded on sides and back.

Toothpick tang

Belt end is carved and glued in place.

Curved belt buckle

Drawing: Clarke Barre

shako to appear to be set back on his head, and so I sanded an angle on the base of the head. I imparted some tilt to Reginald's green tapered miter in the same manner, but with a less pronounced angle. The basic shaping of both the black and the white helmets was complete when they came off the lathe, but Reginald's green miter headdress required further shaping at the back and sides, as shown in the drawing. I formed the three facets on a sanding disc and finished them with a sanding block.

All three helmets are fitted with finials turned from ⅝-in.-dia. dowels. The finial on the bell-shaped helmet is doweled into a hole where the tailstock center had been. The finials on the other two helmets are notched on the base to fit the helmet shape and are mounted near the front. For the white shako you'll need to fill the hole left by the tailstock center if it is not smoothed out when you sand the slight dome on the top. You'll also need to carve a small visor for the shako. To further individualize each helmet, I cut a small insignia badge from pine and shaped it to fit the helmet's curvature. Then I painted the detailed design on lightweight paper, cut it out and glued it to the badge.

The most important detail you will add to your nutcracker is the nose. Copy it from pictures or model it after a nose you know, but don't be afraid to make it distinctive because it is largely responsible for giving an individual personality to each nutcracker. After I carve a nose from pine, I pin it to the face temporarily with a ³⁄₃₂-in.-dia. dowel in order to experiment with placement before gluing.

Uniform details include tunic buttons cut from ¼-in.-dia. dowel for Cornelius and Tobias, drilled through with a ⅛-in.-dia. bit for the latter, and piping cut from ³⁄₃₂-in.-dia. dowel for Reginald. I glued six short pieces of the piping to paper to form the groupings before I painted them. The shoulder epaulets are cut from the wide end of toothpicks and arranged around the shoulder cylinders. The belt buckle is cut from pine with a bit of a toothpick attached as the tang. The belt end is also cut from pine with a small hole drilled for the final notch. Trousers are trimmed with toothpick stripes and ¼-in.-dia. dowel buttons at the boot tops.

The sword and flagstaff are cut from ⅛-in.-dia. dowel and the sword hilt is a miniature bowl turned from ¾-in.-dia. dowel. The flagstaff is cut down the middle just far enough to hold the 4-in. by 6-in. flag. I bought the flags for my nutcrackers from The Flag Shop, 508 Rideau St., Ottawa, Ont., Canada K1N 5Z6. I use a jeweler's saw to cut the flagstaff, but a coping saw or a fine blade in the scroll saw should also do the job. Once the flag has been glued into the staff, I add a finial turned from ¼-in.-dia. dowel. Cornelius carries the maple leaf flag of Canada, and his uniform is painted to match. Although the other two flags are the national banners of specific countries, I chose them to suggest regimental colors, not to make a political statement. When not being held in one or both hands, the flagstaff may be set into a small turned base.

The rapier sword, when not challenging the Mouse King or other miscreants, is slung at the hip in an open scabbard fashioned from a narrow strip of leather doubled back in a loop. I used a short piece of dowel and a toothpick end to hold the scabbard and sword securely against the hip.

Painting—At this point I prepare the parts for painting by giving them all a coat of urethane, except on surfaces to be glued. Most of the nutcrackers I've seen are painted with gloss enamel, but I prefer using artists' acrylics for their color range and surface texture. For the silver and gold metallic accents, I use brush-on lacquer.

Paint the uniform first and then the small details, saving the face for last. By then you'll be familiar with your paints and brushes and will have gained some confidence. Skin color is determined

Sneath turns all the arm parts from a single spindle, which allows enough length to accommodate the overlap at the mortise-and-tenon elbow joint. The sleeve cuffs are in the middle of the spindle and the shoulders are at each end. Above, Sneath marks the point where he will saw the upper arm and forearm apart.

With a round-head carving bit in a rotary tool, Sneath forms a socket on the end of a ⅜-in.-dia. dowel as part of the ball-and-socket wrist joint. After the socket is complete, a ⅜-in. length of the dowel will be cut off and tied to the ball with elastic cord. Then the short socket dowel will be glued into a carved hand.

by the wood you use and I made the rosy cheeks by applying colored pencil and smudging it. The moustache and eyebrows are traditionally painted and their color will be dictated by the material you use for the hair and beard. I paint the facial features directly on the wood, but they could also be painted on paper and then cut out and glued onto the face. For the nutcrackers shown here I used scraps of rabbit and fox fur left over from fur coat alterations and glued them in place. Alternatively, the hair and beard could be made from a number of materials: yarn, carpeting, fake fur or an old toupee.

The nutcracker is now ready to assemble with glue at the fixed points: head to torso, torso to legs, legs to feet, and feet to pedestal. Apply a final coat of satin urethane to add sheen and protect the painted surfaces, and then glue a cork circle to the bottom of the pedestal.

As a postscript, Cornelius Crownheart now gets around in style on a music-box stand, which I gave to my daughter on the Christmas following his arrival. The turned maple music box is painted to match the nutcracker and the musical mechanism plays "Waltz of the Flowers," a composition from *The Nutcracker*, as one might expect. □

Fred Sneath is a retired educator who lives and builds toys and musical instruments on Stony Lake near Woodview, Ont., Canada.

Turned-and-Carved Vessels

Hand-tooled details hide the inside story

by John Jordan

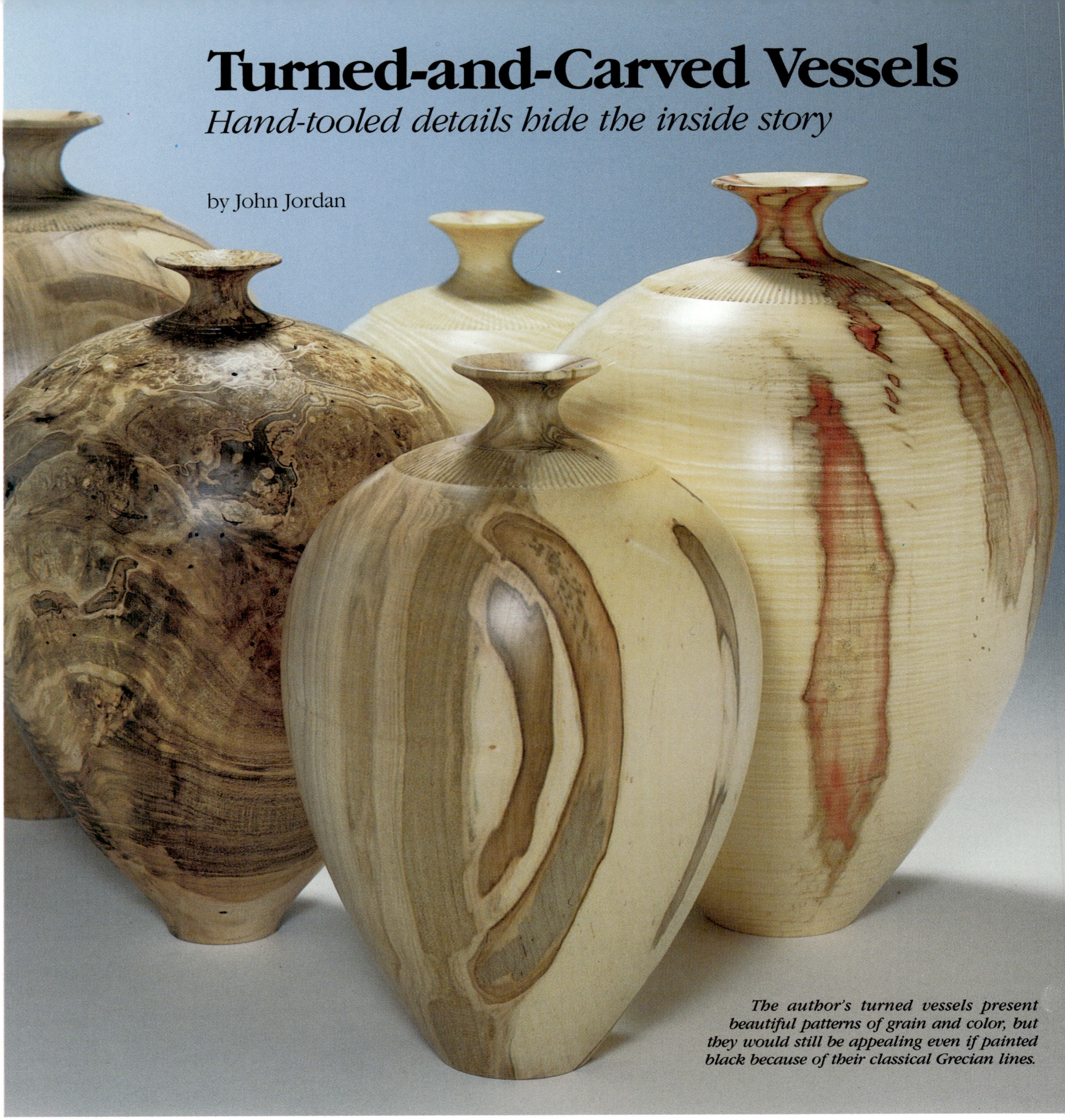

The author's turned vessels present beautiful patterns of grain and color, but they would still be appealing even if painted black because of their classical Grecian lines.

Any experienced woodturner will tell you that the ultimate success or failure of a piece is determined by its form. And while turned objects provide a means to creatively use wood color and patterns, no amount of flashy grain will save a piece that is poorly shaped. Although I adjust my turning blank on the lathe to take advantage of emerging grain patterns, it is the classical form and deceptively simple curves of the vessels shown here that fascinate me.

The first small-neck vessels I made were hollowed through the bottom, and while I was very pleased with the results, rechucking the piece from each end was difficult and time-consuming. In addition, this technique required shaping the inside of the neck, be-

fore the outside shape was finished. This was a difficult procedure that yielded inconsistent results because the tool extended as much as 14 in. beyond the tool rest. Later, while carving one of my vessels, I realized that a decorated area would conceal a glueline. This meant I could part off a piece for the neck and hollow out the inside of the vessel. Then after gluing the neck back in place, I could hide the joint with a decorative carving. Best of all, I can do all of these operations with the bottom of the blank screwed to a faceplate.

The procedures for making one of these pieces are pretty simple, but you must be careful, particularly in the later stages. After the inside is hollowed and the neck is being fitted and shaped, a

From *Fine Woodworking* magazine (November 1990) 85:64-67

Left: When shaping the outside, leave a raised shoulder area around the neck for carving and leave extra stock at the base for support when hollowing the inside. The neck stock is parted off for hollowing the inside and then glued back on for shaping.

Above: A hook tool reaches the inside shoulder area of the vessel for hollowing. Take light cuts because it is easy to catch your tool in the endgrain and ruin the vessel.

slip or a catch can destroy many hours of work instantly. Some of the pieces I turn are fairly large, 12 in. to 15 in. tall and 10 in. to 12 in. in diameter; however, I suggest you try a more modest size until you are familiar with the technique.

Turning the outside—I turn these pieces from straight-grained green wood. Unlike most bowl work, the grain is oriented parallel to the lathe axis, making it easy to manipulate the blank so that the grain and color best suit the evolving shape. Because there is less radial shrinkage than tangential shrinkage in wood, the vessels will become slightly oval; but they are still more stable than most bowls, which are turned on a faceplate with the grain perpendicular to the lathe axis. I cut blanks from a log section, avoiding the pith. Each blank should be two to two and one-half times as long as its diameter. This leaves plenty of stock for the neck and for mounting a faceplate to the bottom.

You should avoid blanks with highly figured or twisted grain, crotch grain or grain that does not run parallel with the lathe's axis because the turning will distort badly or become lopsided. Wood with curly or fiddleback grain is fine, and gets what I think is a pleasing texture as it dries. Also, many burl woods work well and can be oriented for maximum yield and best figure. I like to find wood that has a lot of color contrast, as you can see in the vessels shown here.

I mount the blank between centers, turn it to rough shape and flatten the bottom for fastening the faceplate. During the roughing stage, I shift the blank at either the headstock or the tailstock or at both ends at once to take advantage of emerging figure and color, to align the grain with the lathe axis or to avoid defects. Once the blank is roughed out, remove it from the lathe and screw the faceplate to the bottom with 1½-in.- to 2-in.-long drywall or sheet-metal screws. The sharp threads of these screws provide a much better grip in the endgrain than the shallow threads of regular wood screws.

Remount the blank on the lathe and use a revolving center in the tailstock for additional support as you finish turning the smooth and flowing curves of the vessel. I prefer to do this with a ⅜-in.-deep fluted bowl gouge with the edges ground back, cutting from the large to the small diameter. I rough out the vessels with a pulling cut and then make the final light cuts with the gouge's bevel rubbing against the piece. To make small refinements in the shape and for final smoothing, I employ a technique I learned from Del Stubbs, a California woodworker who turns everything from salad bowls to musical instruments. This method involves using a scraper tilted at an angle to make a sheer cut, which produces a smooth surface requiring little sanding. Clean cuts eliminate the heavy sanding needed to remove tool marks or torn grain that can quickly ruin a good curve or soften details.

Leave a raised shoulder area for carving and a cylindrical section for shaping the neck, as shown in the left photo above. This cylinder will be parted off and later reattached after the vessel is hollowed out. The neck cylinder needs to be long enough to allow flexibility in shaping the neck, as well as for a tenon at each end—one for gluing the neck back to the vessel and one for mounting the neck in a spigot chuck so you can turn the inside to match the interior curve of the vessel. Use a small tool when parting off the neck cylinder because the less wood removed in the joint area the better the grain match when you rejoin the cylinder to the vessel. Also, leave extra wood in the foot area for support when hollowing the vessel. This wood will be turned away after the rest of the piece has been completed. Now turn a 1½-in.-dia. by ¼-in.-long tenon on the end of the neck cylinder to remount it in a spigot chuck, and cut the cylinder off with a narrow parting tool. If you don't have a spigot chuck, you can just part off the neck and glue it to a scrap block for faceplate mounting. Put the neck cylinder in a plastic bag to prevent checking while you work on the inside of the vessel.

Hollowing out—I hollow out the vessel by first drilling a hole from the top to just shy of the finished inside depth. The hole serves as a depth guide for roughing out waste, eliminates the need to cut directly into endgrain and removes the slow-turning center, which is difficult to cut. Begin by cleaning up the parted off surface on top of the vessel with a gouge and make a small dimple in the center for starting a drill. To determine the depth, I visualize the foot area that is not yet turned and measure from the top of the vessel, allowing ½ in. to ¾ in. for the rough bottom thickness. I drill the hole with a long ⅜-in.-dia. electrician's drill held in a pair of Vise-Grips and pushed in by hand, using the tool rest for support. A lamp or shell auger would also work. Push the drill in, pulling back often to clear the chips, until you reach the full inside depth.

Rough out the inside of the vessel, making cuts from the center to the outside, but allowing for your wall thickness. To reach into the shoulder area, you will need either a tool with a bit that can be swung or fixed to the left, or a hook-shaped tool. I prefer Dennis Stewart's hook tool (Dennis Stewart Enterprises, 1383 N.E. 25th, Hillsboro, Oreg. 97124), as shown in the above photo at right, although some people find it awkward. For bigger pieces, I have made larger hooks and longer straight tools that fit in the Stewart handle. It is very easy to catch your tool in the endgrain, however, and so you must work slowly and take light cuts. You should keep

Above: After turning the inside of the neck to shape, align the grain and draw reference marks so you can reposition the pieces when gluing them back together. A good fit is essential for an invisible glueline.

Right: The author uses the tool rest to guide the veiner when carving flutes in the shoulder. For straight flutes, cuts must be made on the vessel's centerline, and for spiral flutes, raise or lower the tool rest.

the pieces fairly small until you have some experience at working with the tool extended some distance over the tool rest.

With the interior roughed out, begin turning the vessel to final thickness by working the tool from the top down, thinning out an inch or two at a time and cutting from the center out; then move the tool lightly up and down the wall to smooth it out. By thinning out in stages, thicker wood supports the cut. Always leave a distinct shoulder where the last cut ends so you can easily feel where you left off and where wood needs to be removed. Stop the lathe often to blow or vacuum out the chips and check the wall thickness. Standard double-ended calipers work well for gauging the thickness of many pieces, but you may need to make your own devices for checking difficult-to-reach places or larger pieces. Once you've been making these vessels as long as I have, you probably won't need to measure as much, but will rely instead on feel, sound and instinct.

As a general guideline, take the walls to a final thickness somewhere between ⅛ in. and 3/16 in. for small pieces and between ¼ in. and 5/16 in. for larger pieces. I vary the actual wall thickness depending on the size of the piece and the density and type of wood. It's hard to define proper wall thickness because it's an intuitive process that is learned through experience. You'll know when the wall thickness is right by the weight of the piece. But this is only revealed after the piece is off the lathe. Since the base area is small, you may want

to leave the walls slightly thicker in the lower part to provide a balanced feeling, but avoid making the piece top- or bottom-heavy.

Fitting the neck—I turn the inside of the neck before gluing it back on the vessel, because this interior profile is somewhat visible through the small neck opening. I also like the neck's inside shape to be consistent with its outside shape. I mount the neck cylinder in a spigot chuck by the tenon that was turned on the end. If you don't have a spigot chuck, mount the neck on a glue block, three-jaw chuck or screw center. Lightly true the outside of the cylinder, and turn a straight or slightly tapered tenon about ¼ in. long and slightly larger in diameter than the opening in the vessel. Drill a ¼-in.- to 3/8-in.-dia. hole lengthwise through the center of the neck and turn the inside to match what will be the profile of the outside lower portion of the neck.

Because the hollowed out vessel is somewhat flexible and possibly warped, you will need to be extra cautious from this point on. Carefully enlarge the opening in the vessel top to fit the neck tenon by taking very light cuts with a diamond-point scraper or skew on its side. A good fit is essential to having a nearly invisible glueline. The neck should fit snugly, but it can split the vessel if it is too tight and forced in place. Align the grain and mark both pieces with a pencil, as shown in the left photo, so they can be

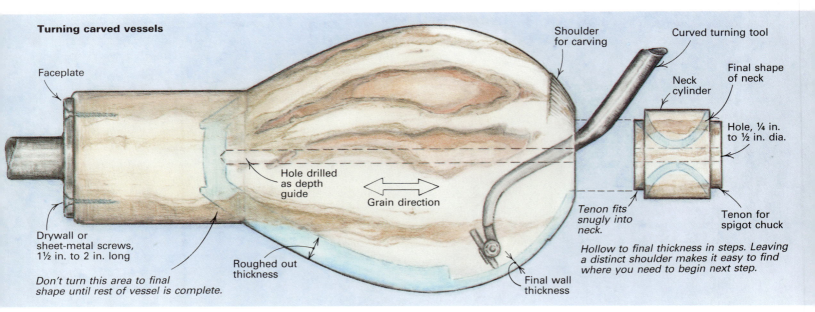

Turning carved vessels

Faceplate

Shoulder for carving

Curved turning tool

Final shape of neck

Neck cylinder

Hole, ¼ in. to ½ in. dia.

Hole drilled as depth guide

Grain direction

Tenon fits snugly into neck.

Tenon for spigot chuck

Drywall or sheet-metal screws, 1½ in. to 2 in. long

Don't turn this area to final shape until rest of vessel is complete.

Roughed out thickness

Final wall thickness

Hollow to final thickness in steps. Leaving a distinct shoulder makes it easy to find where you need to begin next step.

Photos: John S. Cummings; drawing: Bob Goodfellow

Left: Jordan supports the neck of the vessel with his left hand while taking very light cuts with a small gouge to shape the inside of the neck. Any mistakes at this stage can ruin the project.

Above: The bottom is shaped after the vessel is parted off. The tailstock holds the vessel against a padded cone mounted on the headstock so the author can turn a slight recess in the bottom.

repositioned quickly when gluing up. Next, apply a liberal coat of gap-filling cyanoacrylate glue (Hot Stuff) to both surfaces. (Hot Stuff is available from many hobby stores and most mail-order woodworking suppliers.) Align the marks and lightly tap the neck into the bottle, allowing a few minutes for the glue to harden. Bring the revolving-cup center chucked in the tailstock up to the neck for support, and then rough-turn the shape of the neck, cutting away the excess wood to expose a tight glueline. If you are going to carve the shoulder, take a light cut across the raised shoulder, leaving it about 1/16 in. proud of the vessel surface, and stop the cut at the glueline. This creates a step at the glueline and serves as a stop for the carved flutes. If you choose not to carve, then finish-turn the neck, blending it in with the shape of the vessel. For these uncarved bowls, I like to turn three small decorative grooves, one right on the glueline and one to either side, as you can see in the second vessel from the left in the photo on p. 98. You can vary the amount of grooves, but I think an odd number looks best.

Carving the flutes—The shoulder flutes are carved with a small veiner using the tool rest as a guide. Set the tool rest parallel to and almost touching the area to be carved, and adjust the height so the center of the veiner is on the centerline of the vessel. Test the height adjustment by lightly dragging the veiner backward, making a light impression on the shoulder and checking that it is on center. You can also spiral the flutes by raising or lowering the tool rest. Start carving the flutes by pushing the veiner across the tool rest toward the neck, stopping at the glueline and taking care not to cut into the neck. Rotate the vessel backward slightly and cut another flute next to the previous one, as shown in the photo at right on the facing page. Continue until the entire shoulder is fluted, adjusting the width of the last two or three flutes so you don't end up with a half flute or an extra wide flute at the end. Since you are cutting across endgrain, a sharp tool will yield clean cuts with no tearout and there is no changing grain direction to give you trouble. You may choose to carve a random pattern, but I think the symmetrical flutes best suit the style of these vessels. I also use this method when carving large-neck vessels.

Finishing up—Finish turning the outside of the neck using a small gouge, taking care not to cut into the flutes. Move the tailstock back and shape the top recess or bevel inside of the neck, supporting it with the first two fingers of your left hand and guiding the gouge with your left thumb and right hand (see the left photo above). Take light cuts toward the inside, even though you'll

be going against the grain, because this reduces chatter and yields a smooth surface with a sharp tool. You may need a small round-nose scraper to smooth and shape right inside the hole.

To finish shaping the area around the foot, measure the depth of the piece with a dowel or your long drill and transfer this measurement to the base of the vessel. Define the outside bottom with a parting tool and leave enough wood so that when the bottom is recessed slightly, the thickness will be consistent with that of the walls.

Applying a finish—The key to a good finish is surface preparation, starting with clean gouge cuts and ending with proper sanding. Grain that has been badly torn and sanded out will never look right. Sand the neck, as well as the rest of the piece, by hand or with a foam-padded power sander, being careful not to damage the carving. I usually start with 150-grit sandpaper, followed by 220-grit, and then finish up by hand-sanding with 320-grit or 400-grit paper.

I like a minimal amount of finish—just enough to protect the piece from dirt and to bring out the color. On light-colored woods, I wipe on lacquer sanding sealer, thinned enough to totally penetrate the wood. After the lacquer has dried (about 15 to 20 minutes), I polish the piece with fine Scotch-Brite pads or steel wool before parting off the vessel. During this operation, leave a 1-in. stub at the bottom so you can remount the vessel to turn the bottom. Don't try to cut the vessel free with the parting tool; saw through the last 1/2 in. of the stub or you risk having the piece bounce loose and breaking. After the vessel is removed, I apply a coat of tung oil.

To shape the bottom, I remount the vessel between centers after reshaping and padding the waste block as a drive center. First I turn a small cone on the waste block that will fit inside the neck of the vessel and then I pad this cone with thin foam or Naugahyde. The vessel is held against the drive cone with light pressure from the revolving center in the tailstock, centered on the stub left on the bottom of the vessel, as shown in the above photo at right. Be careful not to overtighten the tailstock, as too much pressure will break the vessel. With a small gouge or roundnose scraper, recess the bottom and turn the stub down as small as you can without actually parting off the vessel. Remove the piece from the lathe and pare off the remaining stub with a sharp chisel. Allow several days for the wood to stabilize, and then smooth the bottom rim with a flat sanding block to ensure that it sits flat, and sand the recess by hand or with a 1-in. disc. Apply another coat or two of oil if you like and sign the bottom. ☐

John Jordan is a full-time woodturner in Antioch, Tenn.

Wall Sculptures
Turning big and burly

by Dennis Elliott

The author's wall pieces get much of their visual impact from the orderliness of the circular design being superimposed onto the chaos of the maple burl's natural edge. On this piece Elliott added a turned alabaster center and burned one of the rings with a propane torch.

I've been turning and selling large wooden platters for some time. I suspect that some of them end up as shallow fruit bowls, while those purchased by less-practical folks probably function only as objets d'art. Either way, a big and beautiful wooden plate looks great in the middle of the dining-room table. The only problem is what to do with it when you use the table. Seeking a solution to this problem led me into a new area of turning: wall-hung sculptures.

But wait, I'm getting ahead of my story. My most popular platters are turned from big-leaf maple burls, which I get from a supplier in Oregon. The burl comes in 3-in.-thick slabs that usually measure about 2 ft. to 3 ft. in diameter. Most of the slabs have the rough natural edge partway around the perimeter, as well as one or two straight edges from chainsaw cuts. Normally I bandsaw out a complete circle, which eliminates both the natural edge and the sawcuts, and then turn a platter from the circle. However, a few months ago, a shipment arrived that included several slabs that were cut from a very large and fairly symmetrical burl and were completely surrounded by the natural surface of the burl. Well, there was no way I was going to cut out a circle and throw away the completely intact natural edge just to make a platter. I realized that this was an opportunity for me to make something special: a nice, smoothly turned platter that would show off the spectacular figure of the burl and contrast beautifully with the prickly irregularity of the naturally sculpted edge (see the left photo on the facing page).

So I set about turning these large gems of the forest into decorative platters. They were very successful, both in the satisfaction they

gave me and in the sales department. But I was getting to the bottom of the pile and even though the remaining slabs still had an intact natural edge, they had other problems. For one thing, they had bark inclusions, which would result in irregular holes in the surface of the platter; I find this condition undesirable, even on a semi-functional platter. In addition, I was left with the larger and more irregularly shaped slabs. I think that a 3-ft. platter is a bit overkill, and the remaining slabs were far from circular—more like 35 in. by 25 in.

While thinking about how to use these large, oddly shaped pieces to best advantage, I came up with the idea of making purposely nonfunctional wall pieces. I had already begun to rout a keyhole slot in the bottoms of the natural-edge platters so they could be hung on a wall when not on a tabletop; this combination of functions prompted me to name them "Vertizontals" (see the top, left photo on the facing page). So it was a short mental leap to eliminate the tabletop function entirely and use the larger-than-platter-size slabs to make wall-hung sculptures with no pretense of being functional (see the photo above and the top, right photo on the facing page). Turning these wall pieces is pretty straightforward. Of course you need a heavy-duty lathe to handle the large size and out-of-balance weight of the spinning slabs (see the sidebar). But the actual turning doesn't require any exotic techniques, and I've developed a step-by-step method that gets the job done quickly and efficiently.

Turning irregular burls—After selecting a slab, I decide whether it will be a functional platter or a wall sculpture. Since the slabs
(continued on p. 104)

Photos left and right: Dennis and Iona Elliott

The platter above is a "Vertizontal"; a keyhole slot on its bottom allows it to be displayed (and stored) vertically on a wall when not in use horizontally on a table. The sculptures at right and on the facing page, which are both about 3 ft. at their widest points, are made from burl slabs that were too large or irregular to be used as platters.

A 3,000-lb. portable lathe

I was in the market for a bigger lathe—one that could handle the large burl slabs and whole log sections that I was struggling to turn on my 12-in. spindle lathe. When I saw fellow woodturner David Ellsworth's huge 4,000-lb. lathe, I immediately asked him where I could get one like it. He said that his lathe was custom built by Jim Thompson of Greenville, S.C., and that Thompson had a new, portable model in the works. I wasn't interested in anything portable, but on Ellsworth's insistence I called Thompson to find out more. As it turned out, he was working on a videotape to demonstrate the portable lathe's capabilities. I ordered a copy of the tape and after viewing it, I called and ordered the machine on the spot.

The lathe gets its portability from the ease with which its bed portion can be disassembled from the headstock, motor, etc. Both base sections are made from ⅜-in.-thick steel plate formed and welded into boxes that can be filled with sand. Empty, the lathe weighs 1,500 lbs.; but when filled with sand, it tips the scale at about 3,000 lbs., giving it the stability needed for turning the large-size pieces that it's capable of holding. It will swing an 18-in.-radius piece over the bed and turn 42 in. between centers.

Everything about the lathe is big and heavy, but the machine is designed to be effortless to use. The tool-rest base and tailstock move along the tubular steel bed on precision radial bearings and can be locked to a central feed screw that runs the length of the bed. When locked in position they will not slip, no matter how much pressure is applied to them. But they can be moved along the bed together or independently by turning the feed-screw handwheel. The tailstock barrel can be removed and replaced by a 3-ft.-long boring bar,

which will accept different size cutters. With the boring bar in place, you can advance the tailstock with the feed screw and hollow out the center of even very tall faceplate-mounted pieces. After this initial hollowing, you can move the tailstock out of the way and straddle the bed, as shown below, to complete the hollowing.

The 5-HP, 1,725-RPM motor drives a "Dana" hydrostatic speed variator, which allows you to start the motor under no load and then go from 0 RPM to 1,800 RPM clockwise or counterclockwise with constant torque. You can bring the work to a halt without turning off the lathe by dialing the speed back to 0, or you can stop and start the lathe at whatever RPM you're using. The on-off control is mounted at eye level on a swiveling arm, allowing you to

place the switch wherever you happen to be working on the lathe.

The handwheel is designed to accept any number of small magnets so that with a little trial and error, you can counterbalance an out-of-balance workpiece. However, I must confess that I've never used this feature; I figure that if I can get a 3,000-lb. lathe to vibrate, I should just slow it down a bit.

I could go on about this monster lathe that combines mammoth bulk with hummingbird precision, but I've probably made my point. Of course this dream machine doesn't come cheap; it costs about $11,000. But it delivers what it promises and does it all. For more information on Jim Thompson's lathes, write to him at 1021 Miller Road, Greenville, S.C. 29607.   —D.E.

Elliott sits astride the custom-made lathe that makes it possible for him to turn these large irregular pieces. In spite of its size, the lathe can be made portable by unbolting the bed portion from the headstock. After the lathe is assembled, the base can be filled with sand, which increases its weight to 3,000 lbs.

With a faceplate mounted on what will be the front of the sculpture (above), Elliott cleans up the slab's back side. It takes concentration and a steady hand braced against the tool rest to keep the tool's cutting edge in the same plane while the spinning slab's jagged edge moves in and out of contact with the tool (below).

Below: The author has removed the faceplate from the front of the slab and has mounted a larger faceplate on the back side after turning it true. The aluminum bar with the pointed rod is used to center the faceplate on an indentation that was made with the tailstock center just before removing the workpiece from the headstock.

are cut from roughly spherical burls, all but the center slab have a naturally beveled edge. If the slab is to be used as a platter, I make the finished side the one away from the bevel of the natural bark edge, because this makes it easier to pick up the platter. For the sculptures that are meant only to hang on the wall, I use the other side to take advantage of the natural irregularities that lie just beneath the bark. Since I will need to mount a faceplate on the slab, I often have to smooth the chainsaw marks on the surface with a small power planer so the faceplate will sit flat. Then I pick off all the bark that will yield to a large screwdriver or a pneumatic chisel. This job can be very easy or very difficult depending on what season the burl was cut and on how long it has dried. The important thing at this point is to remove all the large pieces of loose bark so they won't fly off when turning the slab on the lathe. Later, after the initial turning process, I sandblast the natural edge to remove the small pieces of bark tightly embedded in the crevices of the burl's prickly edge.

With the burl flattened and most of the bark removed, I locate what will be the center of the turned portion. This is usually not the actual center of the slab as determined by measurements, but is rather the point of visual balance. To find this point, I just play around with the compass until I find a circle that relates well with the natural edge. I draw this circle onto the slab and mark its center with a hammer tap on the point of the compass. I center my faceplate with the aid of a short length of threaded aluminum bar—a by-product from milling out the faceplate that I salvaged from the machinist. To register the faceplate precisely at the center of my desired circle, I thread the bar into the faceplate and then insert a slender sharpened rod through a hole in the bar's center, as shown in the bottom photo.

I mount the piece on my lathe and flatten the back side, as shown in the top and center photos. I slowly increase the lathe's speed until the overhead switch vibrates slightly and then I slow it down a little. The average speed for turning these burls is about 300 RPM to 500 RPM. You can see from the photos at left that as the slab spins, the jagged edge moves into and out of contact with the cutting edge of the tool. Keeping the cutting edge in the same plane as I work toward the edge of the burl requires a steady hand registered against the tool rest and steady nerves. Make no mistake about it, this type of work can be dangerous. If I'm feeling at all anxious or nervous about anything, I will not turn these pieces.

After cleaning up and flattening the back side, I run the tailstock forward until its point marks the slab's center. This gives me a point of reference for mounting a faceplate on this side at the center of my desired circle. I then remove the faceplate from the headstock, unscrew the faceplate from the slab and mount a larger-diameter faceplate on the just-flattened back side (see the bottom photo). It's not entirely necessary that the new faceplate be larger, but it is critical that the screw holes of the two faceplates do not line up with each other. If the mounting screws in the second faceplate were in the same circle, I might hit them with the tool when making the deep cut to remove the holes left from the first faceplate (see the center photo on the facing page). The circle of mounting-screw holes in my second faceplate has a 1 in. larger radius than those on the first faceplate; this way, these screws will be safely anchored in the raised ring adjacent to the deep cut that removes the first faceplate's screw holes.

Once the work is back on the lathe, I make about a 1-in.-deep cut at the original compass circle and then taper the area outside this circle to the edge, again taking great care as I work into the jagged zone. I then use a ¼-in. (6mm) roundnose scraper (a parting tool will also do) to define and visually separate the center circle from the tapered outer area. Before turning the center section, I shut off the lathe and use the tool rest to lay out the radiating V-grooves that I usually carve in the outer tapered area (see the left photo on the facing page). There's nothing tricky about

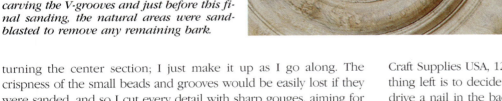

Left: The radiating lines of the carved V-grooves are laid out by rotating the workpiece in small increments and drawing along the tool rest.

Center: Elliott uses a gouge to cut the concentric rings that form the central design. He develops the pattern as he works by alternating wide raised areas with narrow beads and V-grooves. The small ring near the slab's center was cut with a narrow gouge in order to eliminate mounting-screw holes left by the faceplate.

Top, right: When the turning is nearly complete, the author takes the piece from the lathe and carves the V-grooves with a reciprocating gouge, which runs off a flexible shaft chucked into the multipurpose tool in the background.

Bottom, right: A flap sander is ideal for breaking the burl's sharp edges and spikes without altering their basic shapes. After carving the V-grooves and just before this final sanding, the natural areas were sandblasted to remove any remaining bark.

turning the center section; I just make it up as I go along. The crispness of the small beads and grooves would be easily lost if they were sanded, and so I cut every detail with sharp gouges, aiming for clean, precise lines right off the tool (see the center photo).

When I'm sure the turning is about 90% complete, I take the piece off the lathe and carve the V-grooves with a reciprocating gouge, as shown in the top, right photo. The V-grooves draw the eye to the center of the piece and their hand-carved quality adds another texture, one that aptly fills the space between the smooth orderliness of the turned rings and the natural chaos of the outer edge. After carving the grooves, I sandblast the rough burly edges to clean off any remaining bark or paper-like remnants of the cambium layer. Then, the piece is mounted on the lathe one last time so I can redefine the ¼-in.-wide groove between the carved V-grooves and outer ring. I also take this opportunity to add more detail to the central area if the spirit moves me to do so. Now I dull the sharp edges and spikes of the natural areas with a flap sander chucked into a portable electric drill, as shown in the bottom, right photo. Finally, I smooth the raised rings of the center area with a pneumatic sander, being careful not to soften crisp edges.

I've found that I can further enhance the textural variations by oiling only the turned portions (see the finished pieces on pp. 102-103). I carefully apply about five coats of Waterlox oil (available from most building-supply stores) or Sealacell, a two-part finish available from Craft Supplies USA, 1287 E. 1120 South, Provo, Utah 84601. The only thing left is to decide which end is up. I do this by trial and error. I drive a nail in the back at various places and hang the piece off the bench until the center of gravity is just right for the visual balance of the sculpture's abstract shape. I then mortise in a large brass keyhole bracket that I order from Larry and Faye Brusso's Fine Cabinet Jewelry Co., 3812 Cass-Elizabeth, Pontiac, Mich. 48054; (313) 682-4320.

If you have a lathe that can handle a project such as this and decide to tackle it, be forewarned; turning pieces with irregular edges and voids in the surface can be very dangerous. You can't be in a hurry and you should turn at a slow speed. Keep your tools sharp and always wear face and head protection. When the piece is spinning, the outside edge will either disappear or will look like it is completely round; so a large, well-anchored tool rest is essential to support and guide the tool when you're working toward the edge. In addition, if you keep your hands behind the tool rest at all times, you won't risk getting severely mashed knuckles. Don't do this kind of work in an environment that could pose any distractions. Finally, make sure you are in the right frame of mind; whenever I'm turning large pieces, I borrow a line from the old *Honeymooners* television show and run it like a broken record through my head: "If I'm not careful, 'One of these days...pow, right in the kisser'!"   □

Dennis Elliott is a woodturner in the Brookfield, Conn., area.

Multiple-Segment Turnings
Designing with structure and color

by Janelle Lenser

*In Neil Munson's segmented turnings,
design and structure are interdependent.
Clockwise from upper left, "Ovals," named for the
grain pattern of the segments in the center bands; "Thermos," a double-wall vessel with a walnut bowl in an oak outer
shell; "Jewel Case," a walnut box assembled from two separate turnings;
"Chimney," end-grain oak segments glued up on a tapered, Philippine mahogany
block; and "Skyline," a lidded cherry bowl with a handle that represents a city skyline.*

Segmented construction is not new to woodturning. By gluing up various precut wood segments, a woodworker can create a turning blank that is greater than the sum of its parts, the same way that a composer arranges notes into complex and unique compositions. But just as a piece of music can be either monotonous or moving, so too can segmented turnings be boring or appealing. Neil Munson of Lincoln, Neb., knows the difference. His turnings, a few of which are shown in the photo above, demonstrate some of the possibilities if a segmented turning is well planned and constructed with carefully selected segments.

Munson, who recently retired after 41 years as an industrial-education instructor at the University of Nebraska, has been experimenting with segmented turnings for the last 15 years. His responsibilities as a teacher left little free time for his own woodworking, and so he's only produced three or four pieces a year. With this low output, he hasn't worried about sales; nevertheless, his turnings have been purchased as gifts for a governor of Nebraska and a retiring dean at the university.

With most laminated turnings, the contrast between the colors of the parts is the first thing to catch your eye. But Munson is much more interested in the overall structure of the finished turning than he is in just making colorful bowls with contrasting woods. His turnings are carefully thought-out experiments where design and structure go hand in hand. He works out all the details of each turning at the drawing board, beginning with two or three different views of the final shape. The drawings help him determine the number, shape and size of the segments that make up the turning blank. Visualizing the finished turning in this way also guides his selection of wood for each segment, which is based not only on the species or color of wood, but also on the precise grain orientation. This con-

cern with structural details is the thread that runs through all of Munson's work. Each of the turnings shown here represents a unique combination of some of the basic structural elements in Munson's design vocabulary. An abridged dictionary of this vocabulary follows.

Grain orientation—In experimenting with segmented construction, Munson discovered that he could produce patterns and color schemes in the finished work by carefully orienting the grain of the segments. For example, in his turning called "Ovals," far left in the photo above, each of the Douglas fir segments in the two center bands has an oval grain pattern, hence the name. But the ovals did not happen by chance. Referring to his drawing, Munson measured the angle that the surface of the segments would have on the finished turning and then "went hunting" through his stock for just the right grain that would result in an oval when turned (see detail A in the drawing). In "Chimney," front right in the photo above, he cut segments with similar end-grain patterns and centered each segment on the most vertical medullary ray to add an even subtler uniformity (see detail B in the drawing).

The turning that Munson calls "Thermos" (because of its double-wall construction), center in the photo above, illustrates a different way that grain can produce a pattern. Detail C in the drawing shows how Munson glued-up the original three-part oak sections that form the vessel's outer shell. The color difference between the endgrain and the side grain reverses depending on the angle of light reflection; dark areas turn light and vice versa. To make sure the visual effect was uniform, Munson cut all the pieces with the annual rings running straight through the endgrain, thereby also ensuring that the medullary rays ran squarely through each piece.

Grain orientation of segments

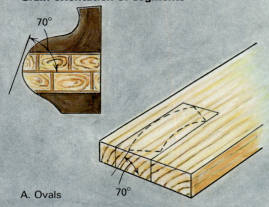

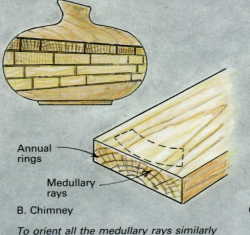

A color difference results from endgrain contrasting with side grain at each joint. The colors reverse, depending on the angle of light reflection.

A. Ovals

Cutting segments from stock where the annual rings are at the same angle as a line tangent to the finished contour, results in a uniform oval grain pattern on each segment. (Slow-growth Douglas fir works well.)

B. Chimney

Annual rings

Medullary rays

To orient all the medullary rays similarly on the finished turning, the endgrain segments are cut to center on a radius line extending from the pith.

C. Thermos

Two types of three-piece segments are glued-up, bandsawn into wedges and glued together alternately to form the outer shell of the vessel. The medullary rays are aligned squarely through each block for uniformity.

Left: To create the tilted plane for the turning "Chimney," Munson mounted a solid block of mahogany at an angle between two pieces of plywood and ran it over the dado blade, repeatedly adjusting the fence until the whole block was tapered. Right: The tapered block becomes the foundation for layers of segments. Using the jig shown in the photo at left, each layer is tapered in the opposite direction from the original block until the blank is once again of equal thickness. The blank is then bandsawn round and turned on the lathe. The small pieces of plywood on the sides of the mahogany block are spacers for the jig.

Mortar around the brick—"Chimney" and "Ovals" share another of Munson's structural experiments: surrounding each segment with a thin band of a contrasting wood, a technique he calls "mortar around the brick." The "mortar" wood can be glued around each individual segment, but whenever possible, the segment stock is selected and glued, surface to surface, onto an 18-in.- to 24-in.-long piece of the mortar wood before each segment is cut out. Then the ends of the segments are disc-sanded to fit the adjacent segments, and a small piece of mortar is glued to one end of each segment (see the right photo above). Because the curvature of the bowl will affect the thickness of the horizontal layers of mortar, it may be necessary to reduce the thickness of a layer if all the layers are to be of equal width after turning.

Removing and replacing segments—In the turning that Munson calls "Skyline," front left in the photo on the facing page, he left certain segments unglued when he assembled the blank, and then removed them before turning the outside shape. When the outside was complete, he shaped and sanded the missing walnut segments and glued them in place so they protruded slightly. Then, he finished turning the inside of the bowl so the reinserted segments were flush on the inside. The handle, which forms the skyline for which the vessel is named, was glued up as a unit from individual blocks and the pieces that form the lid were cut to fit around it.

In "Jewel Case," upper right in the photo on the facing page, removing segments has a functional purpose. The segments for mounting the hinges were fitted but not glued during assembly. The hinge blocks were then glued in place after the outside of the glued-up hollow form was turned. Segments can also be effective

by their absence; leaving them out completely or filling them with other materials, such as stained glass, can add a special effect.

Segments on a tilted plane—"Chimney" is one of Munson's most striking pieces because of the tilted plane of the segments. The left photo above shows how he begins with a solid block mounted on a faceplate, and then tapers it with a jig and a dado blade on the tablesaw. From there he glues the segments onto the block and tapers each layer in the reverse direction from the block so that the last layer of segments brings the blank back to equal thickness (see the photo above right).

Cutting turnings to reveal the shape—Munson thinks that "Cutting a completed turning exposes and verifies its dimensional features, its total shape, in the same way a mechanical drawing examines the sections of objects." The top of "Ovals," sliced to reveal a section view, ultimately provides a glimpse of the shape of the entire piece. Sometimes a turning is cut apart and then reassembled to give it a completely new form, or as with "Jewel Case," to give it a function. But even then, cutting the piece reveals its structure: When the doors of "Jewel Case" are open, they reveal a circular shelf (its edge is visible as the thin lamination just below the pulls in the photo on the facing page), which Munson inserted between the preturned shallow bowls that he glued together to create the hollow form of the finished case. □

Janelle Lenser is Features Editor for the Fremont Tribune *in Fremont, Neb., and a former student of Mr. Munson. Since retiring from teaching, Neil Munson has continued to experiment with segmented turnings in Lincoln, Neb.*

Backyard Timber, Tabletop Treasure

Turning natural-edge wooden bowls

by Joseph M. Herrmann

W hen I turn wooden bowls, I avoid designs that are perfectly round and look lathe-turned. I create an illusion by turning bowls green and letting them dry to an oval shape. Natural edges, with the bark still on the rim of the bowl, further add to the effect.

Burls allow more exotic illusions because of their wavy figure, but they are usually difficult for most turners to obtain. On the other hand, ordinary logs from the backyard or the firewood pile offer an inexpensive way to produce pleasing, natural-edge, oval-shape bowls. Whatever the source, I've found that the greener the wood, the better the bark will adhere. It also is important to work quickly when turning a green bowl because the bowl quickly becomes distorted as the wood dries. I try to turn each bowl in 45 to 60 minutes. If the bowl cannot be completed in one session, it's filled with the wet shavings produced during turning, and then put in a plastic bag to prevent rapid moisture evaporation.

To turn the bowl, I check the blank on the lathe three different ways before I'm finished. First, the green-wood blank, with bark on, is mounted between centers to turn the outside profile. This is a much safer procedure than faceplate mounting, particularly since the initial blank may be out of balance. Also, I can precisely align the grain so that the growth rings are centered about the axis between the tailstock and headstock. The result is a symmetrical turning with on-center growth rings that greatly enhance the illusion of ovalness in the finished piece. Then, I remount the blank to a lathe-turned faceplate that maintains the same central axis for turning the inside. Using a shopmade mandrel, I remount the bowl again, and turn the base for a more finished appearance.

Wood selection and layout—I prefer locust, cherry and ash because these woods have three distinct attributes: pleasing, concentric growth rings that contribute to an oval appearance, sapwood that contrasts with the heartwood and snug-fitting bark that doesn't break off easily. With care, walnut can also be used, but its rough bark tends to break off when turned.

Once you've chosen a log, measure its diameter and then chainsaw or bandsaw a length of it equal to its diameter plus an inch or two. The fresh end cuts reveal the true colors of the wood, checks and other defects. Keep the cuts as square as possible. When working green wood, the greatest chances for radial cracks are at the pith, so I generally avoid this area in my designs. While there is no right way to determine where the bowl should be in the log, I find it helpful to draw bowl shapes on the end of the log with a lumber crayon or chalk. Based on your experience, preferences and inspection of the

From *Fine Woodworking* magazine (September 1989) 78:58-61

endgrain, select the side of the log you think will produce the biggest or the most colorful bowl blank and draw a line directly through the pith. Now draw another line parallel to the first, but 1 in. deeper in the waste side of the log, as shown in the left photo below, and cut along this line with a bandsaw or chainsaw. The extra material at what will be the foot of the bowl gets turned into a tenon that will fit into an auxiliary faceplate. Matching this tenon to a mortise that has been turned into the auxiliary faceplate ensures the bowl will be centered when you reverse it to turn the inside.

Using a framing square, I draw a line perpendicular to the bandsawn surface directly through the pith on both ends of the blank, as shown in the middle photo below. Draw a centerline the length of the blank and locate the center point on that line. Using a compass, dividers, trammel points or a circular pattern, outline the bowl shape on the bark and bandsaw a round blank as shown in the right photo below.

Mounting the blank on the lathe—A center-finding tool (available from Craft Supplies USA, 1287 E. 1120 South, Provo, Utah 84606; 801-373-0917), although not totally accurate on these irregular surfaces, helps me locate the center on the flat pith side of the blank. Then, using a mallet, I drive the spur center deep into the center mark on the bark side of the blank. With thick-bark wood,

such as walnut or butternut, it might be necessary to remove a portion of the bark to allow the spur center to penetrate the solid sapwood. A revolving cup center in the tailstock works best for making the adjustments for centering the blank on the growth rings, which I'll discuss later, because a cone center makes a hole in the stock that could interfere with making a critical adjustment. Move the tailstock into position, centering it on the mark previously made on the pith side of the blank, and you're ready to start.

Because the blank will be out of balance, put the lathe on its slowest speed before turning it on and stand to the side because it may throw some bark. A full-face shield is absolutely necessary for this kind of work because it protects your eyes and face from serious injury if a piece of bark comes loose or the blank itself comes off the lathe. Now I true-up the blank with a bowl gouge, which cuts much more quickly than a scraper and reduces the chances of the blank being thrown off the lathe.

Once the blank has been trued, adjust it on the lathe so that the central axis is in alignment with the center of the blank's growth rings. This is a trial-and-error procedure. Because changing the tailstock position will throw the blank off balance again, I true it up after each adjustment before I check the alignment. I begin by locating the four reference points indicated in figure 1 below in the area where the bark meets the sapwood. With my pencil on

After selecting the section of log for your bowl, mark it off by drawing A-A' through the pith. The cutting line, B-B', is laid out 1 in. to the waste side of the first line.

Connecting lines drawn perpendicular to the base on each end of the blank provide reference points to mark off the bowl blank centered on the growth rings.

The curving profile of the bowl's lip is clear after bandsawing the circular blank. The more round the blank, the better balanced it will be when mounted on the lathe.

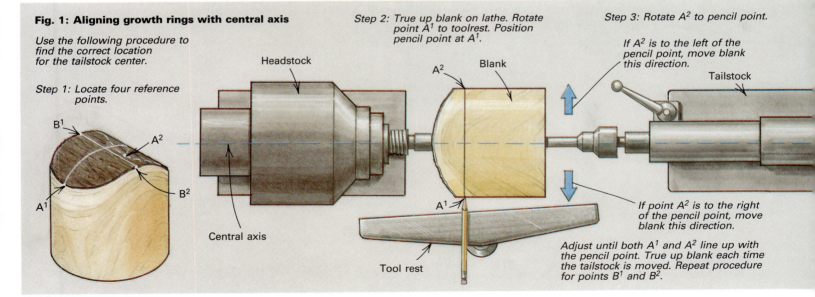

Fig. 1: Aligning growth rings with central axis

Use the following procedure to find the correct location for the tailstock center.

Step 1: Locate four reference points.

Central axis

Headstock

Tool rest

Step 2: True up blank on lathe. Rotate point A¹ to toolrest. Position pencil point at A¹.

A^2

Blank

A^1

Step 3: Rotate A² to pencil point.

If A² is to the left of the pencil point, move blank this direction.

Tailstock

If point A² is to the right of the pencil point, move blank this direction.

Adjust until both A¹ and A² line up with the pencil point. True up blank each time the tailstock is moved. Repeat procedure for points B¹ and B².

the tool rest and the pencil point at reference A^1, I rotate the blank by hand to check the relationship of A^2 to A^1. An adjustment must be made if A^1 and A^2 do not align with the pencil point. Loosen the tailstock and relocate the cup center on the blank, as shown in figure 1. By keeping the center on the same horizontal plane while moving it forward or backward on the lathe, you can bring points A^1 and A^2 into alignment with the pointer. When A^1 and A^2 are in alignment, repeat the procedure with the B points. This will usually go much quicker than the first setting.

Turning and shaping the blank—I prefer the ½-in. Superflute bowl gouge, available from Craft Supplies USA, for turning my bowls. To avoid tearing the endgrain, turn from the smaller diameter to the larger diameter, contrary to the common rule of always cutting downhill. I've ground back the sides of my gouge so I can make this cut, which would be difficult with a square-end gouge. Although the appropriate speed of the lathe will depend on the size of the blank, a good rule of thumb is the larger the blank, the slower the speed. I usually turn around 1,000 RPM for a 6-in. bowl. Don't forget to turn a tenon on the bottom of the bowl, which will be needed for faceplate-mounting the stock, before removing the piece from the lathe.

While there are no specific rules, I've found that woods with a lot of figure or natural-edge bowls look best when simply shaped. I prefer shapes that flare at the rim and curve gently to a smaller-diameter foot, as shown in the photo on p. 108. Experiment to find pleasing shapes that work well with the wood being used.

I make a special faceplate-mounting chuck that recenters the blank to turn the inside of the bowl. The chuck is a circular hardwood block, ¾ in. to 1 in. larger than the diameter of the foot of the bowl and thick enough so the screws used to attach it to the faceplate do not protrude through the wood. Mount the chuck to the faceplate and true-up the wooden circle. Next, carefully turn a ¼-in.- to ⅜-in.-deep mortise in the wood to accept the tenon on

A bottom-turning mandrel is made by stapling a foam pad to a turned 4x4x6. The foam pad serves as a friction drive for the bowl that is held to the mandrel by the tailstock.

the base of the bowl. The tenon should fit snugly without being forced into the mortise. I super-glue the tenon into the mortise, producing a fillet of glue around the base of the bowl for additional strength. Hot Stuff, a cyanoacrylate adhesive available in three different consistencies, works very well. I use Hot Stuff-Super T for faceplate mounting because of its good gap-filling capability, and use the thinner Hot Stuff-Original for gluing bark, a procedure I'll describe later. Hot Stuff is available from almost any hobby shop and several mail-order sources. I order mine from Sheldon's Hobby Shop, 2135 Old Oakland Road, San Jose, Cal. 95131; (408) 943-0220.

When used with the accelerator, cyanoacrylate glue cures almost immediately, but I usually allow an additional five minutes of drying time before turning on the lathe. Then I true-up the outside of the bowl and rough-sand to remove any tool marks before beginning on the inside. Drilling out the center serves as a depth guide and removes the slow-turning center, which is difficult to cut with a gouge. Using a 1¼-in. to 1⅓-in. multi-spur bit, I drill to about ½ in. less than the maximum depth; be sure to measure from the point of the drill. Rough-out the inside with a bowl gouge to a wall thickness of approximately ½ in.

A uniformly thick wall helps to eliminate uneven drying and cracking, although the bowl will probably distort. You should, therefore, continually measure the wall thickness with double-ended calipers to ensure uniformity. Final wall thickness should be about ¼ in. to ⅜ in., depending on the integrity of the wood. Some spalted woods and pieces with large voids will need to be on the thicker side to prevent them from being torn apart by the centrifugal force of turning.

To provide a secure attachment once the bowl has dried, I glue the bark with Hot Stuff-Original super glue because its water-thin consistency gives deep penetration and an invisible glueline. The glue is applied to both sides of the bowl where the bark joins the sapwood. With the lathe running, I power-sand the inside and outside of the bowl using a foam-backed abrasive disc, available from Craft Supplies USA, in my ¼-in. electric drill. I start with 120-grit and work up to 400-grit. When sanding the bowl's interior, avoid touching the rim because it can give you a bad cut. The path the drill takes must be either from five o'clock or seven o'clock to center to avoid the drill being caught up inside the bowl. The next phase involves hand-sanding, with the lathe stopped, until all imperfections are removed. Over-sanding can result in a wavy surface as the softer earlywood is removed more quickly than the more-dense latewood. Further damage can result if you overheat the wood while sanding, causing heat checks. The fruit woods, such as cherry, are more susceptible to this kind of damage than the nut woods.

Finishing and turning the foot—I like a natural finish so I use a simple procedure that is quick, yet seals the wood and provides a soft glow. While the bowl is still on the lathe, and without the lathe running, I liberally brush on a coat of Deft lacquer, which I immediately wipe off with paper towels. After the lacquer dries for 30 to 60 minutes, I pad on a coat of Minwax Antique Oil Finish with a piece of fine steel wool or, especially on light woods, with a Scotchbrite light-duty cleansing pad, available at the local supermarket. The Scotchbrite doesn't cause lighter woods to turn gray or black. Wipe off the excess oil immediately, and then let the finish dry thoroughly. Sometimes I add a light coat of wax to renew the shine. This finish is good for decorative bowls, but for food vessels I would use plain mineral oil.

A bowl with a turned foot has greater appeal than a bowl right off the faceplate. The foot should elevate the bowl from the surface on which it is sitting, but it should not interfere with the visual flow from one side of the piece to the other. A turned

Turning bottoms

by Betty J. Scarpino

The bottom of a bowl, though usually not seen, has a great effect on the way the bowl sits on a flat surface and on how potential customers react to the piece.

After several years of simply sanding the bottoms of my bowls flat, I decided to finish them as professionally as the rest of the bowl, so I came up with a way to tape the bowl to a lathe-turned jig and turn the bottom to follow the bowl's inside contour.

Bottom-shaping: Make the jig from a ¾-in.-thick piece of pine or plywood, the diameter of which is slightly larger than the rim of your bowl. The only additional materials needed are some masking tape and strapping tape. Bandsaw the jig round, center and attach it to the faceplate on your lathe and then true-up the rim with a gouge or scraper. Next, I turn a ⅛-in.-deep groove until it's the diameter of the bowl's outside rim. After measuring the thickness of the bottom of the bowl so I'll know how much material I can safely remove, I masking-tape the bowl to the jig as shown in the top photo at right; for extra security I add a few pieces of strapping tape.

The bottom of the bowl is now ready to finish. Because best results are achieved with sharp tools and light pressure, I remove most of the waste with a round-nose scraper and then finish up with a small skew. The lathe is set at the same speed I would use for bowl turning. Working carefully not to remove too much material and cut through the bowl, I shape the bottom to match the bowl's interior contour. Because the bowl is automatically recentered on the jig, it is easy to untape the bowl and check your progress.

When sanding my pieces, I usually start with 80-grit sandpaper and work up to 400-grit for finish-sanding. Pieces of abrasive from the current grit can cause unsightly scratches, however, if they are left

Photo: Jay Williams

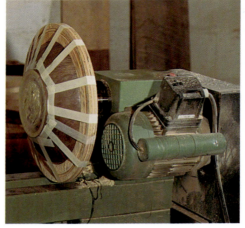

A simple plywood disc screwed to a faceplate makes a jig for turning bowl bottoms, as shown above. The bowls shown below demonstrate the variety of bottoms and professional results obtainable using this simple jig.

on the piece when you move to the next level of abrasive. To avoid this, I frequently wipe away loose grit and dust with a cloth. Also, after I've sanded up to 100-grit paper, I use a sharp tool to touch up fine details that tend to become muted and rounded. Although the sand grits embedded in the wood grain will dull the tool, the result is worth a little extra sharpening.

Removing the bowl from the jig is merely a matter of removing the tape. I've never had a problem with tape residue, but if you run into this problem, try scraping away as much as possible with your fingernail and then lightly sanding. If you are using an oil finish, any remaining residue should be removed by the oil. You should wipe the bowl with mineral spirits, however, if you will be using a lacquer or varnish finish. □

Betty Scarpino, a seven-year professional woodturner, lives in Indianapolis, Ind.

bottom creates a more professional piece, provides a stable base and makes a perfect place to add your signature. Usually waiting several days before turning the base will give the bowl time to do whatever warping it is going to do. Your turned bottom should then remain flat and true.

Using a parting tool, I mark off the bottom of the bowl, leaving enough material to square up the base, and then cut the bowl free from the mounting chuck with a backsaw or on the bandsaw. The bowl is then remounted using a type of pressure chuck, which holds the bowl between the shopmade mandrel, shown in the photo on the facing page, and the tailstock. To make the mandrel, turn a seasoned 6-in.- to 8-in.-long 4x4 to make a cone with a depression. The depression eliminates the point of the cone, which could mark the bowl's interior. The turned end is covered with a piece of foam pad, which protects the inside surface

of the bowl, and creates sufficient friction to secure the bowl while the bottom is turned to shape.

I mark the center of the bottom with a center finder, place the bowl over the mandrel and position the cup center of the tailstock on the center of the bottom. Advance the cup center into the bottom of the bowl to force the bowl tight against the foam pad on the mandrel until the bowl is stable. With the bowl firmly held, I true-up and shape the bottom, cutting a recess and forming a rim on which the bowl will sit. The small spud that is left under the cup center is chiseled off and sanded smooth when the bowl is removed from the lathe. Sign the bowl, apply the finish and you're done. □

Joe Herrmann is an industrial-arts teacher and semi-professional woodworker in Jefferson, Ohio.

The International Turned Objects Show

New signs of the turning tide

by Michael Podmaniczky

When *Fine Woodworking* reviewed the first Turned Objects Exhibition seven years ago, former editor John Kelsey said that one of the exhibitors, Robert Leung, "is at the beginning of a journey, and it will be fascinating to see where he goes." Now that we are well into that journey, not only one individual's work, but the entire craft of woodturning has exploded into something that could only have been a dream at that first exhibition.

There is no better evidence of the ascension of woodturning in the last decade than the 1988 International Turned Objects Show (ITOS) at the Port of History Museum in Philadelphia, Penn. The exhibition is organized by Albert LeCoff and the Wood Turning Center, of which he is chairman. The ITOS is a rich smorgasbord of turned innovations and an important update of what has been going on in the world of turning. The show, which opened concurrently with the American Association of Woodturners Conference in Philadelphia, is scheduled to tour the United States and several countries through 1992.

The ITOS features the work of 39 turners from around the world who were invited by LeCoff, with selection assistance from American turners David Ellsworth and Rude Osolnik. These well-known turners (many of whom appeared in the first show) are joined by another 68 exhibitors who had their work juried by Osolnik, Jonathan Fairbanks, the curator from the Museum of Fine Arts in Boston, Mass., and Lloyd Herman, the founding director of the Renwick Gallery in Washington D.C.

Containing more than 300 pieces, the ITOS exhibit displays an eclectic variety of what the lathe has to offer, both as a primary fabrication tool and as an incidental technique for turning objects made from wood, alabaster, ivory, plastic, metal and other materials. There is a staggering array of different kinds of turned pieces in evidence: vessels of all sorts, tables, stools, pens, boxes, instruments, jewelry, games and objects d'art.

Bowl turning remains the touchstone of the turner's craft in this show, and as far as materials go, burls still seem to command the interest of most turners. Turner Robyn Horn of Little Rock, Ark., emphasizes material over form with her "Redwood Geode," above, by contrasting a rich and lusciously finished interior vessel with surfaces that become coarser in texture and blander in color as the eye moves from the core to the outside.

Box turning has always allowed a lot of design and craftsmanship to be packed into a pint-size object, and there are few disappointments here. A collection of exquisite boxes by M. Dale Chase, a decorative turner from Chico, Calif., are shown above. These boxes are turned from exotic woods and ivory, and their decorative elements are machined on an antique Holtzapffel lathe. Chase's work reminds me of the simply turned, carved and lacquered boxes of the late Japanese master wood craftsman Tatsuaki Kuroda; his work was highly decorative, yet not overdone.

The turned furniture in the show includes Bob Ingram's dining table, above on the facing page, which is made of bird's-eye maple, bubinga and wenge. Ingram, a Philadelphia, Penn., furnituremaker who only does occasional turning, joined the wishbone-shape turned-and-cut-apart brackets to the tapered legs with a jig he designed 10 years ago while building a Shaker-style table.

From *Fine Woodworking* magazine (January 1989) 74:84-85

Using a Holtzapffel ornamental lathe to cut the faceted designs, M. Dale Chase makes small boxes from many exotic materials, including these, left, made of Honduras rosewood, pink ivory wood, African blackwood and ivory. Robyn Horn's 'Redwood Geode,' below left, allows the exterior of the burl to remain naturally rough, in counterpoint to the finished vessel turned on the inside. Bob Ingram turned a 48-in.-dia. disc of bird's-eye maple for the top of his post-and-bracket-style dining table, below. The tapered legs are turned bubinga. After turning a simple ebony vessel, right, Frank E. Cummings III inlaid two bands of ivory with 14K-gold accents. He then carved a delicate openwork pattern of waves and loops around the top to create a lace-like effect.

One of the loveliest objects in the exhibition is by Frank E. Cummings III of Long Beach, Calif., who produced a cup of arresting beauty he calls "Ebony Lace," shown above, right. This is a stemless cup that flows into a remarkable band of wavy, lacy carving around the lip. Around the base and lip, Cummings applied bands of ivory, overlaid by a balustrade of fine gold rods. The bands break up the flow of figure within the Macassar ebony, but the coloration is so strong that the eye cannot help being drawn up from the solid turning into the delicately carved fretwork.

Despite the kaleidoscopic range of styles and aesthetics in the ITOS, one turner's work appeals directly to my tastes. The architectural turnings of Gail Redman, right, embody all the truths of the turner's trade: the simplicity and beauty of wood are unadulterated by a finish of any kind. The results of cutting edge on wood are left naked for inspection. And, the spongy, truculent redwood the San Francisco, Calif., turner chose maintains sharp, crisp corners and surfaces, and it bears not the slightest blemish of catch or tearout or any hint of an unsure hand. What is on display is nothing less than complete mastery of a craft. To me, this is what turning is all about. □

Michael Podmaniczky is a contributing editor to FWW and a furniture conservator at The Winterthur Museum in Winterthur, Del. For ITOS schedule information, contact the International Sculpture Center, 1050 Potomac St. N.W., Washington, D.C. 20007. The ITOS catalog, with pictures of all the exhibit pieces, is available from the Wood Turning Center, Box 25706, Philadelphia, Penn. 19144, for $32 ppd. (softcover) or $43 ppd. (hardcover).

Architectural turner Gail Redman's turned balustrade and newel post, below, shows the crisp and clear tool marks of a deft touch, difficult in the soft redwood she used to make the turnings.

Photos: ©1988 Eric Mitchell

Current Work in Turning

Do high gallery prices make it art?

by Richard Raffan

Of all the objects that can be turned on a lathe, the bowl has attracted the most interest among amateur and professional woodturners. Indeed, entire professional careers have been built on bowls, and there is now enough interest—both aesthetic and economic—in these objects for galleries to mount entire shows devoted to the subject, or at least very nearly. Major shows at two craft galleries last summer, "Masters of Turned Wood" at The Elements Gallery in Greenwich, Conn., and "Works Off the Lathe: Old and New Faces" at the Craft Alliance in St. Louis, illustrated the point. While touring the U.S., I attended both exhibitions.

Both of these shows revealed what I consider to be a disturbing trend in contemporary woodturning: Today, there exists a plethora of turners who are apparently in pursuit of recognition as top artists, as collectible as David Hockney or Andy Warhol. In these shows (as in others I've seen), the favored vehicles for expression are the bowl and the vase, along with their bastard cousins, the Bowl-form and the Vase-form.

The high prices attached to many of the individual pieces in both shows indicated clearly that we must be looking at Art or, at least, at something quite rare, and not a collection of what I thought was largely mediocre work from well-meaning turners not yet in full control of their medium. Art prices should be attached to art objects. But at these two shows, that vital, undefinable spark essential to a true object of art was missing in all but a few pieces. And there is too much of this work around now for it to have scarcity value.

The varying quality of The Elements' show suggested that the gallery was getting into turning, but without a great degree of knowledge or discernment. The press release proclaimed one turner to be a "consummate technician," said that a second "reveals the character of the wood," and noted that a third considers his bowls "works of art." I felt that, between them, these three makers failed to come up with one piece remotely near exhibition quality. I found distorted rims indicating excessive and inexpert use of abrasives in little bowls which I would regard as overpriced at one-fifth the gallery tag. Such work belongs in gift or kitchen stores, not in a gallery claiming to deal in art.

A typical example is a pair of bowls by John Whitehead, shown in the middle photo at right. The piece on the right is visually unbalanced, contrasting sharply with Whitehead's other version of the same idea on the left, which is well-balanced with a good line (though the wood, to my eye, doesn't make this an exhibition bowl either). In the same show, the mundane forms of David Lory's "Heirloom Bowls," with their wavering curves and indecisive rims and bases, are not enhanced by the

Right: This 24-in.-dia. bowl is the latest in a series of lacquered bowls by Giles Gilson. The bowl's interior is sprayed with a rubberized material similar to automobile undercoating. Price: $13,500. Below: Two versions of the same bowl idea by John Whitehead. Each bowl is about 7 in. in diameter and priced at $150. Rob Sterba brick-builds his bowl blanks out of aspen, then turns them on a shopmade lathe. The bowl at bottom— priced at $2,200—is 25 in. in diameter and is finished with nitrocellulose and acrylic lacquer, detailed with silver leaf.

Staff

From *Fine Woodworking* magazine (November 1987) 67:92-95

Top: This walnut burl bowl ($6,500) is a recent example of David Ellsworth's deep, hollowed turnings. Two smaller Ellsworth pieces, above, were shown at The Elements: an 8½-in.-dia. ebony bowl ($1,800) and a 15-in.-tall, spalted Norwegian burl bowl ($1,500).

epoxy finish that renders them dishwasher-proof but not, I could see, scratch-proof.

In the world of turned wood, spectacular wood grain or color is frequently mistaken for art, as is the ultra thin or wany-edge bowl. Praise for the material might often be justified, but should clever manipulation of wood grain really be the basis of a reputation as an artist, unless the object resulting from the use of that wood is of particular merit in its own right? Should a mediocre form displaying technical virtuosity gain entrance into a collection purporting to be of fine art? A mechanical museum perhaps, because such objects are not art, but demonstrations of expertise, despite what exhibition notes might imply.

In the end, no amount of gallery rhetoric will obscure the fact that while most of the objects were well enough made and finished, I didn't see widespread evidence of any real feeling for form in either of these shows. This, combined with a general lack of finesse or exquisite detailing, reveals that too few turners are in control of their material and tools as they struggle to be different in a competitive market.

This, however, is not to say that I found nothing of merit. Far from it. Giles Gilson, for example, has that elusive combination of skill, eye and attention to detail needed to produce a truly remarkable object. With its precise and subtle surface patterns, his large-scale "Sunset Piece" (large photo, above) shown at The Elements is wonderful to look at and to touch. It is almost

churlish to wonder why Gilson left holes in the metal rim ring, but these do detract from an otherwise near-perfect object. The soft iridescent glossiness of the outside contrasts with the black, rubberized undercoating material sprayed on the mysterious interior. Similarly, Robert Sterba's 24½-in.-dia., outflowing lacquered bowl (bottom photo, left) displays a mastery of line rarely matched. I'm not convinced that the silver appliqué is necessary in a form so strong, even though it's a nice example of restrained decoration. Each of these bowls is a technical achievement of both turning and finishing, but that fact is overshadowed by the stunning results.

These two lacquered and polished pieces contrast sharply with a similarly sized walnut piece of classic hollow turning (top photo, above) by the acknowledged grand master of the genre, David Ellsworth. I found the form to be good and well detailed. But what kills any rational thought concerning the piece is the hole near the base. Instantly, this reveals a very thin-walled, impractical object whose insides have been removed through the small hole in the top. The piece exudes technical achievement, and this really overwhelms any aesthetic consideration as it cries out "see how clever I am." I preferred Ellsworth's smaller and much less flamboyant macassar ebony vase which, together with a tall bottle form, are in a different league (bottom photo, above). These forms have no holes to confuse the eye, and there's no indication of their weight until they're handled. Shape

Staff

is the concern and shape is what we see. They are comparatively heavy, woody. No longer is extreme feather-lightness considered an unquestionable mark of skill.

Ellsworth's small pieces have another quality worth noting: the delightful rim details might encourage others to pay attention to this important feature of any turning. Ed Moulthrop, well known for his large-scale bowls, rarely seems to consider rims at all, but his son, Philip, takes a different approach. The tulipwood bowl shown in the top photo at left has a rounded edge that cuts back under, a style typical of Philip Moulthrop's turned work. The bowl, which was shown at The Elements Gallery, springs off the table and could have been a truly exceptional object had the surface been devoid of scratches and other finishing marks. At 14½ in. in diameter, Moulthrop's bowl is diminutive by father Ed's standards—some of Ed Moulthrop's bowls are as large as three feet in diameter.

The best turnery in these shows was on a less monumental scale and more accessible. At Craft Alliance, I gave laurels to Bob Krause for his ebony box (middle photo, left), to Michael Mode's three "Sibling Boxes" in spalted silver maple and ebony (lower left), and to Skip Johnson's highly eccentric croquet set, shown below. Delight in the whimsy of the croquet set masks the display of skill in turning matching balls, mallets and stakes, which is as things should be: appreciation of the object first, then the skills that executed it. His was a delightful departure from vessels. Every lawn should have one. Krause's and Mode's boxes are not only useful, but well proportioned and immaculately detailed, both inside and out, with a flawless finish and well-fitted lids. Although I thought both were rather expensive for what they are, we can all relate easily to such objects and see them inside almost any home.

At The Elements, my favorite piece was undoubtedly Alan Stirt's quiet and understated 8-in. cocobolo bowl (top photo, right). This is a bowl to dream of emulating, if only once in a lifetime. The carving is discreet, harmonizing with the smoother surfaces rather than overpowering them. The inside line is a smooth sweep, and the whole has a balance impossible to convey without picking the thing up. Other pieces involved more dramatic carving but less turning: Michael Hosaluk's fishes and Mark Sffirri's cut-and-colored dish rim each used carving to enhance the turned form successfully. Less successful was Bruce

The $745 tulipwood bowl, above, was turned by Philip Moulthrop, son of Ed Moulthrop. The piece, which has a rounded edge that cuts back under, is 8¼ in. high by 14½ in. wide. Like Ellsworth, Bob Krause also turns deep, hollowed shapes, albeit on a more accessible scale. His ebony lidded box, left, sold for $525 at the Craft Alliance show in St. Louis last summer. A trio of spalted silver maple boxes by Michael Mode, below, sold at the same show for $875. Turning impresario Albert LeCoff, who curated the St. Louis show, sought to broaden the exhibition's appeal by including non-bowl turnings like the ash and cherry croquet set by Skip Johnson, below right. A favorite among St. Louis show-goers, the whimsical set sold for $1,200.

Alan Stirt fluted the outside of his 9-in. cocobolo bowl, above, with a power carver. The bowl was shown at The Elements, priced at $350. Bruce Mitchell's carved, spalted bay laurel bowl at right sold for $2,850. Segmentation is the usual method for achieving patterns in turned work, but in the macassar ebony bowl below, Mike Shuler bandsawed circular segments from a single disc of laminated wood, gluing the segments together to form a conical turning blank. The bowl was priced at $950 at the Craft Alliance show.

Mitchell's "Super Nova" (large photo, above). The carving creates subtle, tactile surfaces, but the form itself is uncharacteristically weak.

I thought those represented in both shows had their best work at The Elements, but the St. Louis show—curated by turning impresario Albert LeCoff—had a wider range of the unusual, including some ornamental turnery by Frank Knox. A leader in the field of ornamental turning, Knox proffered several archetypes, all well-made, highly decorated, traditional forms. Most curious of all was a pair of twisting spiral candlesticks designed by Leonardo da Vinci, who apparently left no clue as to how it was done. My theory is that he threw away any notes to save the world from reproductions. In any case, Knox's pieces were a notable achievement.

In St. Louis, there were a few nice ideas apart from the croquet set. Leo Doyle's "Spindle Bowl"—looking like an upturned multi-legged stool—was certainly different, if not an aesthetic triumph. Identical spindles are set into a base at an angle to create a bowl ideal for large fruit or tennis balls, but nothing smaller. The fine segmented macassar ebony bowl made by Mike Shuler (lower photo, above) is an excellent example of frugality many turners should investigate. There were fun pieces, too, like Joanne Shima's bright, high-tech kids' chair and Hap Sakwa's pedestal bowl full of bright, geometric shapes. Unquestionably a curiosity was Dennis Stewart's highly collectible "Temple of Tri," with an exotic little Easter scene of androgynous figures enclosed in glass cylinders.

The word "exhibition" suggests quality, especially in a gallery.

But time and time again, I've been let down with expectations unfulfilled. More discretion needs to be exercised during the selection processes, both by the organizers and by the exhibitors. I realize people must hustle to earn a living in the arts and crafts, but there are too many pretentious objects passing through these shows, created by turners anxiously hoping to boast of a sale of so many thousands of dollars. Would that the standard could rise, real things might appear to which we might all relate and the price might lower to realistic levels so that more people can afford to have nice, handmade artifacts in their homes.

This should be a reality. After all, turning is a technique for rapid and, therefore, low-cost production. Any efficient and fluent turner should complete a well-made 12-in. bowl or a fine lidded box in well less than an hour. If prices reflect the hours spent turning and finishing, then few of these turners can claim to be either masters or craftsmen as I understand the term. Or are they really earning hundreds of dollars an hour and on to an easy ride? I've always thought I did better than most by keeping the price down to keep sales up and cash flowing. The aesthetics of the end product will depend on whether the turner has an eye for form. Few of us do, so masterpieces will be rare. But the quest for the ultimate curve should produce a good deal of high-quality, competent turnery for a ready market. □

Richard Raffan is a professional turner, mostly mass-producing one-off bowls. He lives in Canberra, Australia. Raffan's book and video set Turning Projects *was published by The Taunton Press in the spring of 1991.*

Malletsmithing
Make your own quality croquet set

by Michael Hanner

Though you may not have the impeccably manicured lawn required for serious croquet, you can make a serious croquet set, like this one by Michael Hanner, with little more than a lathe. (The balls are made by C.P.J. Webber, Ltd., of Exeter, England.)

Fifteen years ago, I drove into Eugene to pick up an old friend who was moving to Oregon from Los Angeles. His luggage consisted of two suitcases filled with games and a croquet set. Within a few weeks, I was hooked on croquet. The game we played was traditional backyard croquet: nine coat-hanger wickets; undersized mallets, often with plastic faces; two broomsticks as stakes and rules that changed by the minute.

As little as ten years ago, I probably could have saved myself from addiction, but I embraced it. Soon we had replaced the wire wickets with ones of bent steel rod. This was getting serious. I tried making larger mallets using pool cues as handles. Bad job, so I bought a lathe and began exploring. Concurrently, I heard of the United States Croquet Association and an advanced form of the game they played, typically described as a combination of chess, billiards and war. A worn phrase, but true.

In the advanced game, it is important to be able to place the balls you control precisely where you want them on the court. For, unlike backyard croquet, you don't send an opponent's ball into the shrubs, but to a place on the court where that ball will be most advantageous to your scoring many hoops during a single turn. Ideally, the game is played as if one were crossing a shallow stream wearing new shoes. You don't want to get the

shoes wet, but you can find only three stones on shore to build a bridge with. So, to cross the stream, you must always pick up the stone (ball) you have just used and place it out in front of you once more. A movable bridge. But if you misplace one, your opponent will steal the other two, and leave you standing alone in the middle of the creek on a stone. And they usually laugh at that point. Yes, it's a foul, fiendish and decidedly nasty game.

The first time you stand on a full-size USCA court and know you have to roll two balls 135 ft. diagonally across court to attack your opponent or else he's going to score ten hoops on you, you realize better equipment is important.

The components of a good advanced croquet set are six wickets, made of ⅝-in.-dia. iron or steel; a 1½-in.-dia. stake; four 1-lb. balls, 3⅝-in. in diameter; four mallets and a variety of accessories. Of these elements, the mallet is the most intriguing design and construction problem, but also one which allows the most freedom in design, as the specifications are brief, and personal preferences rampant. Typically, a mallet weighs 2¾ lb. to 3½ lb. The head, usually of a dense wood, may be square, round or one of several other configurations. The striking faces must be parallel and are traditionally bound in brass. The shafts are usually 36 in.

From *Fine Woodworking* magazine (May 1986) 58:46-49

Brass pipe is ideal for binding round mallet heads (top). Make sure the rabbet is a snug fit; secure the binding with two or three countersunk brass screws. Below, Hanner turns the knuckle on a handle shank. The finished handle behind the lathe is a reminder of the desired profile.

long, bound in leather, bicycle grip, cloth or twine and constructed from ash, yew, hickory or birch.

When building a mallet, I begin with the head. The selection of the wood is critical, as it will affect the overall weight of the mallet and its balance. The most common wood for mallet heads is lignum vitae, for its high density and resistance to impact damage. I also use several species of rosewood, ebony and hard maple.

Most first-quality mallets are square or rectangular in cross section. There are many opinions as to why this is such a popular shape. My view is that a flat-bottomed mallet may be left standing on the lawn while the player heads for the bar. When he or she returns clutching a double martini, no stopping is necessary to retrieve the mallet.

A typical square mallet head is 2¼ in. by 2¼ in. by 9 in. long. I bandsaw the block 2½ in. square and cut it to length, then joint it to the final size. Next, using a router or tablesaw, I rabbet each end for the brass binding. Mallets need not be bound, but binding helps prevent splitting. The brass shouldn't be flush with the striking face—I usually hold it back ³⁄₁₆-in. I most often bind with ¾-in.-wide by ¹⁄₁₆-in.-thick flat brass, attached with flathead brass screws, countersunk flush with the surface. You can bend it around the head without too much trouble. Starting on the center-

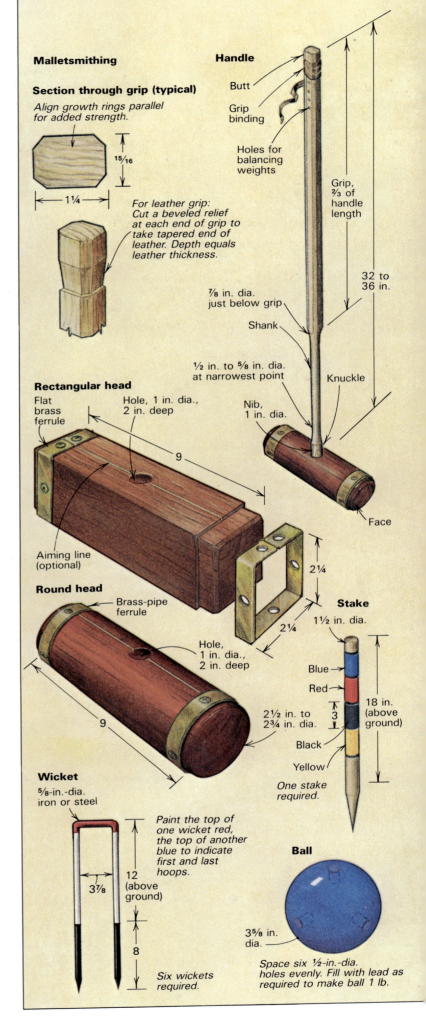

Malletsmithing

Section through grip (typical)

Align growth rings parallel for added strength.

1¼

15/16

For leather grip: Cut a beveled relief at each end of grip to take tapered end of leather. Depth equals leather thickness.

Handle

Butt

Grip binding

Holes for balancing weights

Grip, ⅔ of handle length

32 to 36 in.

⅞ in. dia. just below grip

Shank

½ in. to ⅝ in. dia. at narrowest point

Knuckle

Nib, 1 in. dia.

Face

Rectangular head

Flat brass ferrule

Hole, 1 in. dia., 2 in. deep

9

Aiming line (optional)

2¼

2¼

Round head

Brass-pipe ferrule

Hole, 1 in. dia., 2 in. deep

9

Stake

1½ in. dia.

Blue

Red

18 in. (above ground)

2½ in. to 2¾ in. dia.

3

Black

Yellow

One stake required.

Wicket

⅝-in.-dia. iron or steel

Paint the top of one wicket red, the top of another blue to indicate first and last hoops.

3⅞

12 (above ground)

8

Six wickets required.

Ball

3⅝ in. dia.

Space six ½-in.-dia. holes evenly. Fill with lead as required to make ball 1 lb.

Joint the grip carefully, making sure to maintain symmetry around the turned shank.

Hanner binds a grip with twine on his homemade binding machine. An octagonal wooden chuck holds the butt of the handle and a cradle holds the shank. The device is powered with a sewing machine motor and a variable-speed foot control.

Almost-round croquet balls are relatively easy to turn. Accurate templates are a considerable help in turning truly round balls.

line of the top, mark and drill a pilot hole, then set the first screw. Clamp that section of the brass in place on top so it will maintain a tight corner when bent and make a 90° bend in the brass. Set the second screw and continue around to a butt joint on top, filing the ends to fit tightly.

I finish the head on a belt sander, working from 80 grit to 240 grit and easing the edges of the wood to match the curved brass corners. Last, I sand a 45° bevel on the edges of the face wide enough to include the front edge of the brass as well. Sand the striking faces flat and at right angles to the sides.

Some people prefer a mallet with an aiming line that runs the length of the top surface on the centerline. Before binding the head, you can make a thin saw cut on the centerline and inlay a strip of contrasting wood or paint. You can also laminate the head, sandwiching a thin piece of contrasting wood between two halves. After drilling the 1-in.-dia. by 2-in.-deep shaft hole, I finish the head with light coats of polyurethane varnish.

Round mallet heads are turned from octagonal blanks 10 in. long, which includes ½ in. allowance for waste at each end. When I'm within 1/16 in. of the final diameter, I rabbet each end to receive a brass binding, or ferrule. The thickness of the brass pipe or flat brass bar that I use for ferrules dictates the depth of the rabbets. Using pipe eliminates the butt joint, but requires very accurate turning to achieve a tight fit. (Thick-walled brass pipe is available from plumbing supply houses.) After rabbeting, take the mallet head off the lathe and set the ferrules. (Key a blade on the drive center to its depression on the work so the piece can be remounted later in exactly the same position.) I predrill and countersink for brass screws.

After installing the ferrules, remount the head on the lathe for final sizing and finish sanding. (You can cut a groove for an inlaid aiming line, or sandwich woods together as described previously.) I bore the 1-in.-dia. hole for the handle 2 in. deep using a cradle to hold the head in position on the drill press.

Mallet shafts are usually 36 in. long with the lower third turned and the upper two thirds (the grip) hexagonal. I've had a 30-in. tool rest made for my lathe so I can turn the full length of the shaft, as well as croquet stakes, without resetting the rest.

When I began building mallets, I made a profile template for the shank, but have abandoned it as my eye improved. I still use templates (maple scrap notched to the correct radii) to check the diameters, because certain diameters give good playing characteristics. Obviously, the thinner the shank, the more action or whip it will have, but the more likely it will break. In general, the minimum shank diameter should be ½ in. to ⅝ in.

I begin with 1½-in.-square by 38-in.-long blanks, usually hick-

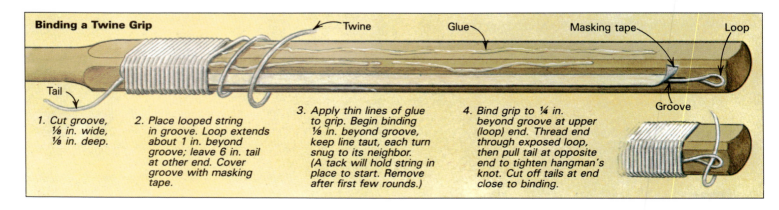

Binding a Twine Grip

Twine — Glue — Masking tape — Loop

Tail

Groove

1. Cut groove, ⅛ in. wide, ⅛ in. deep.

2. Place looped string in groove. Loop extends about 1 in. beyond groove; leave 6 in. tail at other end. Cover groove with masking tape.

3. Apply thin lines of glue to grip. Begin binding ⅛ in. beyond groove, keep line taut, each turn snug to its neighbor. (A tack will hold string in place to start. Remove after first few rounds.)

4. Bind grip to ¼ in. beyond groove at upper (loop) end. Thread end through exposed loop, then pull tail at opposite end to tighten hangman's knot. Cut off tails at end close to binding.

ory. Make sure to use straight-grained pieces—if not, the handle will be more likely to break. Long, thin pieces often require some sort of intermediate support, such as your hand or a steady rest. The profile I prefer starts with a 1-in.-dia. nib, which fits into the hole in the mallet head. Next comes the knuckle, which tapers sharply to ⅝ in., the narrowest point on the shaft, before tapering gradually up to ⅞ in. just below the grip.

After turning the shank, true and finely shape the grip on the jointer to the finished cross-section shown in the drawing. The dimensions are my personal preference and can be varied to suit. Note that the growth rings are parallel to or perpendicular to the direction of the force of a swing, which I've found gives the mallet a more accurate follow-through. Holding the nib of the shaft and pushing with a push stick, as shown in the top photo, facing page, make a few shallow passes on one face to establish a flat base surface. Make sure the fence of the jointer is at 90°, then true three more surfaces, rotating the blank 90° after each. Next, make these four surfaces bilaterally symmetrical about the turned shank, and reduce the cross section to the desired dimensions. Then set the jointer fence at 45° and plane the chamfers ¼ in. wide. During the shaping operations, take care to maintain the symmetry and concentricity of the shaft.

Cut off the tailstock scar and sand the end of the grip to a gentle curve. If you're binding with twine, rout a groove in one of the narrow faces, about ⅛ in. deep and within 1 in. of each end of the grip. The groove prevents binding of the cinchdown cord. For leather binding, cut a beveled relief around the grip 1 in. from each end, as shown in the drawing on p. 119, to allow the leather to finish flush with the grip. I make bandsaw cuts equal to the thickness of the leather around the grip, then chamfer into the cuts with a chisel or bandsaw. Apply the finish before binding the grip; I use polyurethane varnish for the exposed wood of the grip and a shellac sealer coat under the binding.

A well-made mallet must be balanced. Typically, the balance point is one-fifth of the shaft length from the head (that is, about 7 in. from the bottom of the mallet). I balance the mallet before binding the grip, slipping the head temporarily in place to do so. I balance it by drilling a ½-in.-dia. hole axially into the butt of the handle and packing it with lead; or by packing a series of ½-in. holes drilled through the upper portion of the handle just below where the binding begins. These holes are then plugged with wood. (One-ounce lead fishing sinkers with their eyelets snipped off are fine weights.) The binding will affect balance, so I cut a strip of leather or twine of approximate length, roll it up and tape it to the center of the grip area while balancing.

I built a little lathe-like machine to bind handles with twine—with it, a handle takes only a couple of minutes to bind. You can easily bind by hand, too. I use ordinary 18-gauge cotton twine. Start at either end of the ⅛-in. groove cut in the grip portion, leaving the first 6 in. of twine out of the groove, as shown in the drawing. Run the twine up to the other end of the groove and back, forming a loop that extends about 1 in. beyond the groove at the other end. Cover the string-filled groove with masking or drafting tape, and apply thin lines of white glue up and down the surfaces of the grip. (Though white glue is water soluble, it makes removal easier for periodic rebinding.) Starting about ⅛-in. beyond the end of the groove, begin winding on the twine. Keep the line taut, each succeeding turn snug to its neighbor.

Bind the entire grip to about ¼ in. beyond the loop end of the groove. Then cut the cord with 6 in. to spare, insert this end through the loop and pull on the tail at the other end of the groove. (This whole process is rather like a hangman's knot.)

Once the loop has been drawn down into the groove, cut off the tails at each end as close to the binding as possible. The cotton I use needs no finish, but may be sprayed with a stain repellent or periodically rubbed with gymnastic chalk.

For leather binding, determine the amount of leather you'll need (circumference times length plus waste). The width of the binding is a matter of choice, I prefer 1 in. to 1½ in. widths. Cut the leading end of the leather strip on a bias. The pitch of the winding determines the angle of the bias, so experiment before cutting. Epoxy the leading edge into the beveled relief, clamping it briefly. After the epoxy cures, run lines of glue over the grip surfaces and wrap the handle, butting the joints. Apply epoxy to the second end and cut it off with a very sharp knife to fit the beveled relief at the top end. I haven't yet found a good solution for treating the ends of the binding, but a ¼-in. strip of electrician's tape or colored plastic tape works.

Traditionally, the shaft nib extends through the mallet head and is wedged in place. Although I through-wedge new shafts on existing heads (brass wedges work best), it leaves the end grain of the shaft exposed. A croquet mallet often leads a hard life. Once the finish has been breached by a couple of errant hammer shots too close to a hoop, moisture and discoloration follow. Therefore, I prefer a blind hole, attaching woods that do not accept glue readily (lignum vitae and its relatives) with a brass pin set through a hole bored perpendicular to the shaft across the widest portion of the mallet head. I epoxy glueable woods.

For years I've felt there are two great problems in popularizing advanced croquet: the lack of good lawns and good balls. When I began making equipment, I made my own balls, but found the task so tedious that I abandoned it and now purchase the balls that I supply with my sets.

If you want to turn your own balls, begin with a block of hard maple, 7 in. by 4 in. by 4 in. Cut lathe-centering diagonals on each end and bandsaw the blank to an octagonal cross section. Make three accurate semicircular templates, one the right size for a finished ball (3⅝ in.), one 1/64 in. larger and one 1/64 in. smaller—to compensate for the finish. Rough-shape the ball, turning down the spindle ends until they're ½ in. in diameter (my templates are ¼ in. less than a hemisphere to rest on these two "ears" when checking the size). It's easy to get a ball *almost* round. Round is a different matter. To check the final truing, I use the end of a piece of large-diameter pipe, milled perfectly flat. Placing the pipe against the ball will show up any high or low spots—a perfectly round ball will contact the pipe at all points. A hole cut in a flat piece of hardwood will work, too.

A regulation croquet ball weighs 1 lb. As no wood has the proper specific gravity to yield that weight at the prescribed diameter, you'll need to remove the work from the lathe and bore six ½-in.-dia. holes, each 90° apart, and pack them with enough lead to bring the ball up to weight—this usually takes about 5 oz. Glue dowels in the holes, trim them off and finish sand.

I paint balls with a good grade of spray enamel, blue, red, black and yellow. I used to use an opaque primer before painting. However, after the balls have been through a few games (the attrition on paint being high) the primer shows. Clear primer at least shows off the wood when the finish is damaged. □

Michael Hanner is an architect who makes croquet equipment for his company, A.F. Kopp Co., of Creswell, Ore. For more on croquet, write the United States Croquet Assoc., 502 Park Ave., New York, NY 10022.

On Workmanship

David Pye, retired professor of furniture design at the Royal College of Art in London, recently showed an assortment of turned and carved boxes and bowls at the British Craft Centre. He has written two remarkable books about design and workmanship: *The Nature and Aesthetics of Design* and *The Nature and Art of Workmanship.* The work shown here is a small part of his effort to explore and illustrate his concepts of workmanship.

Pye rejects as futile the usual distinction between handmade and machine-made, proposing instead the distinction between "workmanship of risk" and "workmanship of certainty." In the former, the result is constantly at the mercy of the maker, and a single careless move will spoil it. In the latter, once the tools are properly set up, the result is guaranteed. Most woodworking, whether with hand tools or machines, is workmanship of risk.

Pye further distinguishes a spectrum of workmanship: from highly regulated, through free, to rough. In highly regulated work, there is no evident disparity between the idea and the result, as in most mass-produced goods. Most fine cabinetwork would be defined as moderately free—there are always slight discrepancies between the idea and the reality—and most carving, where precise repetition is avoided, is free workmanship. Rough work is just that, although rough isn't necessarily bad.

The small turned boxes shown below are highly regulated, but were nonetheless produced by the workmanship of risk. The pattern is made by ornamental turning attachments to the lathe, but these jigs still must be used with enormous dexterity, gradualness and care to yield the flawless surface. The carved bowls, on the other hand, exemplify moderately free workmanship. Once the bowl has been formed with conventional carving tools, Pye uses a levered arm to guide the gouge through its arc. This jig hardly reduces the risk of spoiling the surface pattern at any moment.

From *Fine Woodworking* magazine (November 1978) 13:84

Turning Segmented Pots
Elegant woods, artful joinery and graceful shapes

by Dan L. Mongold

The author's larger decorative pots are assembled from segments of woods with contrasting color and grain. Specially made jigs ensure crisp joints and speedy construction. After the pots are turned, they're sanded and finished with several coats of a urethane-varnish finish.

W eed pots commonly display dried flowers or perhaps a bloom or two, but my segmented and turned hollow pots are intended to stand alone, as beautiful displays of graceful shapes, spectacular woods and subtle grain patterns. I started making these laminated pots several years ago after seeing some bowls made by Dennis Bodily, a local high-school teacher and woodworker here in Bozeman, Mont. I was taken by the shape and form of his work and the way fine joinery made the turnings strikingly different from those shaped from a piece of wood. My early efforts were dissatisfying: Making the pots was time-consuming, and it was difficult to produce crisp, tight joints and finishes that enhanced the wood's grain and color. The solutions to these problems didn't come rapidly; over time, I've come up with tools and jigs that simplify the process and enable me to make pots in limited quantity.

The construction of my pots, like the ones shown above, is not complicated, but it does involve many steps. Unlike David Ellsworth's hollow vessels (see the photos on p. 115 for examples), which are skillfully turned by working from the outside in through the vessel's small opening, mine are formed from two turned bowls glued together rim to rim. Before assembly, I turn two shallow bowls to the same inside and outside diameter at the rim. Double-face cloth tape holds each bowl to its faceplate while it's being turned. One of the bowls will become the bottom half of the pot; the other becomes the top. The lower half is turned from a single piece; the top often is turned from a glued-up segmented disc made from different woods. The segments are precision-shaped with tem-

plates on a specially designed radial-arm router I'll describe later. After shaping the inner surface of the bowls, I apply a gunstock finish (John Bivens Express Oil Filler, available from Ted Nicklas, 5504 Hegel Road, Goodrich, Mich. 48438; 313-797-4493) to the hollowed-out portion and then glue the bowls together, rim to rim. I clamp up the two halves in my special shopmade press, and after the basic bowl is dry, glue on a decorative 2- to 3-in.-dia. plug in the center of the upper half. The three-piece assembly later is mounted on the lathe, where the center hole is formed and the outer shape of the pot is turned. I complete the pot on the lathe, sanding and applying several coats of the gunstock finish.

Designing the pots—I've tried working with the open form of bowls, but it's the closed-form hollow pot that holds greater appeal for me. Most of my pots are squat, not more than 2 in. to 3 in. high and from 8 in. to 12 in. in diameter. I think their broad surfaces are ideal for displaying the patterns and exotic woods I like to use, such as padauk, bubinga and bocote. I don't have a rigid approach for designing my pots: Freehand sketches, approximately full-size, help me develop pleasing profiles and segment shapes. (Later, the segment shapes will have to be drawn precisely so accurate metal patterns can be machined.) This loose approach usually works well, but occasionally something gets lost in the translation from a two-dimensional drawing to the three-dimensional object. I've made some pretty clunky pots that only the local landfill will ever see.

The simplest pots I make aren't segmented at all: They're made

From *Fine Woodworking* magazine (July 1989) 77:57-59

in the same way as the more complex segmented pots, but because they're smaller and have a one-piece top, I can make them more quickly. These simpler weed pots have created a demand for the larger, segmented pieces I'll discuss in this article.

Making the templates and shaping the segments—Once I've settled on a pot design, I begin working on the templates needed to shape the segments that make up the upper half of the pot. I first tried working without templates, bandsawing the segments directly from a stack of different woods, "mixing and matching" pieces to create a pot's pattern. But the joints between the segments were not tight because the bandsawn edges were not perfectly smooth. Now I

Mongold uses a shop-built radial-arm router to shape segments. The segments, rough-cut with a bandsaw, are firmly positioned on steel templates and held in place by a vacuum chuck. A flush trim router bit guided by a pilot bearing does the final shaping.

This gluing fixture applies uniform pressure in a radial direction. The wood cauls can be modified to accommodate various size discs.

This shop-built thickness sander flattens the segmented disc so it can be mounted and shaped on a lathe. The sander uses a drum made of steel.

use metal templates and shape each ¾-in.-thick wood segment (first roughed out on my bandsaw) on a shop-built radial-arm router using a flush trim bit with a ball-bearing pilot that rides along the edge of the template, as shown in the top photo this page.

To make the radial-arm router, I mounted a Dayton Tradesman router in a steel frame that rides along a steel arm made from 3-in.-sq. box channel. I adapted bearings and other parts from an old Ward's radial-arm saw for this. Two 3-in. angle irons welded together provide vertical support for this arm and a 1-in.-dia. steel bar attached to the end of the arm fits to pillow blocks (bolted to the vertical support) to allow the arm to swivel in a horizontal plane. A machine-surfaced steel table that supports the work is also attached to the vertical support. To create a vacuum chuck for holding the patterns and workpieces, I drilled a hole through the table, installed piping and connected it to a milking pump I bought from a dairy farmer for $50. I'm partial to this tool, but the segments could be shaped using the templates and a hand-held or table-mounted router.

In my setup, which works just the opposite of a pin router (which could be used as well), the workpiece is held stationary in the vacuum chuck while the cutting tool moves, its guide bearing riding along the template's edge, defining each segment's shape. Each template has weather stripping around the periphery of its top and bottom surfaces, forming vacuum seals to the workpiece and the vacuum table. Also, each template has two or three small pins that penetrate the wood segments when the vacuum is applied, to prevent any shifting between the template and the wood while it is being shaped. The patterns are not expensive: Mine, made at a local machine shop, cost less than $100. I like this method of making the segments because it ensures precise and reproducible joinery and is very fast. I can knock out all the segments for a pot in a few minutes.

Gluing up the segments—The next step is to glue up the segments to form a disc. I use a specially made fixture that applies uniform pressure in a radial direction and prevents the segments from sliding out of alignment, as shown in middle photo this page. The push clamps around the circumference of the jig are made from 3-in. channel iron and ⅜-in. by 4½-in. carriage bolts. A small T-handle is welded to the threaded end of the bolt after it is passed through a nut welded to the channel iron. By varying the curvature and width of the wood cauls between the push clamps and segments, I can glue up circles up to 14 in. in diameter. The jig makes glue-up simple and quick, and it's easier to use than the band clamps often used for gluing up discs. With simple modifications, the jig can be readily adapted for a variety of production glue-up situations.

I use Titebond yellow glue exclusively. I've never had a joint failure with it, even with weak endgrain-to-endgrain joints or with the hard-to-glue, dense and oily woods, such as teak or bocote. I don't do any special surface preparation, but I'm careful to glue up the pieces within an hour or so of the time they're machined or sanded. The only other precaution I take is to place waxed paper on the gluing jig's surface, to prevent the glue squeeze-out from adhering.

Turning the discs—The last step before turning the assembled disc is to sand both sides flat with 80-grit paper, as shown in the bottom photo this page. I rely on double-face, cloth carpet tape to hold the disc to the 6-in.-dia. lathe faceplate: A flat surface is essential to ensure good adhesion and to prevent vibration or "chatter," which might cause the disc to pop loose. My shop-built thickness sander uses a 1¾-in. steel drum (other low-tech sanders I have seen use drums made of plywood discs glued together and mounted on a steel shaft). The diameters of the ends are turned down to ¾ in. to fit pillow bearing blocks bolted to the sander's steel frame. The drum is belt-driven by a 1,750-RPM, 1½-HP motor. The table is made from two sheets of ¾-in.-thick plywood hinged together on the outfeed side, and I installed a screw adjustment on the infeed side to raise and lower the table. For dust collection, I built a plywood collector and use plastic hose connected to my shop-vac.

After taping the disc to the faceplate, I turn the disc to within ⅛ in. of the pot's finished diameter with a roundnose scraper. Later, after the insides of both top and bottom halves have been hollowed out and glued together, I'll turn the outside of the pot to its final shape. The goal at this point is to remove as much wood as possible from the inside of the top—I want my pot to be lightweight—while leaving sufficient wall thickness for strength. I also need to form a flat-surface rim for gluing the top to the bottom half of the pot. Again, using a scraper, I take the center of the disc down to about 3/16 in. thickness. Then I work from the center out toward the perimeter to form a slightly concave surface, leaving about 3/16 in. at the outside edge for the rim.

While the disc is still on the lathe, I sand the inside surface with 120 and 220 grit, using a flexible disc sander. Next, I cover the rim with masking tape to protect the gluing surface, and apply two coats of John Bivens Express Oil Filler with a brush or rag. Although the inner surface won't be seen in the completed pot, the finish seals the surface and protects the pot from humidity changes that could otherwise cause it to distort. Also, the smooth, finished inside surface is its own answer to the curious individual who can't resist feeling inside the pot. I remove the piece from the lathe, but leave it attached to the faceplate, and turn my attention to the bottom half.

The pot's bottom half is not segmented, so it's just a matter of turning it bowl shaped with a diameter and rim width to match the upper half I've just completed. The match isn't critical: Any mismatch on the inside won't show; any outside discrepancy can be corrected when I shape the pot's exterior. I use thicker stock for the bottom half: for the smaller pots, 1 in.; larger pots, 2 in. Although I usually rely on solid stock, occasionally I laminate thinner pieces to make the required thickness. As with the upper half, double-face cloth tape holds the piece to the faceplate; after marking the outside diameter (to match the top half) with a compass, I shape the piece with a scraper. At this point, the piece's inner surface is turned to its final shape, but the outside is only roughed out. As with the top half, oil sealer is applied to finish the bottom's inner surface, after the rim is protected with masking tape.

Assembling the turned discs and turning the pot—

With both inner surfaces completed, the top and bottom halves are ready to be glued together. Even though I use only kiln-dried wood, some slight movement and rim warpage occurs in both halves by the time they're ready to be glued, so I return each piece to the lathe and true the rims with a scraper. Finally, I sand the rim of each half for a second or two on a vertical disc sander (80 grit) to make certain each is perfectly flat. I remove the top half from its faceplate but leave the bottom half mounted, to ensure the assembled pot will be centered on the faceplate for finish-turning. The two halves are glued together rim to rim with yellow glue and clamped in a press I built especially for this purpose. The two flat rims form a simple butt joint. Close mating of the surfaces is more important than clamping pressure, and only enough pressure should be applied to squeeze out the excess glue. When the glue has dried, I center and glue a ¾-in.-thick, 2- to 3-in.-dia. piece to the top. This will be shaped to form the pot's rim and center hole. Use the press for clamping here also, as shown in the photo this page.

The glued-up pot, its bottom still attached to the faceplate and its hollow interior now completed, is remounted on the lathe so the pot's exterior can be shaped with a scraper. I complete the shape of the bottom piece, then shape the top to form a subtle dome. The

A versatile shop-built press clamps the top of the pot to its bottom during glue-up. Its external profile is later refined on the lathe.

center hole, which is usually between 1½ in. to 2 in. in diameter, can be bored, but I find that roundnose and squarenose scrapers do the job well and quickly. The center hole's lip is made to protrude slightly upward from the domed top, then its edge is rounded over.

Finishing—Most of the finish-sanding is done before removing the pot from the lathe. I use a power disc sander, and while the pot is rotating, sand with 120, 220 and 400 grit. Finally, I stop the lathe and hand-sand with the grain using 600 grit to remove circular scratches. While the pot is still on the lathe, I apply finish to all the surfaces, except the bottom.

With the pot spinning, I brush on the same gunstock finish I used to finish the pot's inside. This urethane varnish penetrates and seals well, with only slight darkening of the wood (about the same as with lacquer). The finish works well to develop clear, visual access to the wood, highlighting the wood's iridescence, depth and subtle color nuances. I apply as few as three coats, but more often as many as 20 to fill the pores of the wood, buffing the pot's surface between each coat with 0000 steel wool.

The gunstock finish dries in four to six hours; on oily woods, such as cocobolo, bocote and bloodwood, it may take two to three days or not dry at all. Washing these woods with solvents, such as acetone or lacquer thinner, before applying the gunstock finish doesn't seem to help. So, for these oily woods, I spray clear lacquer instead, as it dries on any wood.

The last step in constructing the pot is to remove the faceplate, sand the bottom through 320 grit with an orbital sander and apply the gunstock finish. The trick is to find a way to hold the pot while doing this without damaging the completed finish on the rest of the pot. My solution is to build a vacuum chuck. It's simply a wood box with a 6-in.-dia. hole cut in its top surface and connected to my shop-vac. The pot is turned upside down to cover the hole like a lid, and the hole is lined with foam weather stripping to cushion the pot, form a vacuum seal and prevent damage to the finish. □

Dan Mongold is a full-time woodworker in Bozeman, Mont.

Index